THOSE KIDS,
OUR SCHOOLS

THOSE KIDS, OUR SCHOOLS

*Race and Reform
in an American High School*

Shayla Reese Griffin

Harvard Education Press
Cambridge, Massachusetts

Library of Congress Control Number 2014952433

Paperback ISBN 978-1-61250-766-8
Library Edition ISBN 978-1-61250-767-5

Published by Harvard Education Press,
an imprint of the Harvard Education Publishing Group

Harvard Education Press
8 Story Street
Cambridge, MA 02138

Cover Design: Steven Pisano
Cover Photo: Flying Colours Ltd/Getty Images

The typefaces used in this book are Adobe Garamond Pro and Futura.

To the black women who raised me:

My grandma, Margarette Louise McWilliams Sallee,
who graduated valedictorian of her class in 1946
at the age of sixteen;

My nana, Geneva Estella Brown Griffin, who graduated from
Howard University in 1949;

And my mother, Pamela Denise Sallee Griffin, MS Education,
MAE School Administration—my first and best teacher.

Contents

Part IV: Intervention

Foreword

A half-century ago, at the opening cusp of the American civil rights movement, the United States Supreme Court handed down a unanimous decision in the case of *Linda Brown v. the Board of Education of Topeka, Kansas*, striking down legal segregation in American schools. Popular perception holds that the decision was a moral landmark, that every member of the court recognized that this system of racial categorization was anathema to democracy. In reality, it was a feat of judicial engineering: Chief Justice Earl Warren took the unusual step of privately lobbying his fellow justices, arguing that history would look askance at anything less than unanimity on the matter. The *Brown* decision delivered in May 1954 had such a concussive impact socially that the court waited an entire year before prescribing how the ruling was to be enacted, and then did so by way of an intentionally vague program of desegregation occurring "with all deliberate speed," meaning, literally, to slowly move as fast as possible.

America's chaotic resistance to the demise of legal segregation has been well chronicled. Books detail the intransigence of Southern political leadership; documentaries capture the snarling fury of mobs that gathered to prevent integration in the deep South and the violent opposition to busing in the North. But what is far less recognized is the degree to which integration was as fraught a subject for many African Americans as it was for their white counterparts. Sarah Bulah, the black plaintiff in a desegregation suit in Delaware that eventually became part of the cluster of cases grouped under *Brown v. Board of Education*, faced intense scrutiny from African American neighbors who opposed integration; criticism from black teachers fearful that integrated schools would result in far fewer black educators being hired; and disagreement from her own pastor, who felt that segregation was the best of many flawed options. Their concerns were animated by a common underlying dilemma: in a racially stratified society, do black children fare better in racial isolation or in direct contact with white peers and largely white institutions? The common contemporary presumption is the latter, yet more than fifty years after the court's decision, the racial composition of American schools—which are in many places more segregated now than they were then—remains as complex, intractable, and vexing a concern as it was when Justice Warren was cajoling his peers. The facile, enduring categorization of humanity based simply on skin pigment—a tendency whose foundations lie in superstition, not science—has retained its potency, its capacity to warp our perceptions and thwart our democratic and human aspirations down to the current moment.

In *Those Kids, Our Schools*, Shayla Griffin makes a vital contribution to our understanding of this aspect of race. As her examination of one high school shows, race does not exist as a quantifiable, tangible reality; it is made and remade following familiar precepts and patterns but combined in ways specific to the present. Jefferson High School, with its diverse population and middle-class black population, represents the ideal articulated by men and women who fought to dismantle the structures of segregation and inequality in the twentieth century. Yet, like an adaptive species thrust into a new environment, racism thrives in circumstances we once thought represented its ultimate demise. Blackness is recognized as a marker of poverty by both blacks and whites, even when the socioeconomic realities of the student population contradict this assumption. Moreover, the black population is not insulated from the concerns most typically associated with black students in more economically challenged school districts. Here, too, they are suspended and expelled in numbers disproportionate to their white peers.

In recent years, school districts in Ohio, Connecticut, and New York have brought charges against low-income black parents who enrolled their children in affluent suburban districts rather than the poor, underperforming districts for which they were zoned. That parents have been arrested and in some instances sentenced to jail time for the crime of "stealing" higher-quality education than their child's socioeconomic status would otherwise afford them is morally obscene. That those children may then face the type of social minefield that Griffin elucidates highlights the extent to which race is this nation's most enduring quagmire.

The ongoing problem of racial disparity plagues not only the educational arena—the recent housing crisis disproportionately affected black homeowners, even though homeownership is a primary marker of middle-class status; the criminal justice system is so thoroughly racialized as to not simply feature racial disparities but be defined by them. Yet, Griffin argues, understanding this process in our educational institutions remains particularly crucial. This ethnography yields a window into the ways race and its attendant disparities are re-created through social interaction, "humor," and school policy. As she writes regarding students' allegedly harmless practice of telling jokes based on racial stereotypes:

> When Jefferson students said that "everyone got along" or that they were "beyond race," they meant they were a part of a generation in which white people had permission to say biased, bigoted, prejudiced, discriminatory, and oppressive things with smiles on their faces, and people of color did not have permission to be offended by it. White students had both the privilege of not having to admit the racial prejudice they were perpetuating and of getting to determine whether or not the students of color they were targeting were responding to these attacks rationally . . . The burden of being "beyond race" was on the backs of students of color.

Faced with a rapidly swelling population of immigrants at the turn of the twentieth century, American schools were tasked with inculcating "American values" in the newly arriving children. The American creed of prosperity and social mobility derived its credibility from the schools' capacity to provide their charges with education befitting the manifold opportunities the country offered them. But, as the paragraph above makes clear, our schools have been vectors of social bias too. The process by which the white people's racial attitudes remain beyond reproach while the sensitivities of people of color are disregarded is not specific to Jefferson High School or the once-rural community in which it is located. "Those kids" remain the problem precisely because a half-century of efforts have not liberated them from that category and the implicit bias and skewed perceptions that come with it. Jefferson High School is simultaneously a single ethnography and a microcosm of the phenomenon we might call *Those People, Our Country*. To the extent that we preserve hope for changing this state of affairs, it is vital that we understand the underlying mechanisms. We have yet to devise a schematic for disassembling what critic Wahneema Lubiano calls "the house that race built," yet our best hope for doing so is the diligent, careful, incisive analysis of studies like this one.

—William Jelani Cobb
Associate Professor of History and
Director of the Africana Studies Institute
University of Connecticut

Prologue

A group of ninth-grade African American boys stood outside the main entrance of Jefferson High School. Although school had been out for almost two hours, students—especially black students—often stayed in the building, gathered at the front doors, waiting for rides, well into the evening. JHS, which was located in a once-rural area being rapidly developed, did not provide students with afterschool transportation, nor did the public transit system come far enough into the exurbs to be of service to them.

Cho, one of a handful of Asian students at this large Midwestern high school, walked past the group of boys. Although he had lived in the United States for only a couple of years and still struggled with English, he was fairly popular and had managed to make friends with both black and white male students. The young men he walked by this day were not his friends, though. With no apparent provocation, they began hurling racial slurs at him, calling him a "flat-faced bitch," among other insults. As the students continued to harass him, Cho became more and more upset. In retaliation, he called them "niggers." Enraged, the black students threatened to beat him up for daring to call them the N-word. Cho's white friend Blake, who had a reputation for getting into fights, came to his defense. More racial slurs were flung, as were punches. In broad daylight, with parents waiting in cars and numerous students as witnesses, black, Asian, and white boys from Jefferson engaged in a brawl so severe the police were called.

RESPONSES TO THE FIGHT

The next day, JHS was in an uproar. Students talked about the fight as further evidence of the school's hyperracial culture; administrators went to great lengths to avoid the racial dynamics of the incident; and teachers, left in the dark by administrators, heard only rumors and failed to engage students, or each other, in any critical discussion about race in their school. The different and seemingly contradictory ways in which these three groups responded illuminate some of the struggles of integrated schools to deal constructively with racial conflict and inequality.

In an Intergroup session—an afterschool program I facilitated that engaged Jefferson students in dialogue about issues of race, class, and social justice—a number of students who had witnessed the fight shared what happened:

Victoria (black): I was there after school talking to Blake (white) with Jasmine (black). Cho (Asian) was looking at one of the black guys and he looked at them wrong. It dropped from there, but then the boys were talking stuff.

Kwesi (black): This guy, Cho, they were making fun of him, and he said the N-word to them. He was scared and didn't want to fight, but his friend Blake said he wasn't afraid to fight . . . Blake started taking off his jacket and then someone hit him. And a whole bunch of people jumped in. It moved outside.

Willie (black): Cho hangs out with a lot of black people and he uses the N-word, 'cause . . . his friends think it's okay.

Kwesi: It was one-on-one, and then random people jumped in. It was like fifteen people fighting.

Victoria: And no teacher was there, and parents had to break it up! My mom!

Leah (white): I saw Blake (white) being taken out in handcuffs. And people were saying he should be freed—that it was unfair.

Willie: A lot of the dudes that jumped in, they came back to the school the next day and didn't get suspended. And they were like, "He can't use the N-word! I got my licks in!"

Raymond (black): Cho's not from this culture. He has only been here two years and didn't know the context of the word. So when he said that, he didn't think it would be that big of a deal. And so the other people felt he made them look stupid, so they wanted to make him belittled. That was the only reason for the fight. When Cho uses it with his friends, they say he doesn't know any better.

Curtis (white): They were making fun of his ethnicity.

Kwesi: . . . They didn't have to make an Asian comment—that was totally unnecessary. Cho used the word wrong, but if they hadn't made the Asian comment, he wouldn't have said the N-word.

Madison (white): It all comes back to who's allowed to say it and who's not—either the N-word or other slurs.

Kwesi: I didn't really notice the racial part of the fight until *just now*. I realize now that race is a big problem in our school.

Willie: Me too . . . at the beginning [of the Intergroup program], I said race wasn't a problem at this school, and then this happens!

Nathan (Asian and white): Bottom line—if you're not black you shouldn't say the N-word. And even 90 percent of black people who use it don't even know what they're saying, 'cause they say it like, "What's up?" It's only when someone else says it to you that you feel what it means. So I think no one should use it or "yellow Asian."

Willie: I agree with Nathan—no one should use racial slurs . . .

Gabrielle (white): I just want to know where the people were who are supposed to protect us.

In a structured, racially integrated setting, these high school students talked productively across race about the politics of racial slurs, the usage of the N-word, the realities of racial intimidation, group identity, and the ways in which cultural misunderstandings and prejudice can lead to intense racial conflict. Moreover, they expressed their frustration at the failure of adults to protect them, both physically and psychologically, from racial bullying, discrimination, and violence.

Teachers' and administrators' responses shared none of these qualities. Instead, I watched them gloss over the racial dynamics of the fight and enact punitive measures to punish students. A number of educators reported this approach was due, in large part, to their own fear and discomfort.

Most teachers had heard rumors about the fight, but had received little information from the administration detailing what had happened. Ms. Hill, a white teacher, explained:

> The principal writes this e-mail: "Rumor control. There was this incident and, uh, you know, if the kids are talking about it, don't say anything about it." Like he didn't tell us anything, but created more speculation. And then at the staff meeting, it wasn't really talked about either . . . It wasn't clear at all.

Mr. Collins, also white, agreed that the information teachers had received was "very vague, no detail." Frustrated, he said, "You know, if I have two kids in class that fought, I would like to know. The kids know it. We don't even know!" Though annoyed by the request to keep the incident quiet, teachers largely complied.

In the days following the fight, I sat in on a number of emergency meetings with administrators. School leaders took the violence that had ensued very seriously, but went to great lengths to avoid discussing race.

The first meeting was attended by the principal, Mr. Jackman (white), one of the assistant principals, Ms. West (black), school counselors (all white), the district deputy sheriff (white), and the two community assistants (both black men) who served largely as hallway monitors. The focus of the meeting was on how to immediately secure the Jefferson High School building—especially during afterschool hours—in order to avoid another incident. They talked about changing the bell indicating the start of afterschool activities from 3:00 p.m.—twenty minutes after the school day officially ended—to 2:55 or 2:50 because students had too much free time to get into trouble. When asked if there would be any efforts to deal with the underlying racial tensions, they responded, "Right now, we're dealing with security."

The next day, the administrators held another meeting after a student came forward with a video of the incident. Expressing her frustration, one of the assistant principals said, "At first, we thought it was a cultural thing, that Cho didn't know what he was saying when he said the N-word, but he knew! He used it in exactly the right way. He knew they were making fun of his culture and so he did it back to them." The remainder of the meeting was a discussion of who would be put up for suspension. They did not talk about the possibility of proactively engaging students in conversations about racial slurs, racial bullying, or racial performance.

The third discussion about the fight took place at the tail end of a separate meeting about the school's new disciplinary policy. Ms. West was there again, along with the principal, three of the counselors, the school social worker (white), and the school psychologist (white). As in the previous meetings, the group spent their time brainstorming ways to quickly suspend students for fighting when future incidents occurred. Again, the initial reaction was to punish the fighters, not to think about preemptive or long-term intervention.

These reactions made clear that JHS's top school officials lacked the awareness, knowledge, and efficacy to address race. Even when racial incidents were on full display, they manipulated these events into being about something other than race—miscommunication, insufficient disciplinary policies, low-income backgrounds, and the inaccurate perception that many students were opting to attend Jefferson from other, "worse off," districts.

These efforts to avoid race were confirmed in the third meeting when I finally asked, exasperated, "How are you dealing with your race issues?" Everyone in the room stared at me blankly for what seemed like a full minute. Then the school psychologist responded, "Honestly, we just ignore it. We don't talk about it." The group agreed that perhaps it would be a good idea to consider ways to provide some support and training to staff and students to address the school's negative racial culture, but they were puzzled about what this would look like in practice.

The principal then said, "We can't go to the school board with 'race issues.' They don't want folks to talk about that. What else can we call it?" The remainder of the meeting focused on ways to present a bullying prevention program to the school board that was palatable—one that did not mention race.

WHAT THE FIGHT CAN TEACH US
ABOUT RACE IN SCHOOLS

While the fight was an extreme incident, the issues underlying it are common. Over the past decade, I have worked as an afterschool program director, professional development facilitator, and researcher in many schools where students, teachers, and administrators fail to effectively engage with race. Some schools, like Jefferson, are in integrated suburban and exurban areas, while others are in college towns and racially homogenous cities. In the overwhelming majority of these schools, young people are eager to talk about race but frequently find themselves interacting in ways that reinforce racial hierarchies, biases, and conflicts. And in most schools, adults—though intellectually committed to diversity and equity—struggle to acknowledge that race affects the daily experiences of their students, the climate of their buildings, their disciplinary procedures, their teaching practice, and the outcomes by which they are measured.

Since the passage of the No Child Left Behind Act in 2001, school stakeholders have been acutely aware of the continuation of racial inequality in the American education system—reflected in test scores, college attendance, special education placement, suspension, expulsion, and graduation rates, among other things. There are numerous reasons why these racial disparities persist. However, one of the most overlooked is that we—teachers, students, administrators, policy makers, parents, and community members—have not been willing to address race directly. Nowhere is this more evident than in our daily interactions in schools.

For too long we have operated under the faulty assumption that it is possible to eliminate racial disparities in education without addressing the experiences, relationships, and interactions of those on the ground in our schools. We have been trying to solve a problem whose roots we pretend not to see. And while we remain entangled in webs of avoidance, cultures of silence, and games of omission, students, teachers, and administrators in our schools have been engaging with each other in ways that reinforce racial stereotypes, cultivate racial tensions, and consecrate racial hierarchies. As a result, even schools like Jefferson, whose diverse demographics seem to represent the dreams of a generation past, are more often than not places in which racial divisions and disparities are created, reinforced, and sustained.

The Continuing Significance of Race in America's Integrated Schools

> The black parents, they're just so happy to be here, so happy to be out of [the city], out of [the factory town], they don't say anything . . . You think when you run out to the suburbs it's better, you'll have more stuff, but is someone there to nurture your soul? Your child's soul? 1+1 will always equal 2 wherever you go, but it's the soul part that's not everywhere.
>
> —Black staff member

I first visited Jefferson High School with two university colleagues on a sunny day in June, six months before the fight. We were hoping to expand Intergroup—an afterschool program that brings students from diverse backgrounds together to discuss issues of diversity and justice, which we were already running at two other high schools. I drove behind a slow-moving green and yellow tractor down a two-lane country road past three subdivisions of newly constructed homes. To the left stood a big red barn, a massive cornfield, and a subdivision advertising available lots; to the right, the sprawling Jefferson campus.

While the Jefferson district seemed rather rural, I quickly learned that it represents a growing number of integrated, middle-class, suburban and exurban communities across the country. Such communities are places where tractors and farms—the latter quickly being bought up by

1

developers—mingle with shiny new cars, big new houses, and diverse families in search of the American Dream of economic prosperity. They are places where black and white families have surprisingly similar income levels. Nonetheless, the schools in these communities still have significant racial gaps in achievement and discipline, not unlike the majority of schools in the country. Unfortunately, education reformers—focused on the failure of large, urban, low-income, majority-minority schools—have largely left places like Jefferson out of the school improvement conversation.

When I arrived at JHS, the principal, Mr. Jackman, and one of the assistant principals, Mr. Janz (both white men), welcomed me (a black woman in my mid-twenties) and my two colleagues, a white woman and a Pacific Islander man, with warm smiles, strong handshakes, and crisp ties. After giving us a chance to talk about Intergroup, the principal looked me in the eye and said, "Diversity is our biggest strength. But it's also our biggest challenge." Despite having a student population that civil rights activists had only dreamed about, Jefferson struggled with issues of race, not just in test scores and student achievement, but also in the relationships between students, staff, and community members. He continued that many (white) community members, holding on to notions of "the Jefferson way"—nostalgia for the racially homogenous community of years past—had not been able to view the increasing racial diversity of the school as an asset. These administrators regularly witnessed racial tensions between students, teachers, parents, and the larger community. Nonetheless, they did not feel confident in addressing these tensions. Like so many school administrators, their intellectual commitment to diversity was not enough to lead them to action that would create a more equitable school.

Jefferson was the kind of place I was interested in both as a practitioner committed to helping students and teachers navigate racial difference and also as a researcher. I wanted to know how students, teachers, and administrators were making meaning of race in the school. I wanted to know how they thought about and talked about race. I wanted to know how race shaped their relationships and interactions. And I wanted to know if Jefferson was a place where the trend of black underachievement could be interrupted. The administrators graciously allowed me to spend the next three years looking for answers to these questions and helping Jefferson become a place in which diversity was truly a strength.

LOCATING THE EXURBS

In the past few decades, there have been two seemingly contradictory demographic trends in U.S. schools: *resegregation* of urban schools, which has garnered significant attention,[1] and increasing *integration* in America's suburbs and exurbs, which has received significantly less.[2] As white people have moved further away from urban centers, African Americans with the means to do so have followed.[3] Today, the majority of Americans live in suburbs or exurbs.[4] According to Myron Orfield and Thomas Luce's report, *America's Racially Diverse Suburbs: Opportunities and Challenges*, as of 2010, almost half of all suburban residents live in communities that are 20–60 percent nonwhite. They note "racially diverse suburbs are growing faster than their predominantly white counterparts," with diverse suburban neighborhoods outnumbering diverse urban centers "by more than two to one."[5] In the report *Melting Pot Cities and Suburbs*, William Frey similarly finds that over a third of the country's largest cities have suburbs in which 35 percent or more of residents are people of color. In fact, "the share of blacks . . . living in suburbs rose from 37 percent in 1990 . . . to 51 percent in 2010."[6] Perhaps not surprisingly, as suburbs have started looking more "urban" in terms of racial demographics, the white middle-class is moving even further out to surrounding exurbs, or what Deirdre Pfeiffer defines as "areas of new, low-density, and rapid housing development located beyond the contiguous swath of postwar suburbia but within its community-shed."[7] Black families once again are following.

Exurbs, which some call *outer ring suburbs*, are the "the fastest-growing type" of suburban community, according to Orfield and Luce.[8] Citing data from the Urban Institute, Nate Berg reports that "the exurbs . . . have been growing faster than the rest of the country in recent years, even amid the housing bust and economic recession." In fact, in just ten years, from 2000 to 2010, the number of exurban residents in the U.S. "grew by more than 60 percent, from about 16 million to almost 26 million."[9]

While they remain the whitest of all suburbs, exurbs are rapidly becoming more diverse.[10] Moreover, Pfeiffer finds, there may be less economic stratification by race in exurbs than in other communities. As she writes, ". . . it is possible that urban expansion over the past few decades may have produced more diverse communities [and enabled] more equal neighborhood conditions among racial groups."[11]

In many ways, schools in exurban communities embody the hopes and dreams of America. They are not the poor, inner-city, majority-black institutions that are so often the focus of social science research, nor are they upper-middle-class, majority-white districts. They are a kind of hybrid space, whose existence many hope will prove that black, white, Asian, and Latino children can live and go to school together in thriving communities without disparities. Within the walls of exurban schools, we are given a unique opportunity to investigate how students, teachers, and administrators are navigating relationships across race and to learn much about the realities of race and racism, the future of our education system, and the fate of our democracy. Jefferson provides a particularly poignant case study.

THE JEFFERSON SCHOOL DISTRICT

The Jefferson School District (Jefferson Schools) was founded in the 1920s when five predominantly white, one-room districts were consolidated. From the 1920s through the early 1950s, most Jefferson families were farmers. By 1950, while many families still farmed in some capacity, 75 percent of students in the district came from homes in which their parents also worked in factories. The life of Ms. Flournoy, a white teacher, is the quintessential Jefferson story:

Ms. Flournoy: My family's been in the area for over one hundred years. My mom used to live on a little dirt road up here and she'd walk to a little school house . . . My grandma went to Jefferson when [it] was K–12. My great-grandma actually went to the schoolhouses. There's a gas station on the corner . . . There used to be an old farmhouse, and my grandmother grew up there with like nine of her siblings.

Shayla: What kind of farmers were they?

Ms. Flournoy: Just corn and soy, just the basic mass production.

Shayla: And you didn't end up in that industry?

Ms. Flournoy: No—well, they also worked at [a factory]. Yeah, my grandma retired and my grandpa worked there and they farmed. I'm the first one to graduate college . . . I didn't want to work in the factory.

At the time of my study, while most families were no longer farming, many adults continued to work in factories.

In the 1970s, Jefferson Schools annexed a portion of a nearby rural district that was predominantly black. As one black employee recalled:

> Most of them, the black Jefferson kids, had no running water, they had outhouses. But they never missed a day of school. The stuff I did back in those days would be illegal now . . . One boy . . . I knew he was living hard, so I brought him home with me. When we got there, he got in bed with all his clothes, shoes, coat, everything. He had been sleeping cold at home.

The incorporation of this area increased both the racial and economic diversity of Jefferson Schools and contributed to the notion that blackness and poverty were inextricably linked. This ideology would permeate race relations in Jefferson even after middle-class black families began moving into the area.

In the 1990s, housing developers saw an opportunity to capitalize on Jefferson's location between a major college town and a major city. They bought farmland and quickly built 1,500- to 3,000-square-foot single-family homes in a number of adjacent subdivisions. In addition, they constructed smaller mobile home communities. Between 1990 and 2009, the number of homes in the district almost doubled, from 5,850 to 11,564. New residents quickly followed the new construction. Twenty-six percent of Jefferson residents moved into their homes between 1990 and 1999. Another 60 percent moved in after the year 2000. Most of these new residents were homeowners.

The new homes were strikingly similar two-story houses, built with aluminum siding in neutral colors, on small but immaculate lawns. The subdivisions, boasting names like Jefferson Elms, Willow Lake, or River

Oaks, were quiet, with culs-de-sac, sidewalks, and in some cases, wooded trails. The more expensive homes had brick facades and arched entryways. In 2009, the median home value in the area was $187,400—$40,000 higher than the state median. More than 43 percent of homes in the Jefferson school district were valued at over $200,000, and almost a third were worth over $300,000.

However, the blue-collar background of many Jefferson families, combined with the deindustrialization of the previous two decades and the collapse of the manufacturing industry,[12] made the class positions of Jefferson residents rather precarious.[13] By December 2011, more than one hundred homes in the area were in foreclosure. In turn, it was likely that Jefferson was an example of the reality that ". . . today's [middle-class] exurbs may be tomorrow's [struggling] suburbs."[14]

Between 1990 and 2010, middle-class African American families flocked to Jefferson, transforming the small exurb into a rapidly diversifying, middle-class community. Despite the national economic crisis, which disproportionately affected African Americans, black families in Jefferson were doing relatively well (table I.1). More than 50 percent of families,

Table I.1

Family income by race of householder

Income	Jefferson district		Major city district		College town district	
	Black	White	Black	White	Black	White
Total households	1,399	6,283	152,631	27,967	2,603	24,339
Less than $30,000	23.80%	12.30%	44.4%	40.75%	31.5%	9.7%
$30,000–$49,999	7.36%	14.10%	21.9%	21.8%	22%	11.3%
$50,000–$74,999	17.80%	23.00%	16%	17.05%	14.5%	15.3%
$75,000–$99,999	22.30%	21.40%	9.3%	8.3%	11%	14.7%
$100,000–$124,999	10%	16.00%	4.4%	5.3%	5.3%	12.6%
$125,000–$149,999	7%	6.66%	2.1%	2.0%	7.0%	9.0%
$150,000–$199,999	8.79%	4.85%	1.13%	2.6%	6.4%	12.8%
Over $200,000	2.79%	1%	0.67%	2.2%	2.3%	14.6%
Median income	$64,858	$68,730	$29,128	$30,230	$32,716	$60,215

Source: 2005–2009 American Community Survey, five-year estimates.

Table I.2

Rates of poverty by race and age, Jefferson School District

	Living in poverty	
	White	*Black*
0–14 years old	23%	14%
15–17 years old	11%	12%

Source: 2005–2009 American Community Survey, five-year estimates.

black and white, made over $75,000 per year in 2009—almost $25,000 more than the national median income, and almost $30,000 more than the median income for the state. Moreover, 12 percent of black families, compared with only 6 percent of white families in the district, made over $150,000 per year. In fact black families in Jefferson were some of the best off in the region. They had higher earnings than their counterparts in the college town and the nearby city, where the median income of African Americans was just half of those in Jefferson.

Nonetheless, Jefferson's black families were also disproportionately poor when compared with its white residents. However, the rates of poverty for high school-aged youth were about the same across race, with blacks slightly less likely to live in poverty (table I.2). Black adults in Jefferson were also slightly more likely to have a college education than white adults (figure I.1).

The growth in black families was especially apparent in the racial makeup of Jefferson Schools, where the percentage of African American students more than doubled between 1992 and 2010, growing from 12.5 percent to 31 percent. In the high school, where this study took place, the proportion of black students grew from 14 percent in 1992 to 35 percent by 2008, where it remained through 2012 (see figure I.2). This growth was due not only to the influx of upwardly mobile black families but also to a new cycle of white flight. Meanwhile, as in most U.S. schools, the changing student population was not matched by an increase in teacher

Figure I.1 Educational attainment of population over twenty-five, Jefferson
School District

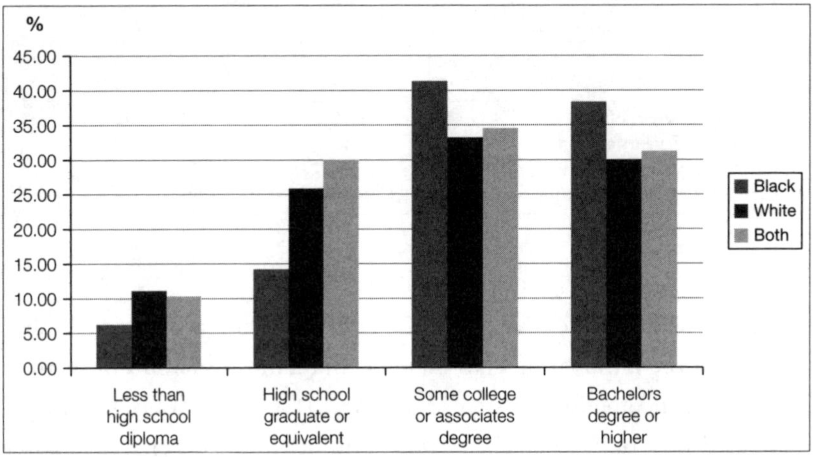

Source: 2005–2009 American Community Survey, five-year estimates.

diversity. Teachers in Jefferson remained over 90 percent white, the majority of whom were women.

Although the majority of black families in Jefferson had attained middle-classes success and highly valued education, as evidenced by their own degree attainment, the graduation rates of their children, which were 10 percent higher than those of white youth, and dropout rates, which were lower (table I.3), black students still underperformed on every subject area of the state standardized test when compared to white students (table I.4). Moreover, although black students made up less than 35 percent of the student population at JHS, they made up almost 50 percent of suspensions. In 2006–07, over half of all black students in the school had been suspended during their high school career. In contrast, less than 30 percent of white students had been suspended. This trend also held true for expulsions, for which black students constituted over 50 percent. For black youth, middle-class status was not enough to interrupt disturbing racial gaps in achievement and discipline.

Figure I.2   Student population by race, Jefferson High School, 1992–2012

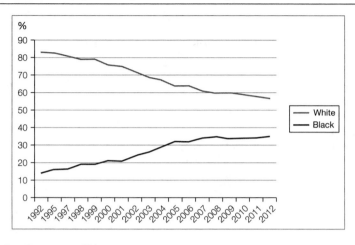

Source: State Department of Education.

Table I.4

Graduation and dropout rates, Jefferson High School, 2009–10

| | Jefferson High School | | State | |
	Four years/ graduation	Dropout	Four years/ graduation	Dropout
Black	83.74%	8.13%	56.43%	20.42%
Male	77.78%	11.11%	48.58%	24.50%
Female	90%	5.00%	64.41%	16.29%
White	74.09%	14.09%	81.69%	8.07%
Male	67.70%	16.53%	78.19%	9.47%
Female	81.82%	11.11%	85.43%	6.58%
Economically disadvantaged	46.34%	34.15%	—	—
Total male	70.62%	14.43%	70.82%	13.30%
Total female	85.37%	8.54%	79.89%	9.25%
Total students	77.30%	11.73%	75.23%	11.33%

Source: State Department of Education.

Table I.4

State merit exam by subgroup, Jefferson High School, grade 11, spring 2009

Subject	Meets/exceeds standards	Doesn't meet standards	Total students tested
English			296
Black	39%	61%	99 (33%)
White	55%	45%	181 (61%)
Male	46%	54%	142(48%)
Female	54%	46%	154 (52%)
Economically disadvantaged	35%	65%	69 (23%)
Math			296
Black	31%	69%	99 (33%)
White	49%	51%	181 (61%)
Male	51%	49%	142(48%)
Female	36%	64%	154 (52%)
Economically disadvantaged	23%	77%	69 (23%)
Reading			296
Black	53%	47%	99 (33%)
White	64%	36%	181 (61%)
Male	56%	44%	142(48%)
Female	64%	36%	154 (52%)
Economically disadvantaged	49%	51%	69 (23%)
Science			297
Black	45%	55%	99 (33%)
White	59%	41%	182 (61%)
Male	59%	41%	143 (48%)
Female	51%	49%	154 (52%)
Economically disadvantaged	32%	68%	69 (23%)
Writing			296
Black	33%	67%	99 (33%)
White	46%	54%	181 (61%)
Male	34%	66%	142(48%)
Female	49%	51%	154 (52%)
Economically disadvantaged	32%	68%	69 (23%)
Social Studies			297
Black	73%	27%	99 (33%)
White	82%	18%	182 (61%)
Male	83%	17%	143 (48%)
Female	77%	23%	154 (52%)
Economically disadvantaged	72%	28%	69 (23%)

Source: State Department of Education.

A NATIONAL CRISIS

Disparities between black and white students are not unique to Jefferson. Since the 2001 No Child Left Behind legislation began requiring that schools disaggregate standardized test score data by race, we have been able to document concerning and significant gaps in achievement, as well as discipline between black and white students nationwide. In 2014, a report by the U.S. Department of Education, which surveyed all ninety-seven thousand public schools in the United States, found that black students are three times as likely as white students to be suspended or expelled—a trend that begins as early as preschool.[15] The data show that these gaps persist not only in racially segregated, low-income, and poorly resourced districts but also in integrated, suburban, middle-class communities like Jefferson—districts in which black children are not supposed to fail.[16]

For almost a decade and a half, U.S. education reformers and politicians have attempted to address these racial disparities, to no avail. Their efforts, which have primarily focused on market-based approaches, "standards," and "accountability," have falsely presumed that treating schools more like businesses through choice, competition, and punishment will improve the educational experiences and outcomes of racially and economically marginalized students.[17] As Charles Payne notes in *So Much Reform, So Little Change*, the standards-based movement seems to be focused on "pretend[ing] to do on a grand scale what we have no idea how to do on a small scale."[18]

While the obsession with such things as standardized testing has revealed troubling trends in education that fall along lines of race, it has uncovered no root causes and offered no effective solutions. Moreover, it has ignored one of the most obvious points of entry: contending with how race works on the ground in schools. As Ms. Mitchell, a white teacher at Jefferson observed, "Many of our problems are not the causes but more the effects. They're symptoms of something larger and nobody ever wants to talk about it."

A number of ethnographers, anthropologists, sociologists, multicultural educators, and other social justice scholars and practitioners have been thinking deeply about how race shapes students' school experiences and outcomes since the 1950s. They have concluded that in addition to inequitable resources and disparities in wealth, racial biases, prejudices, and miscommunications—overt and covert—are major impediments to improving educational outcomes for students of color.[19]

Studies have found that students of color often do not feel connected to their majority-white teachers; they are too frequently targeted as "out of control" and profiled as uneducable by educators; their experiences are rarely reflected in what they are learning or how they are learning it; they are not given opportunities to think critically about inequality or injustice, particularly as it relates to their own lives and experiences; and they are often bullied because of their race and other social identities by their peers.[20]

The sum total of these experiences is that despite the hopes of many reformers—and parents who have moved their children to the suburbs on faith that they will receive a good education—the day-to-day experiences of students and teachers, even in integrated schools in the suburbs and exurbs, are often highly racialized in ways that tend to reinforce rather than interrupt racial hierarchies. Rather than being "the great equalizers," schools often privilege those students who already have "the right stuff"—the "right" ways of speaking, acting, dressing, behaving, looking, and thinking—or what researchers call *capital*.[21] Unfortunately, black students are significant less likely to have these advantages.

Although discussions of race and culture have been a part of the education discourse for decades now, policymakers have never taken seriously the possibility that race, bias, and relationships might actually influence the experiences and outcomes of black students in schools. There has been no prominent national or state initiative to address how teachers, students, and administrators contend with race. There have been no efforts to interrupt biases that lead to patterns of discipline and achievement that fall along racial lines. Our schools of education and professional development offerings have not addressed the need for educators to be reflective about how race shapes their practice and the outcomes of their students or the need to create classrooms that are multicultural and socially just. Curriculum has never adequately reflected the histories, contributions, and learning styles of people of color. There are no nationally recognized movements focused on ensuring that marginalized students are not subjected to discrimination at the interpersonal, cultural, or institutional levels in our schools. While we have given much lip service to the continuing significance of race in education, we have given virtually no attention to race in our efforts to effect change.

It is this gap that *Those Kids, Our Schools* seeks to fill. My time at Jefferson was committed to understanding how racial inequality manifests in schools, not just in test score data and rates of suspension, but in the broader school culture through the daily interactions, beliefs, and biases of teachers, students, and administrators.

ENTERING JEFFERSON

I worked at Jefferson for three years. During the first year of my study, I lived in a multiracial subdivision in the Jefferson community and went to the high school every day, often arriving early in the morning and leaving after school. I continued going to JHS three to four days a week during the second year, and went once or twice a week during the third.

I spent my time in multiple spaces within the school. I sat in the administrative offices, talking to the principals and secretaries and watching as students came and went for various disciplinary infractions, illnesses, and pick-ups. I roamed hallways and lunchrooms during the school day, standing at the most crowded junctions during passing periods. I observed classrooms and spent time in the teachers' lounge. I sometimes acted as an assistant, making copies, putting together packets for parent nights, wiping off tables in the lunchroom, putting chairs on desks at the end of the day, checking students in on the first day of school, and chaperoning school dances and convocations. In most of these spaces, I carried a small notebook and scribbled fieldnotes as I observed who was saying what, where, and to whom.[22]

As a petite, young-looking, brown-skinned, Black American woman, I had a unique position in the building. I was seen as not quite young enough to be a student and not quite old enough to be a teacher. Although I worked to dress more like the adults than the students and never intentionally mislead JHS educators, some staff thought I was working on an undergraduate project. For the better part of a year, one of the secretaries thought I was a nineteen-year-old college student, when in fact I was a twenty-seven-year-old PhD candidate. The assumption that I was a young college student motivated many of the adults to help me with my research by allowing me to observe their classes and interview them. Similarly, I often went unnoticed by students when walking the hallways, which allowed me to be privy to conversations I may not have been otherwise.

Nonetheless, being a black adult in a building with so few African American staff meant that I did not "blend in." Many black students and staff saw me as a much-needed ally—someone they could talk to about their frustrations working and attending school in a place in which they were in the minority. For white staff, my blackness made me simultaneously suspicious and credible. Some staff wondered about my motives in studying race—something they did not consider to be a problem at the school. One white teacher confessed to a white colleague that she believed I had come to Jefferson to "prove that we're all racists just because we're white!"—a sentiment other educators possibly held as well. Other teachers who were interested in thinking and talking about race told me that *because* I was black, they thought I had credibility and authority on the subject and were excited that I was open to having such conversations with them.

By the end of my research, I came to know and have positive relationships with many of the teachers, administrators, and staff as well as a significant number of the fifteen hundred students. Some Jefferson staff openly admitted that, while they had been suspicious of me at the beginning, they were impressed with my commitment to this project.

Over the course of the study, I conducted semiformal interviews with over fifty teachers and more than seventy-five tenth-, eleventh-, and twelfth-grade students from diverse racial and economic backgrounds. I unofficially interviewed almost every staff member in the building, including custodians, cafeteria workers, a few bus drivers, secretaries, para-professionals, administrative staff, the school psychologist, the school so-cial worker, and many more students than those captured on tape. These conversations took place during the school day in classrooms, at apart-ments, houses in the countryside, fast-food restaurants, and coffee shops.

In addition to my role as a researcher, I ran Intergroup for three years, and developed Race in the Classroom, a ten-hour professional develop-ment series for teachers that took place in the second year of the study. I also conducted over twenty one-time dialogues on racial slurs and stereo-types in the English and social studies classes of four different teachers.

The students and teachers who participated in these programs became the particular focus of my research. I interviewed many of them more than once—both in my initial qualitative research in the fall of 2009 and the following year. In this way I was a true "participant observer." I was both a part of the school system—an adult who was charged with "teach-ing" students and providing professional development for teachers—and very much outside of it as a researcher observing the dynamics of race at multiple levels of the system. This dual role gave me great insight into both the challenges and successes of Jefferson and provided me with a deeper understanding of the work it takes to truly reform schools around issues of race.

A FEW NOTES ON RACE, CLASS, LANGUAGE, AND NAMING

The study of race is always a complex and challenging endeavor, in large part because the concept itself is so contested. While the notion of race as a biological reality has long been debunked, the social realities of racism remain salient. Racism, according to Leith Mullings, ". . . is a set of prac-tices, structures, beliefs, and representations that transforms certain forms of perceived differences, generally regarded as indelible and unchangeable, into inequality."[23] In other words, it is not biology that gives race signifi-cance, but rather the ways that we have grouped people and the decisions we have made as a society about which groups are valuable, whose history is important, whose story will be told, and who will have full access to opportunities and resources.

For the purposes of this book, I conceptualize *racism* as a largely structural phenomenon—as a *system* that privileges and oppresses certain groups. Consequently, I often talk about the exchanges between students and teachers as *racial* rather than *racist*—denoting that for the most part, they are not intentionally contributing to a system of inequality even if the sum of their actions ultimately does. When I refer to individuals as *racist*, I am doing so in the more colloquial way to indicate that those from a racially privileged group have expressed *conscious* and *overt* disdain for people from different racial backgrounds.

While this book is not a study of class, it does seek to move forward our understanding of how race and class intersect. It reveals that even when black students are not poorer than whites, our racial frames suggest otherwise.[24] As Sherry Ortner writes, "[T]here is no class in America that is not always racialized and ethnicized, or to turn the point around, racial and ethnic categories are always already class categories."[25] This project explores the how race and class are confounded in schools in ways that maintain racial hierarchies.

The N-word is used throughout this book. Its prominence in popular culture, mass media, and U.S. history has given it a complex and often contradictory status. Depending on how it is said, when, and by whom, this word can be highly offensive to some and a term of endearment to others. I use the phrase *N-word* because I believe it is such a loaded term that it is almost impossible to use productively in a way that moves the conversation about race forward, even when one intends to do so. However, when students or teachers say the word in interviews, conversations, or fieldnote observations, I write it out in an effort to retain the authenticity of the racial discourse at Jefferson.

Similarly, I have chosen not to grammatically correct direct quotes from students, teachers, administrators, or myself. The ways in which we speak and the ways in which we might write are often very different. Verbal language gives us insight into the cultures, norms, backgrounds, and comfort of those speaking. It is important to me to honor what the participants in this study said and the ways in which they said it.

Because of my close relationship with Jefferson teachers, students, and administrators, it is my hope that this book is a fair reflection. What is written is not meant to represent Jefferson in its entirety; rather it is a deep exploration of how a school that seemed idyllic struggled to interrupt racial hierarchies, discrimination, conflict, and inequality. Nothing written in the pages that follow is unique to Jefferson. The school is unique only in its willingness to be a case study to illuminate the challenges faced by so many places like it. As a result, all of the names, including "Jefferson," are pseudonyms, and some revealing details have been modified to protect the identities of the people who were so generous in sharing their stories. In cases in which a topic seemed especially sensitive or an informant seemed particularly easy to identify, I did not use a name at all. This was often the case for African American staff because they were so few.

OVERVIEW OF CHAPTERS

Those Kids, Our Schools is divided into four sections. Separately, each section provides a window into the unique circumstances faced by students, teachers, and administrators regarding issues of race. When read as a whole, the chapters tell a multilayered story of the challenges and possibilities of creating an integrated school culture that serves the most racially marginalized students.

Part I illuminates the prominence of race in the lives of Jefferson students. It investigates the ways in which students' hyperracial interactions reinforced racial hierarchies. Chapter 1 explores the prevalence of discriminatory racial humor targeted primarily at students of color. While young people claimed their interactions were evidence that they had moved beyond race and were now living in a post-racial community, these "jokes" were a thin veneer over deeper racial conflicts, biases, and divisions not so different than those of a generation past.

Chapter 2 finds that students had clear ideas about what it meant to "act black" or "act white." Whiteness was associated with being calm and boring, while blackness was associated with being hype, loud, and obnoxious. Students' ideologies of racial performance led to a culture in which black youth were generally perceived as ghetto and gangster and were harshly judged by their white peers and themselves. These narratives held strong even in a school in which black students were middle-class and in which there was clear evidence that, as one student said, "white kids are bad too!"

Chapter 3 investigates the phenomenon of racial intimidation between black and white students. It finds that some black students purposely pushed their white peers in hallways as another form of "joking." However, unlike the verbal bullying that happened primarily at the hands of white students, these exchanges were not seen as joking by those being targeted. Rather, they served to reinforce negative stereotypes about black people as violent, dangerous, and to be feared. In reality, black students were much more dangerous to each other than to their white peers.

Chapter 4 finds that despite students' claims that they had moved beyond race, most lived racially segregated lives at school and at home. Moreover, white students were navigating racism in their communities, where they were frequently exposed to racial prejudice and negative stereotypes about people of color from the adults in their lives.

Part II of the book explores why, despite decades of national discourse on racial disparities in education, teachers are scared to talk about or take action around issues of race. Chapter 5 investigates teachers' lack of preparation and efficacy in interrupting racial conflicts between students, incorporating racially diverse curricular content, or working through their own racial biases. Their silence, motivated by fear, allowed the school's negative hyperracial culture to go unchallenged.

Chapter 6 reveals the "cycle of mutual disrespect" between some black students and some white teachers. While teachers ignored hyperracial student interactions, they were having their own highly racialized exchanges with young people in which students often accused them of being "racist" in ways that were simultaneously joking and serious. This game was a cover for real tensions between white teachers struggling with their own racial biases, and black students, who felt discriminated against.

Chapter 7 explores the specific mechanisms white teachers used to avoid acknowledging race in a climate in which racial conversations, tensions, and disparities were so prominent. It finds that teachers with various racial ideologies—from the color-blind, who claimed not to "see" race, to the color-conscious, who could intellectually discuss racial disparities in achievement—adopted the same frames that prevented them from considering how they might improve their practice with students of color.

Part III addresses how the Jefferson school board, superintendent, and principals suppressed and avoided discussions of race in ways that set the tone for the district. It illustrates how school district, dealing with reform pressures, a stratified community, and the biases and fears of leaders, maintained the racial status quo through informal policies and practices.

Chapter 8 argues that Jefferson's hiring and promotion practices failed to cultivate a racially diverse staff. As a result, there was "no one at the table" to advocate for students and families of color. African Americans in positions of leadership were expected to discipline black youth, who were seen by many in the district as poorly behaved and in need of control. When administrators of color attempted to engage in conversations about disproportionate suspensions and other racially inequitable outcomes, they were scapegoated by many white staff as "reverse racists" who had caused the district's racial tensions.

Chapter 9 explores what some called "the Jefferson way," in which race was made taboo by those in positions of power nostalgic for the days when Jefferson was an all-white small town. The Jefferson way, combined with the punitive sanctions of the national school reform movement, led administrators to avoid using accurate, disaggregated data to inform practice. As a result, many white staff falsely presumed that the majority of African Americans in the district were low-income "outsiders" who were Jefferson students only because of state-level school of choice policies. This notion that *those* (black) kids had infiltrated *our* (white) schools was a dominant theme that made it more difficult to address race at even the most basic, celebratory levels.

Part IV shows what can happen when we provide teachers and students with a structured, facilitated space to engage in conversations about and take action around race. It follows seven white teachers who participated in the Race in the Classroom professional development series, and twenty students from diverse backgrounds who participated in Intergroup. This approach targets the major outcomes we are concerned with—how students do academically, how they behave, and how prepared they are for an increasingly diverse, multicultural world—not from the top down through federal sanctions and state mandates, but from the bottom up through the relationships and interactions that students, teachers, and administrators have with each other every day.

Unlike many school ethnographies, this book is not about the worst among us. It is not about the most urban, most underfunded, most destitute, lowest-income school. Instead it is about the kind of school that many Americans want their children to go to, in the kind of community where many Americans want to live. I went to Jefferson hopeful, knowing that it did not face entrenched black poverty, a crumbling tax base, or other problems that can make it feel impossible to achieve success in schools. Moreover, Jefferson is located in a state that has enthusiastically adopted the most recent reform strategies—Common Core curriculum, school choice, charter school expansion, high-stakes testing, and merit pay for teachers. However, while Jefferson had done everything "right," it had not achieved racial equity.

In 2010, I was interviewing a black faculty member. Reflecting on the experiences of black students in the district, he said, "You think when you run out to the suburbs it's better, you'll have more stuff. But is someone there to nurture your soul? Your child's soul? 1+1 will always equal 2 wherever you go, but it's the soul part that's not everywhere." This staff member seemed to be saying that the suburban and exurban communities, where so many feel the American Dream has been achieved, are often dangerous for black students in intangible but disturbingly familiar ways.

The students, teachers, and administrators at Jefferson offer a revealing glimpse of the disservice being done to everyone—young people and adults, black and white—when we fail to critically interrogate issues of race in schools. Like the overwhelming majority of schools in the nation,

Jefferson was not intentionally reinforcing racial hierarchies in which white students did well and were seen positively and black students were not. In fact, most teachers, administrators, and even students viewed themselves as actively working against the pull of racial stratification. Nonetheless, as Frederick Erickson writes, "domination and alienation of the oppressed does not simply happen by the anonymous workings of social structural forces. People do it."[26] In the following chapters, I shadow some of the people doing the maintenance work. I explore their relationships with each other across race, with the hope of illuminating how racial hierarchies might be understood and interrupted.

PART I

Students

CHAPTER ONE

Racial Humor

Two competing narratives about race circulated among students at Jefferson High School. The first told of a rapidly diversifying school in which students, rich and poor, black and white, were successfully building relationships across difference. Students used their humorous cross-racial banter and budding interracial friendships as evidence that racial discrimination was a thing of the past. In this narrative, many students claimed that "everyone got along" at Jefferson and said their school was a model of a new, post-racial America.

The second narrative was of racial discrimination and bullying. In this narrative, the humor was a smokescreen for the perpetuation of prejudice, and racial jokes and slurs were thrown around in ways that revealed an awareness of the lines being crossed. If the first narrative was one in which Jefferson High School was beyond race, the second highlighted Jefferson's culture of *hyperracial* discourse entrenched in prejudice. Although most Jefferson students I talked to said they wanted to believe their school was a place where diversity was welcomed and celebrated, in practice they expressed an uncomfortable ambivalence in which they struggled to balance these contradictory narratives in their interracial interactions.

"BLACK JOKES"

Q: What do a black person and an apple have in common?
A: They both hang from trees.
Q: What's the difference between a bucket of shit and a black person?
A: The bucket.

The first way students engaged in hyperracial discourse was through racial jokes. The racial diversity of Jefferson—which included a significant white and black population, as well as small numbers of Asian, Latino, and Arab students—created an environment in which young people from various racial and economic backgrounds "had fun" with race in order to connect with one another. As Winnie (black and white) put it, at Jefferson "racism is like a huge joke" that, according to Harrison (white), "happens every day, like breathing."

Most of the racial jokes exchanged by students, like those above, were "black jokes," told in integrated settings by "mainly white kids" according to Madison (white). These black jokes ranged from what Salim (Arab) referred to as "just the super-stereotypical black jokes like they like chicken and watermelon and all that good stuff," to depictions of black people as sexually deviant, violent, dangerous, and academically, economically, and socially inferior.

Black jokes called upon stereotypes of black poverty, like the following relayed by Brielle (black): "There's this one that people say about black people taking showers or taking baths using dish soap and that shows how poor you are or something"; historical racism, such as one Jada (black) described referencing lynching: "I hear a lot of them, and it's like racial jokes that some white people might say are like racist . . . One joke is like your family tree or something about like being hung, I guess"; jokes that framed black men as violent and dangerous like one Jasmine explained, that students of color were likely to rob gas stations; and jokes that freely used the N-word, such as one told relayed to me by Raymond (black), a middle-class student who had lived in a subdivision in the district since early elementary school with his parents and his older sister, a college student at a university in the area: "He [a white male student] said, 'How does chainsaw start?' And he said, "Run-nigger-nigger, run-nigger-nigger, run-nigger-nigger."' For the most part, these jokes were told in ways considered amusing, lighthearted, and illustrative of interracial camaraderie.

Crystal (black), who had transferred to the district from another state to live with her grandmother, explained how racial jokes often happened: "Let me give you an example from my fifth hour. It was this [white] guy in my fifth hour and every day he comes up and he says, 'You want to hear a black joke?' I'm like, 'No, not really.' He's like, 'You sure?' I was like, 'Okay, tell me the black joke.'" Exchanges of this nature were common. White students asserted their right to tell race jokes in interracial settings, and black students acquiesced, ultimately laughing along, in part because of the social pressure to be able to "take a joke" and in part because their laughter was evidence that "everyone got along."

Matt, a white student being raised by a single father, was in advanced classes, although his anxiety made the courses difficult for him. In class, he was usually quiet and focused, never drawing too much attention to himself. However, when with his friends—a number of other white male students—he could be very loud. He gave me an example of the highly offensive nature of racial jokes:

Matt: Racial jokes, um okay, how do you stop five black men from raping a white woman?

Shayla: Did you say raping?

Matt: Yeah, how do you stop five black men from raping a white woman?

Shayla: I don't know, how?

Matt: Throw them a basketball.

Shayla: Alright . . . throw them a basketball . . . So that's the kind of jokes that you would tell black guys or that you tell to each other?

Matt: I . . . have some black friends that are comfortable with that, and like I guess it's those people that kind of bond everybody together in a way.

Shayla: Oh. Say more about that.   → US vs. them mentality

Matt: It's um, there's this, um . . . my friend Devon (black), he dresses like—I guess you would say like as a white person who likes Scene or listens to like Death Metal and stuff. At the same time, he talks like, I don't want to . . . like he talks like a black person, I guess.

Shayla: So is that a joke that people tell him or that he would tell?

Matt: Both. Like he would tell it himself. Like even among black, um, minorities like they themselves sometimes will make like jokes about their own race. But it's really accepting here.

As Matt's example reveals, black students were not only targets of racial jokes, some also sanctioned these exchanges through their participation.

Although students often talked about racial jokes as evidence of inter-racial camaraderie, the jokes were not always told in integrated settings. White students also told racial jokes in racially homogenous groups—especially those they considered to be most offensive. This disconnect between students' professed ideology that racism was "a joke" and their awareness that some of the jokes were so problematic they had to be told privately demonstrated the ambivalence of students, even those who most confidently expressed the post-racial narrative.

Black jokes were so common at Jefferson that virtually nobody found them remarkable. In the following exchange, I was talking to Danny (white), who had lived in the district since he was born. Danny split time between his divorced parents, both of whom were upper-middle-class. I went to interview him at his father's house, a two-story, newly constructed home on a large plot of land off a country dirt road. We were sitting on the front porch when I asked him where the racial jokes circulating in the school came from:

Danny: [People] either just make them up or they're all over the internet. They're everywhere.

Shayla: So people go home googling [racial jokes] and take them to school the next day?

Danny: Yeah, you can look them up, but they're pretty well known. Everyone pretty much knows black jokes.

Shayla: I don't know them!

Danny: You don't? You don't know any black jokes? You're lying!

Shayla: I'm telling you seriously. I have on occasion heard racial jokes, but I haven't heard anything like this until I got to this school. I've never seen anything like this.

Danny: That's weird. I don't know what to say about that. I've always pic- ~~façade of normalcy~~ tured it as normal. Just across the board as something that like everyone does.

Danny was not alone. Many students reported that they thought racial jokes were the normative mode of cross-racial communication not only at their high school, but in society more broadly. For instance, Alan (white) said racial jokes were "more socially welcome because of Obama, and like how he's uniting everyone . . . We're following that into the school." For him and his peers, the election of a black president sanctioned such interactions.

This "pride" in the ability to tell and take racial jokes was repeated over and over again by Jefferson students from diverse racial backgrounds who believed racial humor was an illustration of racial progress. Raymond (black) explained:

> If you can go up to somebody and tell them a racial joke about their race and have them tell one about your race . . . then that shows how much America and everybody in society has grown. Because in the '60s, if somebody did that, somebody else would be ready to fight . . . Why can't we just like make jokes about it? We're beyond that. I don't think it's a problem. It's good to see that we can all just make jokes about each other. I mean . . . that's cool.

Molly (white) agreed: "I think we make a lot of jokes. I'm glad that we do, 'cause I think it's breaking down barriers maybe that we can all laugh at each other and not feel like, 'What did you just say to me?' and not get mad about it. I think it's kinda cool."

The conviction of both black and white students that racial jokes were "cool" was a part of a hegemonic system in which racial hierarchies were upheld through the seemingly neutral everyday practices of individuals.[1] In this case, the practice of denigrating people of color through "disparagement humor"[2] was normalized and maintained not only by white students from the racially privileged group, but also by the students of color being targeted. As Shannon (black and white), explained, "A white person can tell a joke about a black person and they'll all be laughing." Black students were also likely to make fun of peers who seemed to embody "blackness." I overheard African students being called "African booty-scratchers" and dark-skinned black American students being called "black gorillas." Hegemony and internalized racism—the belief of the group being targeted that they are deserving of the oppression they face—made it normal, taken for granted that black people would be made fun of and discriminated against.

While racial jokes and slurs were most commonly about black students, who made up 35 percent of the student body, other ethnic minorities were also targeted, particularly Arab and Latino students. Palestinian brothers Salim, a twelfth-grader, and Khalif, a tenth-grader, the eldest two children in one of only a few Muslim families in the district, were especially harassed. They had lived in a Jefferson subdivision with their parents and siblings since Salim was in seventh grade. For the six years they had been in the district, their classmates had "jokingly" called them "terrorists." According to Pamela (black and white), a student who took advanced placement classes with Salim, "His nickname that someone came up with like a year ago is Tick-Tick because he's Middle Eastern and it's like a bomb. That's his nickname, so it'll go to that point."

I sat in on one of the classes that Pamela and Salim took together. When the teacher gave students time to work independently on an assignment, a white male student sneakily stood up, walked over to the chalkboard on the side of the room, wrote Salim's name, and then drew a picture of a bomb next to it. A few students giggled. The picture stayed up for the remainder of the class period without the teacher intervening or seeming to notice. When I asked Salim about the incident he quickly laughed it off as well:

Salim: It was a joke. I didn't really care. It was all in good fun, I guess.
Shayla: And what was the reference he was making?
Salim: Um, Arabs are terrorists, I guess. That's usually what the jokes are around.

Shayla: And that doesn't make you feel bad or anything?

Salim: No.

Shayla: Do you make jokes like that too, about Arabs being terrorists?

Salim: Sometimes. You know, I'll add on to it, but it's all in good fun at the end.

Shayla: I also hear you had a nickname that they came up with last year.

Salim: Yeah, Tick-Tick. That was one of them. Would you like me to explain? I don't know, it was all in good fun . . . It was just a nickname, but I don't really care.

In part, Salim believed the terrorist jokes were acceptable because they happened between friends and because he so frequently made jokes in return:

> We play around with [race]. Like they make a Arabic joke, I make a black joke, or a white joke, or a Chinese joke or something like that. You know, it's all fun . . . It's usually the people that make the jokes, you know, I'm friends with them, or I've hung out with them before or after school or something like that.

Raymond (black), who was friends with Salim and lived in the same subdivision, similarly described their racial banter:

> Me and [Salim], we go back and forth with racial jokes and it's funny . . . 'cause we know that these are stereotypes that are true, some of them. And some of them are just off the wall. Like he'll tell me, "Hey, man, why don't you go steal something?" And I'll tell Salim, "Man, why don't you go blow something up?" And we'll . . . laugh about it 'cause we know like that's not us. That's those other people that chose to do that, and those are bad decisions that our races made and we're just making fun of each other for it. It's not that big of a deal.

Raymond and Salim were both high-achieving, college-bound students with no disciplinary problems. They believed they could make these jokes because they were ultimately about *other* black people, *other* Arab people, not about them. Yet Salim admitted, "Sometimes I do find myself taking it too far, but you know, at the end we laugh about it."

Other students admitted that they worried about the ramifications of their jokes—especially those directed at Salim and Khalif, who were at a decisive disadvantage because there were so few Arab students. Pamela (black and white) reflected, "I don't think he [Salim] shows it, [but] I think he might be offended . . . I don't know." Jasmine (black) said she often heard Salim complaining about the fact that so many students would refer to him as "my Arabic friend, Salim." She said:

> He'll be like, "Stop calling me that." It's so funny 'cause I can like picture his face. He's always just "the Arabic guy." He seems okay with it, but I don't think he's okay. I mean, if I was just like one of the few little speckles of black children in a really, really big group of kids, I wouldn't be too happy about it. I think I would feel awkward.

Khalif, who participated in the Intergroup program, was much more critical of these hyperracial interactions, which challenged his brother's claims that what was happening was "good fun." For Khalif, the racial jokes were daily attacks that he had learned to navigate but that still hurt him deeply. This struggle to balance the competing narratives of fun and offense produced contradictions for many Jefferson students.

"COOL" WHITE KIDS AND THE N-WORD

The second way in which students engaged in hyperracial discourse was through the regular usage of the N-word by white students. Most of the white students who publicly said it were those whom black students described as "cool." These students challenged what many black youth I interviewed believed to be the default white position—overtly racist. Cool white students were likely to say things like, "Everyone gets along" or "I have lots of black friends." At school, cool white kids laughed and joked with their black classmates and maybe even worked on class projects across race. However, for the most part, these white students had only surface relationships with students of color. Their close friends—those they hung out with on the weekends and talked to on the phone—were white. The bar for "coolness" was not high. White students did not have to be racially progressive or conscious to be cool; they did not have to have close black friends. They just had to hold some vague notion that overt discrimination was "bad." In other words, the large majority of white students at Jefferson were cool.

These students used the N-word as a way of greeting friends, to amuse their peers, and, as Ryan (white) described, to signal, "I'm cool with the black kids." Danny (white) was one of these students. He said, "I use the N-word sometimes. Just usually messing around. I never say it like seriously and I never use it like as a term of endearment or like calling a friend like, 'What up, nigga?' like that. I'll just be joking and I'll just use the N-word or something." Brittany (white) said that when white students used the word, "Sometimes, they're being funny, like they'll use it with the *a* at the end, you know. And like some black kids are okay with that and they'll be laughing too."

According to Menna (black), "A lot of white people are like okay with calling black people the N-word. It's more like, 'Oh, what's up?' You know what I'm saying?" Brandy (black) said, "I guess they just picked it up like it was cool, like it meant 'homey'. I hear one girl and she always refers to a white person as, like, 'where my N's at?'" In most of these cases, white students distinguished between *nigger*, a racist slur, and *nigga*, a term of affection. By using the term with an *a* at the end—not so different from how their black peers used it with each other—they felt they were momentarily appropriating black culture in a way that was amusing.[3]

Like racial jokes, cross-racial slurs had become so common at the school that students were desensitized to them. Harrison (white) said there were often:

> white people saying stuff to black people, black people saying stuff to white people, and a Latino will jump in. I don't think they hate each other. It's just the words are used so often we don't think much of it anymore. Like love and hate, really strong words. Once you say "I love you" to somebody, to everyone, every day, it loses its meaning. Same with like the N-word and cracker and whatever racial term is for a Mexican.

While Harrison was right about the prevalence of racial slurs, the N-word was by far the most common. White racial slurs like *cracker* were

[handwritten margin note: use of the N word]

occasionally used at the school, but it was the N-word that served as the center of both joking interactions and racial hostilities.

White students not only had to be cool to use the N-word in integrated settings, they also had to be "cool enough with" the black students they used them around to avoid conflict. Raymond (black) described the ways in which racial slurs were exchanged at Jefferson and how he felt about these interactions:

> I mean now, like white people and black people can play around with each other, like call each other names. Like a white kid can call somebody, a black kid, a nigger or something and then the black kid will just be like, "Alright man, chill out." They won't like be all in their face like, "What you call me? I'm ready to fight." I think they really don't care anymore because like, I mean, if a white kid came up to me that I didn't know and called me like the N-word, I'd be pretty upset and like nobody goes that far unless you know them, unless like you're pretty cool with them. I have white friends that are cool with me that'll like say it just like to see my reaction, like see me laugh, and I just like shrug it off. It's not that big of a deal . . . Usually black kids don't initiate the slurs. It's usually the white kids and black kids they'll re-taliate, say the C-word. They'll have a big laugh about it . . . It's surprising, I know, I know. It's surprising, 'cause I'll look at my parents and it's become socially acceptable. From like the perspective of like an adult, right, I can imagine adults thinking that their goal was civil rights. Their goal with all this social justice stuff was not for the kids to start using those words against each other jokingly, but for actually not using them at all. [But] . . . it's okay because . . . I think we as students have grown up.

Raymond illuminated the ambivalence students felt about the ex-change of racial slurs. In the same breath, he admitted being offended when white peers he did not know called him the N-word and approving of its usage by white students he was sufficiently "cool with." He thought the N-word symbolized a new racial reality—one in which it had be-come mocking social commentary rather than an expression of racism. Although he knew his parents would not understand or approve of these interactions, he saw his ability to let his white peers call him the N-word without becoming angry as evidence of individual maturity and social progress.

Kwesi (black) was a tenth-grade student who lived in one of the older housing developments in Jefferson with his younger sister and his parents. His family had moved to the United States from Africa before he was born. His small stature, combined with his recent African heritage, made him a frequent target of racial jokes. Although he got along well with a number of his teachers and wanted badly to do well academically, the social pressures to fit in and the bullying greatly affected him. By the time he was a senior, he had transformed from an inquisitive, eager student who often sat in the front row to one who got in trouble all of the time, was frequently suspended, and ultimately did not graduate with his class. One-on-one, he was one of the most insightful and reflective students I met. He similarly described the importance of white students being "cool enough with" their black peers to call them the N-word:

> You just have to be really cool with the person calling you the N-word, like really, 'cause I don't care if [my white friend] calls me the N-word. He be like, "Okay, nigga," or he be like, "That's what's up," you know, just for show. That's it. But they don't use it often. [You have to] know you're cool with them. If it's a group of random blacks and then some white guy comes up and says, "What's up, niggers?" you're gonna get in trouble. You have to know the person . . . If they come up to you like, "Hey, nigger" and with a serious face, I mean, they're just trying to be racist.

The line between cool enough to use the N-word and not quite cool enough was thin, making engaging in racial humor a risky endeavor that Pamela (black and white) said was "not very clear sometimes." If the white student using the slur had never talked to the black student before, if he or she was perceived as actually biased, or said the word with too much *er* and not enough *a*, there was the possibility of conflict, as seen in the fight that opened this book.

Students like Danny (white) were aware of the fine line they were treading and even admitted being cautious about how they engaged in such behavior:

> I definitely know that there's some [black people] I don't want to say [the N-word] in front of . . . Usually it's easy to tell 'cause they look kind of like they're just thugs and they're ready to kick your ass 'cause you just said the

N-word. Or they'll get really offended or they'll get up in your face, and I don't want to deal with that 'cause I'm a tiny white kid.

Rather than talking about racial humor as evidence that students were getting along across difference, Danny indicated his knowledge of the problematic nature of his comments and the deeply seated biases and stereotypes he held about race. If black students were offended by his use of the N-word, he framed them as "thugs" irrationally attacking a helpless white student. Although he initiated racist slurs, his story was one of white, not black, victimhood.

And yet, despite Danny's supposed fears, he and students like him continued to "test the racial waters." They simply could not resist the temptation of breaking taboos. As Willie (black) framed it, "Some people like to take things far to see how far they can get." There was something thrilling about "tak[ing] a heated subject and mak[ing] it funny, mak[ing] it lighter," said Victoria (black), not only because it challenged traditional notions of what was offensive, racist, and discriminatory, but also because these interactions were inherently all of those things.

For Alena, a popular African American student, it was not so much the "coolness of" the white person or their "coolness with" her that made the exchange of racial slurs acceptable, but rather the coolness of her entire generation. She said she was not offended by the N-word because, "Everybody is pretty much cool nowadays. So you can be like, 'Man, shut your white tail up.' And they be like, 'Okay, blackie.' You know stuff like that, and I think that's cool." Jada (black) had similar feelings:

> I haven't been no slave working on no farm so I just don't feel like I've been offended by [the N-word]. But a lot of black people are like, "They can't call me that, they can't say that, they white, they can't say that." And it's like they try to say, "Well, when we was in slavery . . ." You were never in slavery! Like maybe your ancestors thousands of years ago might have been, but you weren't.

Like so many of her peers, Jada talked about racial oppression as part of a distant and irrelevant past, rather than something that permeated her own daily interactions. The post-racial narrative was strong enough that although, like her ancestors, Jada was being called the N-word openly and publicly by her white peers in a school environment in which black students were more likely to be suspended, expelled, and placed in special education, she viewed her experience as distinctly different. She did not see the use of racial slurs as indicative of continued racial biases or hierarchies that affected students like her.

"THERE'S NO WHITE JOKES"

It was not altogether surprising that students were telling disparaging racial jokes and using racial slurs. The prominence of race in popular media, the racial discourse surrounding the election of President Obama, which happened just before this study began, and the racial history of the region and the United States all shaped the experiences of Jefferson students and their understandings of cross-racial relationships. But the more I overheard white students use the N-word and tell black, Arab, and Mexican jokes, the more it became apparent that something in these exchanges was missing. A nagging question developed in the back of my mind: *Where are the jokes targeting the inadequacies of white people?*

If these jokes had been universal, if they had been exchanged between equals, if students from all racial backgrounds were equally targeted, then perhaps they might have symbolized a kind of racial progress, or at least the beginnings of a conversation in which racial stereotypes were being challenged and called out. However, that was not the case, primarily because, as Danny (white) explained, "There's no white jokes . . . It's weird. There's just absolutely no white jokes."

Most students were completely unaware of the dearth of white jokes until I brought it up. Logan (white) was one of the first people I talked to about this. I asked if he had any examples of white jokes, since students so often told me that jokes at the school went "back and forth." He thought for a while, and then responded, "As bad as it sounds, I've never heard a white joke. I don't know how you can make one, besides calling a white person like, a honky," something that students admitted happened rarely. Lauren (black) agreed: "I haven't heard black people making fun of white people"; as did Salim (Arab): "White jokes? I don't know. I don't got any white jokes." Over the course of the study, student after student said they had not heard, could not think of, and did not make, white jokes.

In the two years I was at Jefferson, I heard only two white jokes. The first Danny (white) told me: "There's one like, what do you call a thousand white people falling down a hill or something? An avalanche. 'Cause they're white and it's snow and they're falling down a hill. Like, that's hilarious." Danny's sarcasm was not hard to catch. According to him, even when the occasional white joke was told, it was not funny, largely because it was not an attack on the character, culture, or morality of white people, but rather on their skin color.

The other focused on white men's athletic ability. Raymond (black) recited it: "'What do you call five white people sitting on a bench?' And they'll be like, 'What?' And we'll say, 'The NBA.' Get it? Five people sitting on the bench? They don't play in the NBA!" While this joke perpetuated a stereotype that white men were physically inferior to black men— that they "can't jump"—it also perpetuated a stereotype about black men's supposed physical prowess which has been used to justify their depiction as "violent thugs."

Beyond these two instances, white people only appeared in racial jokes to illuminate the inferiority of black people. Jada (black) gave an example, "[We might say] well, you white, go be a lawyer. Just something stupid like, go be a lawyer at NYU." The white student would then retort, "You black go rob a liquor store or something like that. And they go back and forth like that."

Black jokes reinforced narratives of black inferiority that have existed since the founding of this country. Fallon, a black student who came from a large two-parent family in which her parents were retired, explained, "We're loud, we were slaves back then, so they have a lot of jokes on us." In contrast, the racial history of the United States is one in which white people have historically held power that the students I interviewed could not figure out how to effectively mock. They believed only "bad" things were funny and they thought only people of color were "bad." Nathan (Asian and white) explained:

Nathan: I feel like because there's a majority of black people [at JHS] and since there's no other racial groups, they just talk about black people.

Shayla: Are there white jokes?

Nathan: Not really.

Shayla: Why not?

Nathan: I feel like this is how jokes start. If a racial group does something and someone else looks at it, they'll make a joke out of it. A majority of people look at white people like, "Oh, they don't do anything [bad]." So if they don't do anything [bad] they can't make a joke out of it. And black people seem to do more crime and do things so [we're] like, "Oh, they're bad." We make jokes about it, that's why there's more. They do more bad things . . . The majority of black jokes that I know, they take something that black people do that no other race does and they make their joke.

Nathan deemed white to be a racially neutral identity. Only the black students were perceived to "have" race, so only they could be made fun of racially. As Paula Rothenberg writes in *White Privilege*, "As long as race is something only applied to non-white people, as long as white people are not racially seen and named, they/we function as a human norm. Other people are raced, we are just people."[4] It was from this position of racial privilege—in which white went unnamed, unseen, and treated as the norm—that one-sided racial jokes emerged.

The fact that there were no white jokes was particularly interesting given the relative class positions of black and white families in the district. Because so many of the white students were poor and lived in trailer parks, it seemed that black students could have easily demeaned their economic positions or places of residence. However, there seemed to be a taboo against disparaging whiteness, regardless of class position. As Beverly Daniel Tatum writes, "What it means to be White is a story of achievement, success, and of being in charge."[5] This story held firm even in a school district in which the majority of white students did not have parents who graduated from NYU or who were lawyers and in which many black families did.

Racial jokes were ultimately rooted in a collective belief in white superiority. Although most crime in the United States is committed by white people, the majority of welfare recipients are white, and the majority of drug users are white, students saw criminality, poverty, and drug usage as inherently black traits—as things that "no other race does." For example, Kwesi (black) explained a joke recited to him by his white friend: "He was like, 'What do you call a white man in a suit? Successful. But what do you call a black man in a suit? At trial.' It's funny because it's 75 percent true." Because Kwesi thought the joke was a fairly accurate reflection of the different social positions black and white men inhabited in the United States, he did not find it problematic. In fact, Kwesi argued that the white perpetrator was, "not trying to be racial," evidenced by the fact that "he has some really racial jokes that he didn't even want to say cause that's racist."

If followed up with a more critical exchange, this joke could have been an opportunity to discuss structural inequality and the unfair criminalization of black men.[6] But there were no spaces in the school or in these students' lives where they had the opportunity to consider things like how the education system, the criminal justice system, the health-care system, and others give white people advantage while denying it to black people and Latinos. As a result, these jokes served to reinforce inaccurate stereotypes in which people of color were made out to be terrorists and criminals. White privilege allowed students to erase the poverty, violence, stupidity, and ignorance, equally present in white populations, and frame these behaviors as inherently "black." It allowed students to claim that these exchanges were in "good fun" and that they went "back and forth" when, in fact, they were only targeted at students of color. These jokes were acceptable not because they were "ridiculous stereotypes" as Raymond (black) argued, but because students believed they were true.

More disturbingly, as Danny alluded to, many of the black jokes students told came from white supremacist websites that JHS students were frequenting. These sites allow people to "enjoy the fun of the lynch mob without moving from their computer."[7] Students at Jefferson were, knowingly or not, a part of this mob.

SHOULD WE BE LAUGHING?

Humor can act as a form of racist rhetoric for serious racism and thus should not always be seen as "just a joke" or as fundamentally harmless.

—Simon Weaver, "Jokes, Rhetoric and Embodied Racism"[8]

Any persons or groups who are the butt of jokes thereby suffer discriminatory treatment and are indirectly being relegated to inferior status.

—John Burma, "Humor as a Technique in Race Conflict"[9]

The majority of students at Jefferson sanctioned the school's hyperracial culture either through their own participation or their tendency to laugh along. However, behind closed doors, many black and white students admitted feeling conflicted. Brandy (black) was one of the highest-achieving students in her class and a star athlete who was offered a number of college scholarships for track. She got along well with her peers, never got into trouble, and had close relationships with many of the staff, teachers, and administrators in the building. When I asked how she felt about racial jokes and slurs, she said:

Brandy: I guess . . . I guess I don't care.
Shayla: But you seem bothered.
Brandy: I am, but I feel like if I show that I care, maybe I'm gonna seem like I'm being a B-word about it, I guess. If other people don't care, I'm just gonna be the odd girl out the bunch.

Brandy's ambivalence was palpable. When reflecting on hearing white people make racial jokes, she said, "Sometimes, I'm like, 'Ugh, you just disgust me. Like why would you . . . where . . . who would tell you this type of joke for you to know this type of joke? Somebody had to make up a joke like this.'" However, she went on to say, "Sometimes it's funny. I think it's good that like you feel comfortable [enough] with somebody [of] a different race that you . . . crack little jokes." When asked what the difference was between racial jokes that were offensive and those that were funny, she said, "The little joke is a nudge and a laugh and you move on to the next subject. A big thing is, 'You want to hear a black joke? You want to hear another one? You want to hear another one? You're black, I'm white, duh, duh, duh, duh.' Like, the longer it carries on, the more tired of it you get."

This distinction indicates that the jokes, as originally told, were problematic; they were simply easier to laugh off in small doses. Ultimately, Brandy said she had been forced to get over being offended, "because it started becoming so common. It was like, I can't stop it, they're gonna do what they do regardless, and I have to be around it every day. So I said if everyone else is cool with it I guess I have no choice but to be." Brandy's resignation revealed the immense pressure in the school to go along with the status quo. The prevalence of racial jokes and slurs wore down the defenses of students of color whose internal barometers told them something was amiss and they were targets.

While the majority of black students were resigned to accept racial humor, some retained their anger about it. This was especially true for black students who had previously attended majority black schools. Dwayne and Shawn had spent their formative schooling years in the nearby major city. Dwayne moved to Jefferson at the beginning of middle school because he often got into trouble at school and his mother wanted to give him a fresh start. He lived in one of the more popular subdivisions in Jefferson with his mother, stepfather, and three younger siblings. Shawn transferred to the district at the beginning of eleventh grade. He had gone to another suburban school the previous year because his mother was dissatisfied with the environment and school system in the city. Like Dwayne, he lived with his mother, stepfather, and a younger sibling. Although Dwayne and Shawn were similar in many ways—race, gender, educational history, city of origin—their connection ended there.

Dwayne was a popular student who struggled academically but excelled socially. He was also fairly well off financially, with access to a car, new clothes, and other material markers of wealth. While he was not a large young man, he was undeniably perceived as intimidating. He did not smile easily or form connections with those different from him, and he had a piercing gaze. To many white students—and teachers—he looked like trouble from a mile away. He was also very homophobic.

Shawn was one of the few openly gay black students at the school. He performed his racial identity much differently than Dwayne. He smiled much more freely and always looked inquisitive and open. Because everyone in his previous high school was also African American, Shawn did not feel the pressure many black Jefferson students felt to dress or act in a certain way in order to prove his racial identity.

For both of these young men, hearing the N-word come from the mouths of white students was shocking, angering, and difficult to understand. Dwayne's reaction was one of rage:

> I know some white people that be saying "nigger." I mean they just say it! I mean, if you say it over here I guess people don't really care, but if you go down to the city and go to the schools I went to and you're a white person and you say that, you going to get your head beat. You going to get beat up. [Here] they [white kids] be like, "What up, my nigger?" I don't know why they calling us that. Nobody going to call me that though, so it don't even matter. Because, I mean, "You white, you know what you did, you know what the slaves did. You know what they used to call us, so why are you still calling me that, 'cause I'm not your slave ?" . . . I mean they can't say nigger to me, cause I'm *not* their nigger.

Dwayne felt that students at Jefferson lacked the racial consciousness that students at his former school had possessed. However, his time in Jefferson ultimately caused him to acquiesce to the cultural norms of the community. When asked how he would respond if white students directed the N-word at him, he said, "I mean, if I was in the city I would've hit him. But if I'm out here, I'm not going to do nothing, because my momma told me not to." In practice, he was no more likely to interrupt white students than black students who had been in Jefferson their whole lives.

Shawn described similar surprise at the ways in which students at Jefferson interacted across race:

> Like the white kids will say "nigger" and the black kids will say "honky." I don't say it, though. I find it sort of degrading, making fun of each of the

races, even though like they're playing, but I don't get into that. It's not something to play about because of the history . . . Like, my fourth-hour class, it's some pretty rough white kids in there . . . It's like, they look like they came from the 'hood, and those white kids will say it and I just find it weird. Like, it's okay. And then the black kids will interact with them saying the word. I can't do it. They interact with them saying the N-word! I don't know, I guess because they grew up with them . . . they really don't care . . . A black kid, he said, "I mean, it's okay. We're friends, we grew up together, so why not?" I guess because I didn't grow up with them and I really don't know them. I still don't think they should use the word.

Unlike students who claimed that the N-word was no longer rooted in any substantive history, both Dwayne and Shawn called on the history of the word as the foundation of their anger. Their time going to majority black schools had given them a very different kind of racial consciousness—arguably a healthier one—than their black exurban counterparts whose integrated schools and communities had taught them to tolerate racially oppressive language.

Students who had moved to Jefferson from out of state were similarly surprised by the racial culture they found in their new school. Robyn (white), who moved to Jefferson her sophomore year after living on the East Coast and in the South, where she had attended schools that were predominantly black and Filipino, said her experience at Jefferson was unique:

> I've noticed up here, like, although everyone says down in the South they're more racist . . . I've noticed there's a lot more racial slurs and racial favoritism, and like people stereotype. They'll stereotype by the way a person talks or the way a person walks or the way they sag their pants. And then . . . like, the white people, they'll make jokes and whatnot towards them [black people] and it's like, "Dude, you don't know them" . . . Like they'll [white kids] say like really mean remarks. Like for instance, "slavery" and like "monkey," and like—you don't say that kind of stuff, ever!

Perhaps because she had been in environments in which people of color were the majority and realities of racism were more easily remembered, Robyn had felt that claiming you were "joking" did not excuse racist comments.

Crystal (black), who had also come to the district from a state in the South, agreed. She said that the boldness of white students at Jefferson was unlike anything she had ever experienced:

Shayla: So did y'all do this kind of stuff at your old school?

Crystal: No, no, no! It was not even, it was not even cool, like for real, for a white person to crack a joke about a black person.

Shayla: So why you think it's different here?

Crystal: I have no idea. I have no clue. It's kind of like—I don't know—I guess 'cause, you know . . . slavery, you know; black people came up here, the white people up here [in the North] were trying to save black people blah, blah, blah. I don't know.

Shayla: So these are different kinds of white folks?

Crystal: Right. These are different white people.

Shayla: What kind of white people are these?

Crystal: These are very brave white people (laughter). Very brave white people.

While Crystal was making many new connections, including dating a white boy, and wished for the world to be a melting pot, she also believed white students in Jefferson were playing with fire.

Dwayne, Shawn, Robyn, and Crystal challenged the narrative that integrated suburban and exurban schools are the ideal places for students of color to learn. Instead, their experiences suggested that within these schools, students of color are being targeted in unique and highly problematic ways.

Many black students were aware of the assaults they faced and struggled to deal with their anger while maintaining Jefferson's dominant postracial narrative. Fallon (black) gave a particularly poignant example when discussing her reaction to discovering her white friends used the N-word when they were in all-white spaces:

I was talking to three white students. I always play with my friends, like, "Oh, that's racist." We just be playing around, and she was, like, "I don't want to sit by you." And I was like, "Oh, so you racist? It's just 'cause I'm black." But then my friend . . . brought up the subject of like, "Oh, what's up, my N?" and all that. And I'm like, "Excuse me?!" I just don't like it when white people say the N-word. It's not right. It doesn't sound right coming out they mouth . . . Because, okay, like back in the day, it was only meant for black people. A nigger, meaning ignorant. So, if you say that, then basically you're calling your friends ignorant. [So] I told my friend, "Don't say that," and he was like, "Oh, I say it all the time." And I was like, "Why would you say that?" and he was like, "I say it all the time." I was like, "No, you don't." He was like, "Yeah, I say it all the time around my friends." I was like, "Say it." He was like, "Nah." I was like, "Why not? You just told me you say it all the time. Why can't you say it around me?" [He said], "Oh, 'cause you're going to hit me." Then I told him that their people used to say that to us back in the day, calling us ignorant and all that stuff, so don't say it now. And I was like, "Just say it now," and he said it real fast, but I didn't catch it, but I told him to say it again and he said, "No." Then the other boy, he said it and I jawed him. I punched him. I punched him in his chest.

Fallon's experience captured the ambivalence of many black students at the school. She was "cool with" white students and engaged in racial joking with them, but was upset when they crossed the line, even though she partially encouraged them to do so. Her response was equally confounding. She told her white friend she was angry, while laughing along, then punched him. It was clear that black students were struggling with how to make sense of their relationships across race in an environment where attacks on their racial identity were regular occurrences.

DON'T BE TOO SENSITIVE

Although many students were bothered by racial humor, they almost never interrupted or challenged what was happening. Both Brandy (black) and Willie (black) related instances in which they failed to interrupt racial humor because they did not want to be perceived as being overly sensitive. Brandy told the following story about feeling immobilized when a white student used the N-word toward a group of black students:

I know this one [white] girl—she's really cool, I love her to death, but one day she came up to a group of African American students, we were in a circle, and she came up to us and she said, "What's up, my N's?" and I guess it took us a minute to realize what she had just said and we kind of all just looked at each other, and then we looked at her like, "Did you really just say that?" And, I don't know, I guess we really didn't want to fight, beat her up or nothing, but we didn't know what to say. We didn't want to seem like, old school and say, you know, "Don't say it." It seems like we should have said something—and we all should have like said, "No, that's not cool, you took it too far," but we didn't. It was weird.

Although all of the African American students were offended by the white students' use of the N-word, none of them felt comfortable expressing their feelings. They were more concerned with protecting the feelings of cool *why is that?* white students who engaged in offensive behavior than protecting their own. While Brandy ultimately concluded that she should have "said something," her initial perception of her options was to either do nothing or fight. She could not conceive of having a conversation with her classmate to express her concern. Since black students were not prone to physically attacking students from different racial backgrounds, their default response was silence.

Willie also struggled to navigate how he should intervene when white students engaged in racial humor. He said, "I feel like I should say something, but then I feel like they'll just say, 'Oh, I'm just kidding,' or 'I'm just *don't know* playing' . . . I feel I shouldn't or it's not that serious or something." If white *how to approach* students claimed to be joking when they used racial slurs or made derogatory *conversation* tory racial comments, black students felt they had no recourse—they also *about it* had to find humor in these interactions or, as Brandy put it, they would seem like they were stuck in a racial past that "cool" white students had supposedly moved beyond.

I pushed Willie to consider what would happen if he said something. He responded, "I don't know. If I said anything to them like, 'That offends me,' or 'That offends people,' I think they wouldn't say it or do it anymore." When asked why he didn't try this method, since he seemed to think it would be effective, he said, "I don't know." Brandy and Willie knew they did not like these interactions, but did not feel they had the power, skill, or efficacy to interrupt them.

Even white students struggled with how to intervene in racial humor. A number reported that when they challenged racial humor, their white peers were defensive. Madison (white) said she had attempted to interrupt her white peers who used racial slurs, to little avail. She recalled an incident in which she asked a white friend not to use the N-word around her, "He said that I am not his boss and he can say whatever he wants to say."

In general, those who were offended by racial humor, rather than those who were the perpetrators, were seen as the problem.[10] Students were expected to brush things off, to assume nothing was a big deal, and to find humor in denigration, especially when it was targeted at those who had historically been marginalized. This made it very difficult to challenge racial humor in a way that did not negatively reflect on individuals who couldn't "take a joke." As Bethany (white) explained, "I don't think anything is racist. Nothing in the world. Like, who's actually being serious about something like that these days? . . . They're just jokes. Laugh. There's no reason to be offended and if you are offended, sorry. Like, why were you here?"

While Danny (white) acknowledged that some people were offended by his comments, he saw this as an individual shortcoming." Yeah, definitely, a lot of people get offended," he said." I just don't associate with those people 'cause it's an . . . irrational thing . . . 'cause they shouldn't get offended at it. I'm obviously not serious. I obviously don't want to kill black people. I'm just making a joke . . . They take things too seriously."

A number of scholars have found that humor that disparages people based on race has negative social impact.[11] As Mark Ferguson and Thomas Ford argue, "By making light of the expression of prejudice, disparagement humor communicates a message of tacit approval or tolerance of discrimination against members of the targeted group."[12] Others have found that racial humor is often the serious expression of bias on behalf of racially intolerant individuals and groups.[13] Despite the claims of jokers, humor is not devoid of hatred, nor is hatred devoid of humor. Rather, Michael Billig contends, there is "an intrinsic link between extreme political hatred and the realm of jokes."[14] Humor often provides cover for racists who can "be brave without acting. They can be murderers in their imagination."[15]

By re-appropriating racism as humor, students were pushing the boundaries of acceptability. Leon Rappoport calls this experience the "joy of transgression"—an act that "gives us license to be spontaneously bad, to violate the rules of conventional morality . . . like the feeling of joyous abandon one may have when jumping fully clothed into a mud bath."[16] He suggests that humor of this nature could provide a mental break in otherwise serious efforts toward equity and justice. However, students at Jefferson did not have another realm in which they were trying to "make the world a better place." They were not having more reflective conversations about race and bias with their teachers, parents, or peers. Nor were they engaged in an equitable exchange in which ". . . minority groups also enjoy a great deal of . . . jokes aimed at the mainstream majority."[17] Instead, in this rapidly changing, racially diverse, exurban context, there were no white jokes and there was no social justice project.

When Jefferson students said that "everyone got along" or that they were "beyond race," they meant they were a part of a generation in which white people had permission to say biased, bigoted, prejudiced, discriminatory, and oppressive things with smiles on their faces and people of color did not have permission to be offended by it. White students had both the privilege of not having to admit the racial prejudice they were perpetuating and of getting to determine whether or not the students of color they were targeting were responding to these attacks rationally. They could make offhand remarks about wanting to kill black people and then accuse the black people upset by these remarks of being overly sensitive. The burden of being "beyond race" was on the backs of students of color. If they could not find humor in these hierarchical, hyperracial interactions, it was their problem for being stuck in the past. White people had moved on, ironically, by perpetuating racist narratives through humor.

The negative racial culture of Jefferson's students did not form in a bubble. It was not the product of Jefferson alone. Rather, it was developed and cultivated by young people from diverse backgrounds with various experiences who, like all Americans, were wrestling with the continuing dilemma of "the color line."[18]

From 1990 to 2010, Jefferson grew exponentially. Families moved into the district from all over the state and country looking for bigger homes, better schools, and safer neighborhoods. When placed in an integrated public school environment, these students—some who had been in Jefferson all of their lives, many who had not—collectively developed norms of behavior about what would and would not be acceptable, which words could and could not be said, and what kinds of racial jokes were and were not funny. Students from a range of backgrounds, from racially liberal families and from racially conservative ones, found themselves engaging in hyperracial behavior—making a little joke, acquiescing to the request of a peer to "test out" the N-word, laughing along at the drawing of a bomb on a chalkboard next to the name of an Arab student. "Diversity" unmediated led to both increased interactions across difference and increased opportunities for the perpetuation of discrimination and conflict.

CHAPTER TWO

Racial Performance

It is now commonly accepted by scientists that race is not biological in the ways we have historically believed. Recent analyses of human DNA have revealed that there is as much genetic variation within racial groups as between them. Although race is not biologically "real," it remains very real socially and culturally. One reason is because of the ways in which race is performed. How we speak, dress, walk, talk, and act are all a part of cultural traditions that have been racialized. These performances of race have been assigned value in our society, a place in a hierarchy in which some are generally interpreted as good and others as bad. As John Hartigan writes, "By starting with basic cultural dynamics, it is easy to show how race both inflects and is shaped by judgments Americans make about whether or not certain people appear to be nice, or friendly, or hardworking."[1]

In the U.S. racial hierarchy, the speech patterns, styles, and ways of being that are predominantly associated with African Americans and Latinos are generally regarded as problematic, unprofessional, or dangerous and used to justify discrimination and oppression. In contrast, cultural performances often associated with white people are seen as normal, ideal, and the standard against which everyone else is measured.

Racial identities are culturally performed by those within a racial group, and are also interpreted by observers outside of the group. Erving Goffman

[handwritten margin notes: "how race is performed"; "black? latino vs white cultural performance"; "cultural meanings"]

51

conceptualizes these differences as *expression* and *impression*—"the expression that [one] *gives*, and the impression that [one] *gives off*."[2] Similarly, Carla O'Connor distinguishes between *reflection* and *refraction*—how individuals experience their own identities versus how they "experience social identity as a consequence of how others . . . make sense of and, subsequently respond" to them.[3] These works suggest that race is as much about how individuals self-identify as how they are identified by others.

At Jefferson, students had very clear ideas of how they should perform their racial identities and distinct opinions about the racial performances of those from other groups. Black students thought of themselves as "hype," a positive term that conveyed a commitment to having fun, being silly, and displaying cultural richness. They told me that in comparison, their white peers were "lame" and "boring." In contrast, the white students I spoke with often viewed their black peers as "loud" and "obnoxious," and saw themselves as calmer and well mannered.

These cultural performances served as both symbols of racial difference and sites of racial conflict. While both groups agreed that black students were the social center of the school and the markers of "coolness," white students' interpretations of racial performance held more weight. Black students' positive explanations of their behavior—the ways in which they viewed their cultural performances as capital[4]—did not buy them much in the larger school narrative, even among themselves. Instead, differences in racial performance reinforced notions of black inferiority and cycles of racial prejudice in the minds of white and black students alike.

ACTING BLACK

The majority of literature on racial identity performance in secondary schools has focused on how "acting white" affects academic achievement for black students. These works have been primarily concerned with proving or debunking the theory that black underachievement is a response to the fear of being labeled "white."[5] More recently, scholars have attempted to disentangle cultural performance and academic achievement.[6] In her

[handwritten margin note: how view themselves & how others view them @ Jefferson]

book *Keepin' It Real*, Prudence Carter argues that "'acting black,' 'acting Spanish,' or 'acting white' connotes more about perceived ethno-racial cultural styles and tastes than about an opposition to education . . ."[7] Similarly, students at Jefferson used the terms *acting white* and *acting black* to signal cultural performance and group belonging, rather than academic achievement or intelligence. Black students at Jefferson were largely unconcerned with what it meant to "act white" or with whether or not they were at risk of doing so. They had given much more thought to what it meant to embody blackness.

"Cool"

When asked to describe how those from different racial groups dressed, behaved, spoke, and acted, students at Jefferson always started by describing "black kids." They said black kids had a kind of cultural swagger that made non-black students envious. As Harrison (white) put it, "[Black kids] tend to dictate what the popularity curve is." Similarly, Brielle (black and white) believed, "People rather be black than white. I know I would rather be black than white. I don't know, I just think that black people have a certain beauty . . . I know a lot of white people that want to be black just cause it's . . . the hot thing." Marcus (black) succinctly explained that African Americans were cooler than whites, "'cause we are. Like, we just are."

[margin annotation: black "cultural swagger" is "cooler"]

The social prominence of black students was evident in the pool of candidates who decided to run for homecoming court. In the 2009–10 school year, although almost 60 percent of students were white, only three white students campaigned for homecoming queen, compared with eight black students. It was also clear in students' estimations of the racial demographics of their school. Most white students thought the black population was larger than it actually was. For example, Harrison (white), said, "In this school I feel like there is a lot more black kids than there are other students. I feel like they're the majority of the school." Brittany (white), who had previously lived in an all-white community, estimated that 70 percent of the students at Jefferson were black. When she realized she had overestimated by 35 percent she said, "I thought there was more

African American than there were white, maybe because I don't really see everyone. When I first came here I was, like, 'Oh my word, there's so many [more] black people than white people here.' Like, I wasn't used to it, you know."

Charles Gallagher's 2003 study found that white people often over-estimate the number of black people in social and institutional settings. White people are accustomed to living in a world in which they see themselves represented frequently in media, in positions of power, in the work-place, and in schools. As a result, when white people are in integrated spaces, racial difference becomes hypervisible in a way that Gallagher found "breeds ignorance, hostility, and discrimination toward racial minorities."[8] This was particularly true at Jefferson, where a minority of black students were seen as the face of the school and racial prejudice flourished.

"Hype"

Black students commonly used the adjective "hype" to describe their ra-cial performances in hallways, classrooms, and lunchrooms. According to Shantel (black), black kids "just like to have fun. Like, they just like to play around and joke with their friends and stuff." Hype was something that black students performed communally. You could not be hype alone. As Brielle (black and white) described, "I think black people feed off other black people. So like if one person's hyped, then they all get hyped."

"Hypeness" was particularly apparent in the schools' two cafeterias, one of which was original to the building, and commonly thought of as the "white" cafeteria, the other added as part of a more recent renovation, and commonly thought of as the "black" one. Stella (black) explained, "When I first came here, the first thing I was told during lunchtime was, 'The new end is the hype cafeteria.'" According to Farrah (black), "The black cafeteria, like that's like the cafeteria to be in. It's always fun in there. And the old is, like, not. The gothics and, like, the white kids and the preppies and all that go to the old one." Marcus (black) agreed that when it came to cafeterias, "basically all the 'lame' people go to the old lunch and all of the cool people go to the new lunch." He described the "lame" people as the "typical punk rock, band geeks." Pamela (black and white) similarly referred to the old cafeteria as "like the weird one where all the rejects go." Or, as Louis (black and white) put it, "I guess all the like really popular kids and stuff eat in that new side and then all the kids who aren't so popular eat in the old." Inherent in this assessment was that by nature of being black, students were cooler, more popular, and more likely to eat in the new, hype cafeteria.

The hypeness of black students was also present in many other spaces within the school. Alena was a very popular African American student. She smiled a lot, talked quickly, had an infectious laugh, and was a self-described "class clown." While teachers generally found her amusing, they were also annoyed by her inability to be quiet or stay in her seat. She said "[Black students] make a party wherever we go." She found this to be especially true when compared with white students."We're just [more alive], we just have more [life] in us," she said. Alena gave an example of the dichotomy between the hypeness of black students and the boring-ness of white ones: "A class meeting, have you been to one of those?" she asked one day when we were chatting. I nodded that yes, I had been at the most recent meeting." You saw it for yourself!" she continued."The whole middle row was black, and what were we doing? Talking the whole time! Everybody else was quiet."

Because there were more white students in the school, many black students felt Jefferson lacked energy and liveliness. According to Denise (black), "We always say our class is so 'lame', 'cause like when we go to our meetings, it's mostly the white people who are the laid-back ones. And so it's like they don't want to get hype with us. So it's like, 'We're so lame.'" Black students frequently categorized the places where they were dominant as exciting and cool, and spaces that were white-dominated as boring and uninteresting. While some black students believed their white peers were more likely to achieve mainstream success—for example, by becoming lawyers and doctors—they saw their potential futures as more culturally rich, more colorful, more stimulating, more fun.

[handwritten margin note: different views on where their lives will go & what success is]

[handwritten in margin: how white students view black students' "hype"]

Obnoxious

Many white students saw the hypeness of their black classmates as a negative trait. White students wanted to be seen as cool by their black peers and wanted to be "cool enough with them" to engage in racial joking; however, they also thought that when black students acted hype by "rapping in the middle of class or in the hallways and . . . getting loud and like dancing," as Robyn (white) described, or "bouncing up and down," as Madison (white) described, they were being "loud and obnoxious."

According to Madison (white), "A lot of white people think that black people are just, they're just ignorant and they're just loud and crazy and stuff like that . . ." Molly (white) said while she sometimes found it "funny when [black kids] do stuff in the hallways, it gets frustrating when I'm in class, and I feel they're being really obnoxious." Danny (white) explained that this was a common sentiment among white students." Sometimes white people find black people annoying," he said." The way they act and like the popular culture and all that. Just like the loud ghetto music walking down the hallways being really loud and kind of just like you're the boss and stuff."

Some black youth were particularly bothersome to some of their white classmates in the hallways. There were a few hallway junctions in the school that got especially crowded during passing periods. Many white students believed the reason for this congestion was that, as Leah (white) explained, "a lot of the black kids tend to just like congregate in masses like around this one spot, and it's like hard to get through to get to class." Logan (white) was especially annoyed by black students "just like doing stupid stuff in the middle of the hall. Just standing in the middle of the hall. That's the worst thing that bothers me is just standing right in the middle of the hall . . . Just hanging out and chillin' in like a big circle. I just don't think they like care. They just talking to everybody and they don't realize what they're doing."

While it was true that black students often socialized in larger groups than white students, most white students admitted that in general black students did not purposely block hallways, nor did they do anything particularly bad or "stupid" when standing in them. I once observed a group of thirteen black male and female students gathered in the hallway between second and third periods. Some were sitting on a bench while others stood over them talking. They were not loud or disruptive in any way.

Nonetheless, many white students struggled to rein in harsh judgments of their black peers—even in cases in which they admitted that white students behaved similarly. Matt (white) explained:

> Like some of the [white] kids, we call the black people slow 'cause they block the hallways. But at the same time, like we don't have any room to talk 'cause I'm pretty sure there's a lot of us that do the same thing. But like, when . . . they're like being loud or obnoxious or like acting cocky, like, you know, just singing along and acting mad, like even though we do the exact same things, it's like we kinda develop more of an annoyance and . . . we kind of like group them together as "the black people," as jumping, loud, and arrogant and obnoxious.

[margin note: student recanting stereotype]

Matt's comments highlighted how racial bias and cultural performance map onto each other. The ways in which black and white students acted in the hallways were often not so different, yet when black students stood in groups and talked—perhaps loudly, perhaps not—they were viewed as collectively deficient in ways that white students were not. Often, it seemed that it was the very presence of black students that white students found annoying, not their specific behavior. Interestingly, Matt described his own idea of fun in ways that sounded very similar:

[margin note: us vs. them mentality]

> I'm white. Like, what we consider as funny is like, you know, um, overreacting, shouting. Or at least in my group, we overreact, we shout, we overexaggerate things and we just bullshit each other . . . It's kinda making fun of each other. It's like poking fun and just like adding on top of it until it gets to a point where it's completely ludicrous and sounds stupid.

Black students were not oblivious to how their white peers viewed them. Some worried that their modes of interaction led to problematic depictions of blackness. Fallon (black) said, "Some of us, our black people, we overdo it too much by being loud and all that stuff. We need to calm that down. We have other people looking at us different and stuff. Like for me when I see a loud [black] person I [am] like, he just embarrassing our race, making us look bad." Black students like Hampton acknowledged that while "not a bad thing," these performances "help the white people make stereotypes." For black students, hypeness was both a source of pride and a site of embarrassment and misbehavior. Black students were constantly balancing their desire to have fun with their awareness that the ways in which many decided to do so were inherently problematic in the eyes of their white peers.

"Ghetto," "Gangster"

> We had a class meeting yesterday after school and like—I don't want to say it's like—it's pretty much the Brittany (white) group . . . [She's] class president . . . And they're like . . . it was an open meeting, and I hear Katie (white) and Brittany (white) and Riley (white) talking. They're like, "We shouldn't have made this meeting open. Like it's so ghetto in here right now and everybody just won't shut up. We should have just kept this to ourselves." I'm like, "What are you talking about? We're a class. We need to do things together," and I was really mad she said it was ghetto [because] there were two sides of the room, like it was super divided. There was the Brittany group and . . . there were like a lot of African American students . . . they were trying to get their points across and like she is sitting on the left side of the room and she pointed her hand towards the right side where all the black students were. She's like, "It's so ghetto in here," and I'm like "Did that girl just . . . ?" I caught myself, I caught myself, I didn't start nothing . . . I silenced myself . . . 'cause I knew if I said something . . .
>
> —Jasmine, black student

The subtext of many comments about black students being "loud" and "obnoxious" was that black youth in Jefferson were perceived as "ghetto." This perception was largely rooted in stereotypes and biases rather than actual realities of poverty. As Benedict Anderson writes in *Imagined Communities*, "Communities are to be distinguished, not by their falsity/genuineness, but by the style in which they are imagined."[9] At Jefferson, black youth writ large were imagined as, and imagined themselves to be,

[margin handwritten note: black students being "loud" & "obnoxious" = ghetto by white students]

urban, poor, 'hood, and gangster, despite their parents' relatively high incomes and their newly constructed two-story homes.

Riley (white), a student who had been in the district her entire life, said her white peers frequently talked about black kids at Jefferson as ghetto: "[White] people say like, 'Oh, that person is black, they're not good, they're a ghetto.'" Logan (white) described what it meant to be ghetto: "Just saggy pants and talking with a slang and acting loud and obnoxious." Ghetto was connected to how you spoke, how you acted, the music you listened to, what you wore and how you wore it.

According Jasmine (black), *ghetto* was "a common word that gets associated with loud and black. Like loud and black usually equals ghetto. Ghet-toe," she sounded out. She said ghetto people did things like:

> Talk about eating fried chicken all the time, just like things usually associated with loud, ghetto black people. Like just talking about ghetto things like, "Oooh, I got to go home and take my tracks [hair weave] out, girl," like stuff . . . that you don't share. Like walk around with big ol' bags of chips and two liters [of pop], coming to school with a head scarf on, and pajamas, knowing you're about to get sent home for [breaking the dress code] and just be like, "Ya'll just doing this because I'm black!"

Ghetto was simultaneously affiliated with being overly materialistic and so unconcerned with social conventions that you were willing to come to school in pajamas. Ghetto students shared what Michael Herzfeld calls "cultural intimacies"—those facets of identity that at once informed ingroup solidarity and caused embarrassment when viewed by those beyond the group.[10] In short, *ghetto* meant failing to behave in ways that were aligned with white, middle-class norms, and doing so publicly.

Ghetto was not a label reserved for a select group of impoverished black youth. White students viewed black students collectively as ghetto— even those whose parents were well-off financially. Brittany (white), the senior class president whom Jasmine spoke of in the opening quote, said when she first got to Jefferson, "I kind of judged [the black students]. I kind of thought they were ghetto. Like in the hallways, they like be singing or something, and then I see like everyone wearing that sag in their pants . . . and I'm like, 'Oh my word.' Like I never like saw it before, you know."

Ironically, in order to read as ghetto in Jefferson, one could not *actually* be poor. To be ghetto, students had to have enough disposable income to wear the latest name-brand clothing—like South Pole, Baby Phat, and Rocawear—which was generally quite expensive. Black students who were unable to afford these clothes were considered "lames" and "nobodies"— like white students. Nonetheless, white students often described their ghetto black classmates who wore these expensive clothes as "dressing poor," by which they meant "dressing black." As Harrison (white) said, "They're not poor, but they dress and act like it. Why? I don't understand it." He was aware that many of his black peers came from economically stable homes. However, he read their styles, which were different than his, as reflective of a lower-class position.

The inability of white students to separate black style from poor style was particularly notable because it suggested that blackness was not only a racial identity, it was also a class marker.[11] Despite the fact that so many of the white students struggled financially—even Brittany's family almost lost their home to foreclosure during this study—and so many of the black students did not, middle-class status was reserved for whites.[12]

On one hand, many of the white students I spoke with viewed their black peers as ghetto writ large. But they were also highly critical of their black peers for being "fake wannabes," who they felt were only pretending to be ghetto. Gwen (white) said some black students talked about being in gangs: "They talk like the Bloods and the Crips and they have these hand signs, and it's like you're not even part of them! They're probably middle-class [and] are living in, you know, nice houses." Curtis (white) was annoyed, almost to the point of anger, by what he perceived to be inauthentic performances of identity. He said that many black students:

> try to act hard and ghetto when they live next to a farm. I mean, come on now, you live right by . . . corn. You have a cornfield! Look out your window, there's a cornfield right there! . . . You're not ghetto, dude, so don't act like it. I mean, they're being stupid. And I hate people that act like that. That aggra-

[handwritten margin note: blackness = class marker]

vates me . . . Trying to act like you're someone you're not. Like they're from the 'hood or something. Like they live in complete poverty when they don't.

The deep aggravation Curtis expressed was common among white students at Jefferson. For example, Ed was a lower-income white student, although he thought of his family as fairly well off because they lived in the country on a large plot of land, worked on old cars, and had four-wheelers. He was a popular athlete who was praised by teachers as a "good egg" but he struggled academically and had a history of disciplinary issues. He described black students in Jefferson as:

> just a lot of people who think they're gangsters and stuff, like a lot of wannabes. They play the part of a gang and stuff and they get out in the streets and they start acting like that and they meet a real gangster and then they're just nothing, and they get scared. A lot of people claim they are [in gangs, but] like who's gonna let a sixteen-year-old kid in a gang? I mean, it happens, but I just think that we're out in the sticks pretty much.

Laughing, he described them as "stick gangs."

But even as many white students described the ghetto and gangster personas of their black classmates as "fake," they also assumed these very identities were innate to their black peers. For example, although Logan (white) was annoyed by his "wannabe" black classmates, he said, "once [middle-class black kids] come here, they just turn into this ghetto wannabe thug at this school." He gave an example of Trevor (black), an A-student who came from a two-parent home in which his mother was working on her PhD: "Trevor's got money. I know he does. I've been in his house. It's nice—with white carpet, glass. When his mom comes in the school, 'cause she does sometimes, he just sits there and does his work. He's not his normal self, [which is] just like a normal black kid here, just ghetto, wannabe ghetto." Logan was frustrated that Trevor did not act like "himself" when his mother was around because he believed that being ghetto was "normal black." He did not consider that how Trevor behaved with his mother was as authentic as his school persona. Moreover, he did not see Trevor's high academic performance, his mother's involvement in his education, or his nice house as evidence that Trevor was something more than ghetto. All he attended to was Trevor's style of dress and his hype persona, even though he denigrated these as "wannabe."

White students were not completely erroneous in their assessments of their black peers. Some black students lived up to these cultural stereo-types of being "ghetto" and wannabe gangsters, particularly a number of black male students who felt pressured by norms of race and masculin-ity to adopt a "gangster posture."[13] Scholars have long noted the ways in which black male youth sometimes take on a "cool pose"[14] to cope with how they are marked as "inferior, deviant, or dysfunctional" by the main-stream.[15] Kaleem (black) said this gangster posture was exhibited by some black students "going around, you just [like], 'Man, I'm the hardest nigga here.'" Some even claimed to be gang members. However, most students at Jefferson did not take gangs very seriously. Dwayne (black) explained, "I mean, some people will be saying they Bloods, Crips, and all that junk. To me, I think it's fake, 'cause I don't see nobody doing nothing. People walk down this hallway with a blue flag and a red flag, and they might be friends."

In addition to the friendships across "gangs," black students cited the lack of gang violence as evidence that they were not particularly sig-nificant. Kaleem compared the supposed gang members at Jefferson to those from his previous high school in another state. He observed that, at Jefferson, it was hard for him to take gangs seriously because they "don't have guns, you know." His assessment of the gang phenomenon was that there were simply, "a lot of fake people, especially the black kids. Like some of them like to act tough and stuff like that. They act fake, just to get along and stuff." As these remarks reveal, most black youth were not actually "hardcore"; they were just "hardcore wanna-be" or "hardcore enough" to convince their white peers.[16]

Some scholars have argued that black students in integrated middle-class communities may be particularly at risk of feeling pressure to act "hard" because they are in an environment in which they are seen as in-ferior and in which they are in the minority numerically.[17] Black youth in

"wannabe gangsters"

Jefferson were part of a new generation of upwardly mobile African Americans trying to find authentic racial identities. But their models were often the most stereotypical versions of blackness—what they saw on TV, what they heard in music, the content of the jokes that were told at school—in which black youth were presented as poor, tough, and dangerous. And so they became all of these things. While these cool poses and gangster postures may have been "fake" to some extent, to students in Jefferson they nonetheless denoted a lower-class black cultural identity that reinscribed racial biases within the school.

CULTURAL RACISM

Although many white students made harsh jokes about their peers of color, used racial slurs, and negatively judged their black peers for being ghetto, they claimed it was not black *people* they disliked, rather it was their *culture*—the "obnoxious," "loud," "gangster" ways black youth spoke, dressed, and acted. Many white students believed strongly that it was wrong to judge people by the "color of their skin," but ultimately felt it was acceptable to discriminate against the label on their shirts, a kind of bias Eduardo Bonilla-Silva calls *cultural racism.*[8]

Brittany (white) explained racial bias among her white peers: "If the black people are wearing the nice clothes too, then they're okay . . . [I]f there was like a loud black kid and he wore Hollister [a clothing brand more likely to be worn by white students] . . . I'm pretty sure no one will be racist against him. But if he started . . . sagging his pants and wearing those do-rags and putting in a gold tooth—you know what I'm saying— then they'd probably be racist."

Interestingly, the styles Brittany pointed to as causes of racism among students were almost totally fabricated. In two years at Jefferson, I never observed a black student wearing a do-rag or a gold tooth. In fact, the only tangible difference between a "nice" Hollister, Abercrombie, or Aeropostale T-shirt that a white student might wear and the T-shirts most black students wore was the brand printed on the front. Yet these very stereotypical depictions, which she more likely got from television than the suburban black students in her school, were what Brittany used to justify the prejudice of white students.

Matt (white) used similar criteria to dismiss his white classmates' anti-black biases:

> A lot of times I've heard like, "I hate black people" [from white people]. But like I understand. They don't hate them because they're black, they hate them because they're loud. It's not because they're black most of the time, 'cause I'm pretty sure there's some hardcore racist people here. But from what I've heard or from what I've interpreted, it's just, they just hate them because they're loud and they're annoying.

Most white students I spoke to believed that if only black students were quieter, wore different clothes, and did not act so obnoxious and ghetto, they would not be viewed negatively. Brittany and Matt's perspectives illuminated that black students had to erase virtually all cultural traces of their blackness to be held in high regard by many of their white peers. They could not escape racial bias unless they became "white." Because most black students were unwilling to do this,[19] white students told me, it was acceptable to dislike them.

[handwritten margin note: White students only liked black students who were "whitewashed"]

INTERNALIZED RACISM

Cultural racism was not the purview of white students alone. Many black students exhibited internalized racism as well. They believed black people were culturally deficient, and thus inherently deserving of prejudice. Fallon (black) observed: "[Black people] are bad. Well, I think everybody knows black people are bad . . . Always selling weed, stealing stuff, shooting, killing people . . . Like on the news, you see like a black person they killed a white person. Now you see, I bet you they whole [white] family probably racist now." Fallon said she witnessed the deficiencies of black people every day at school; "[Black students at Jefferson] are loud, they're bad, and they always getting in trouble . . . I don't know why. It seems like the white people is like calm . . . Like half of the people in this school

[handwritten margin note: not representative in the media]

that are getting suspended and, you know . . . ISS [in-school suspension] and getting written up, and stealing is mostly black people." Willie (black) agreed that black students caused more trouble in the school: "If you think about it, it's mainly the black kids doing something wrong."

Fallon and Willie's observations were not inaccurate. They were based on the fact that racial disparities in discipline were so stark at Jefferson they had been investigated by the American Civil Liberties Union. The resulting report confirmed that black students were significantly more likely to be suspended and expelled than their white counterparts.

However, while Fallon and Willie were right about these measurable outcomes, their analyses did not fully reflect the causes. Researchers have repeatedly found that bias significantly contributes to racial disparities in discipline. For example, Edward Morris's study of white students in a majority-black school found that race mediated discipline in ways that systematically disadvantaged students of color: "Race and gender in this case triggered some educators to interpret white boys as docile and appropriate and black and Latino boys as irascible and aggressive even when both exhibited similar behavior and dress." He found that for teachers of all racial backgrounds, "black and Latino boys received the strictest and most persistent discipline."[20]

Unfortunately, Fallon and Willie did not have this critical perspective, nor was there any place within Jefferson's environment in which they were invited to think about the causes of the racial trends they witnessed. As a result, they believed that if black students got in trouble more than white students, it was their own fault; and if white students negatively judged them, it was deserved. The irony was that white kids were obnoxious too. They were bad. But when they were bad, it had a different impact and came with different consequences.

"WHITE KIDS ARE BAD TOO"

Lots of times, I find that the white kids are just as bad. I think it really depends . . . You can say some black kids are rambunctious, but you can say some white kids are . . . just as disrespectful as any black person.

So I don't think it's really fair to say it's only black kids who are out of control . . .

—Winnie, black and white student

Some black students were more disruptive than their white peers. This was especially true in classrooms that were majority African American. Although there were significantly more white students in the school, tracking and student choice in courses resulted in some classes being disproportionately black. On more than one occasion, I witnessed black students in these classes behaving in ways that seemed inappropriate. For example, in one of Ms. Davis's (white) classes, which was about half white and half black, black students playfully yelled across the room at each other. One student in particular was a ringleader. He repeatedly made jokes and side comments to his peers. After the class was over, Ms. Davis told me that when black students behaved as this particular group had, it was easy for white people to think, "See, this is how *they* are." She reported that a couple of her white students had approached her after class to complain about the distracting behavior of their black classmates.

However, the feeling among white students and teachers that "those kids" were the problem obscured the ways in which white youth were also bad. There were many examples during my time at Jefferson of white students behaving in "loud," "rowdy," and "obnoxious" ways that were very similar to the black students they criticized. Some of the most glaring examples took place in a different hour of Ms. Davis's class in which black students were not in the majority. I observed two white male students loudly making fun of a black male student. The first white boy said, "Yeah, the person we're talking about is stupid!" and then laughed. When I asked him if someone was sitting in the chair behind him so that I could have a seat he responded, "Naw, girl!" and waved his hand jokingly, trying to sound like a black girl. The second white boy turned to me and said sarcastically, "If you're doing a study of how students are behaving in this class, I just want to say that I'm the best student here . . . And write in your notes that [the first white boy] is stupid." The first white student then got up and walked across the room to show his cell phone to a third white male student who was sleeping in the front row. He kept walking around the room while the two white male students in the back of the class laughed at him. He was clearly putting on a show for them. Through all of his antics, the teacher did not say anything to him. Finally, this student announced loudly, "I need to clear my mind!" stood up, and started packing his bag although class was not yet over. The second white student said loudly enough for the whole class to hear, "and your bowels!"

As both of these cases reveal, neither class was one in which there was a lot of order. Small groups of both white and black students, particularly boys, regularly treated class as a time to joke around, socialize, and amuse themselves and their peers. However, only the black students warranted comments from the teacher and their peers about their behavior.

shouldnt teach they teachers about their biases to try to prevent this from happening

Students also gave many examples of "bad" white kids. For example, Kaleem (black) reported:

> In our class we have a lot of Caucasian kids. They just like are nuts, you know. They drive the teacher nuts, and I try to tell them to listen and then sometimes I be getting along with them and we be ganging up on the teacher and stuff like that. They don't listen, they always talking, their iPod on, and they be making stupid noises . . . They're always late to class and they don't really care.

While Kaleem admitted that he occasionally joined in with his white peers, he felt that white students were responsible for the majority of classroom disruption. Brandy (black) expressed similar feelings. She said, "I don't act up, but I know it's a few Caucasian kids that act up, such as Marissa. She cusses, she's always talking loud, disrupting the class. In [another] class, these two white boys they're always just talking, disrupting, disrespecting [the teacher]." Brandy said white youth generally did not get in trouble for their behavior. *this means students are aware of their differential treatment*

Students consistently reported that the most glaring difference between the behavior of black and white students was that when white kids misbehaved, they were more likely to get away with it. Logan (white) was a good example of the ways in which middle-class whiteness made misbehavior permissible. I was motivated to talk to him because I frequently saw him wandering the hallways during class time. I asked him on several occasions why he was not in class, and he always flashed a big smile and delivered a witty comeback. One day, he confessed, "I get to do whatever I want in this school." He explained:

> I have this school wrapped around my finger. I feel like I can do anything here . . . [I can] leave school when I want. Skip when I want. Walk around the school when I want. I mean when I'm hungry I [leave], or when I want to go home, I go. I [can] walk in from Wendy's or something.

Although Jefferson was a closed campus—students were not allowed to leave during the school day—Logan said that he came and went as he pleased. Moreover, he claimed that teachers and administrators were aware of his behavior.

On one occasion I saw Logan wear a hat all day long, a violation of the dress code that regularly resulted in disciplinary action for black students. When I asked him about the hat at the end of the day, he said not one teacher had asked him to take it off. In fact, he claimed that some adults in the building facilitated his freedom by giving him money to buy them lunch and covering for him when he skipped other classes. Logan acknowledged that his race and class gave him privilege to break school rules without consequence:

Logan (white): Black kids, I would say, get in a lot more trouble than white kids. I would say so, in some classes that I've been in. Like the black kids get picked on more for doing wrong stuff. Like a black kid does something wrong and you get yelled at. And then the white kid does the same thing wrong and then he gets like, "What are you doing?" . . . and like jokingly . . .

Shayla: Are these like wealthy black kids, middle-class black kids, poor black kids?

Logan: There's definitely higher-end black kids [too] . . . They're watched more . . . is what I think it is. Just like . . . in a store.

Logan also believed that perceptions of class influenced how students were disciplined. He said that he did not think he could get away with his behavior "if I was poor." He continued:

[handwritten margin note: perceptions of class influential regarding discipline]

Just like different way of dressing and how they respond to how you look and stuff . . . It depends on who you are and how you get treated . . . I've seen [teachers] taking a lot of kids down to the office . . . and they're like saying, "I didn't do this" . . . but I mean, who knows what they were doing, but it's . . . always a lot of poor kids I see going down to the office. They're watched more, is what I think it is.

Logan was observing that black students and students perceived to be poor were more likely to get in trouble with adults at Jefferson. Unfortunately, racial performance worked so that many middle-class black students were perceived to be poor by their white peers and teachers. If middle- and upper-middle-class status, combined with whiteness, provided students with the freedom to break rules without consequences, black students were inherently more likely to be targeted for disciplinary infractions. When middle-class white students talked back to teachers, skipped class, sat on desks, or walked around during class, they were thought of as "witty" and "precocious" rather than disrespectful. When white students were disruptive, it was not necessarily viewed negatively, nor was the behavior of a few individuals used to make sweeping judgments about a racial group. In short, hypeness was obnoxious, was bad, only when it was black.

The ways in which students at Jefferson conceptualized differences in racial performance provided further evidence of the stereotypes and biases they held. Rather than adopting a position of cultural relativism in which the diversity of racial performance they witnessed was just different, not bad, many students held deeply entrenched negative beliefs about black youths' style of dress, patterns of behavior, and even their ways of congregating in the hallway. Both white and black students told me that if only black kids would dress better, talk better, and act better, they would not be thought of as threatening, domineering, obnoxious, and aggressive. These judgments reinforced all students' notions that black people, even those from "good homes," were to blame for the racial discrimination they faced.

CHAPTER THREE

Intimidation and Fighting

Many black students felt they had only their "cool" personas to give them validation. They wanted to be seen as hard and intimidating because they had been shown few alternatives of how one might be black. Their educators, almost all of whom were white; curriculum, which did not reflect the significant history and contributions of people of color; the school's pedagogical approaches, which denigrated their tendencies to be "hype"; the disciplinary system, which punished them more harshly; the daily comments made by their peers that they were killers, drug users, and thieves; along with almost everything they saw in the media about themselves failed to provide them with a vision of blackness that would have challenged the racial status quo. And thus many held tightly to their identities as loud, ghetto, and gangster, even in instances in which these performances directly contradicted their economic and educational backgrounds.

failure in our education system

One of the biggest complaints white students had about black students was that they intimidated them, particularly in the hallways. Chapter 2 discussed the ways in which black students were unfairly targeted as being more likely to stop the flow of traffic in Jefferson's hallways. This relatively innocuous contesting of space was played out more threateningly in a second racial phenomenon in the hallways: physical pushing between black and white students.

I first presumed that the occasional jostling in the hallways was a natural occurrence in a school of fifteen hundred students. However, students said hallway contact was a part of the larger school culture of racial conflict. Dwayne (black) explained:

> Black people known as the bully of white people. Because we stronger than them. Like, we'll push them around sometimes. Like if a white person was in our way, we'd probably push them. It depends on who you with, though. 'Cause if I was to like walk in and there was a whole bunch of white people and I'm not with my friends and I pushed that white person, they probably going to do something to me.

When asked why he pushed white students, Dwayne responded, "'Cause they in my way and they littler than me . . . But, I mean, sometimes people be playing around though. Like they'll push somebody just to be playing around. 'Cause like people will laugh at stuff like that."

According to Dwayne, black students engaged in this behavior for two reasons. The first was simply to assert their authority in the space, to make sure that white students knew who was boss. Ironically, although Dwayne definitely had a hard edge, he was not large; in fact, he was one of the smaller male students in his grade. His assertion that he could push white students around because they were "littler" was a figment of his imagination, as well as the imaginations of his white peers, facilitated by stereotypes about race and aggression.

The second reason why some black students bumped into white students was because it was humorous. If being hype was about having fun, pushing white students around created just the sort of entertainment that made some black students laugh. Like their white peers who made bullying racial jokes, black students were cautious about when and where they engaged in actual physical contact. They too recognized their actions were somewhat risky. However, unlike racial jokes, which the black students I interviewed felt obligated to laugh along with, white students did not find it so funny when their black classmates pushed them and called it a joke.

Taken out of context, Dwanye's admission that he purposely pushed his white peers sounds inexcusable. However, he was the same student who was furious that his white peers regularly called him the N-word and made racial jokes at his expense, who said, "I'm not their nigger!" who was enraged by the verbal bullying he faced, but felt he had no recourse because fighting was not an option. And so, while he did not beat up the white students who targeted him racially, he did push them and laugh about it.

Although pushing was often thought to be initiated by black students, others argued that white students were the instigators. For example, Logan (white) said that when black students blocked the hallways in large groups he would often, "push their backpack out of the way." Denise (black) said some white people, "just feel like they can just be disrespectful any time they want to be." She gave an example: "I was walking and a black [girl] bumped into a white [boy] and so the white [boy] pushed [her] and said, 'I don't like black people, so don't touch me,' and stuff like that. I was like, ugh." It is unclear if the black girl had purposely bumped into the white student to be funny or intimidating, or if the bump was an accident. What is clear, though, is that the racial dynamics of the school were such that a white male student felt justified in putting his hands on a black female student and openly telling her he did not like people like her.

Farrah (black) believed the reason "black people push through everybody like 'Get out of my way,' and everything like that," was ultimately "'cause of anger or something." As these stories reveal, there was real conflict between black and white students at Jefferson. Students spent their days in a racially hostile environment where their only outlets for real anger were jokes, slurs, and shoves.

Trevor (black) astutely explained the dynamics of interracial conflict. When it came to hallway pushing, he said, "I'm not gonna say 'racist' 'cause I don't know them personally, but I know that I do get bumped in the hallway by white people for no apparent reason." He continued:

[But] you can't always blame that on white people because maybe, you know, somebody did something to them so they're just taking it out on the first black person they saw or the first male they saw, you know, depending on what happened. So you can't really group them together and say, "Oh they're racist," . . . 'cause you never know.

Trevor's analysis challenged the assertion that black students were the primary culprits in hallway conflict and spoke to the complicated nature of racial hostility. Beyond physical contact, Trevor also said he sometime heard white students loudly making angry comments about black people during passing periods. He told me, "The other day, somebody just said, 'All these black people in the hallway are in the way!' [And] I'm like 'Whoa, where did that come from?' That was just so random." White students were able to use the cover of quickly moving crowds in the hallways to make derogatory comments that they would not have in other settings.

Despite these experiences, Trevor believed that white students could not be solely blamed for their actions. Rather, they were caught in a cycle in which black and white students were both offenders. Maybe black students had pushed first, or maybe white students were the initiators all along. Trevor recognized that in these instances, he was simply in the line of fire in a battle that was far greater than any specific interaction between any two people.

"WHITE KIDS ARE WEAK"

There was a cadre of black boys at Jefferson who deliberately picked on their white male peers, whom they viewed as small, weak punks, unless they proved otherwise. According to Kaleem (black):

> The black people mostly are looking for the trouble, and the white kids fear them because the black people talk too much, they're ignorant, and sometimes . . . they try to take advantage of people and stuff like that. The white kids fear the black kids. Not all of them, but most of them.

A number of the white male students reported having particularly poignant experiences in which they were targets of racial intimidation. These students often called on perceptions of size as evidence of their victimhood. For example, Danny (white) told of the following interaction he and a white friend had with black students:

> My friend, he was in the hallway . . . and these three big black people walk up to him and take his iPod and just start like passing it between each other

like, "I don't have your iPod," and pass it to their friend. And he's like, "Come on, just give me my iPod back," and they won't do it. And the only reason he [took] it was because [Danny's friend] was white and he was just smaller than them. He got it back. [The teacher] came to the rescue . . . I don't think they would give it back [if she hadn't].

The black male students in this incident took advantage of two students whom they perceived to be physically vulnerable—likely due to the fact of their whiteness, rather than their actual size. When the teacher interrupted, they quickly returned the iPod and likely thought nothing much of the interaction. However, for the white students, this event felt like an assault that reinforced the negative perceptions they already held about black people.

whiteness makes them weak, not actual physical size [handwritten marginal note]

Curtis (white) recounted a similar experience, although he reacted much differently:

Last year, I was sitting in the auditorium with my girlfriend and it was really like messed up how this kid [was] just like pretty much saying I'm soft 'cause I'm white. 'Cause like he kept poking me in the back of the head. And I told him I was going to tell him three times and that's it, and then we're fighting, 'cause he had to provoke me a lot. Like, I'll give you three warnings and then it's, whatever. But he kept poking me in the back of the head and I kept telling him not to do it. And I was like, "Dude, I'll tell you one more time, if you do it again, we're going to be fighting." He's like, "You ain't going to do nothing, you little white boy." And then that's when I—yeah, went off on him . . . Yeah, he stopped.

In some ways, the school experiences of these two students explained their different reactions. Curtis had gotten into a lot of trouble in his life. He was lower-income and had problems at home. In addition, he had previously attended an all-black, low-income school. Compared with Danny, an upper-middle-class student whose friends were all white, Curtis had more knowledge of how to respond to black students who were being aggressive, and more confidence in making threats. Moreover, because of his background, his threats had merit. Curtis was not simply saying he was going to fight the student who poked him—he meant it. Danny did not have the same kind of recourse.

Ryan (white) explained what he thought was happening between black and white students in the school:

I feel like they [black students] think that they can like run the school maybe. Because they're like more loud and like [white students] are intimidated by them. I think sometimes black people like look at white people and like sometimes like think that they intimidate us or like they could like walk all over us . . . That's definitely not [true], especially not for me. Like the other day, this black kid tried to like get in my face, and I wasn't afraid to step back up and be like, "You have no idea what you're talking about, you just need to shut up and sit down," and like I had no problem. I think that when white people like retaliate, [black students] are like, "Whoa!"

Ryan believed that black students purposely intimidated their white peers because, "I think a lot of white people like are afraid of them." However, like their white peers who told racist jokes, black male students were not harassing white people because they actually wanted to get into fights. Rather they capitalized on the fear of their classmates to prove their own superiority and to amuse themselves in ways that they perceived to be harmless. When white students defended themselves, black boys backed down.

White male students were not the only ones who feared their black classmates and viewed them as physically intimidating, white girls sometimes did as well. Victoria (black) relayed the following story:

Like there's this girl in one of my classes, and we were all talking one day . . . and she said that she was actually scared to walk to her car by herself 'cause she's just a little white girl and she has to pass a bunch of black people [in the school parking lot]. She said in the hallway when she's like walking by herself she actually gets a little nervous. Like she said she bumped into some black girl or something and like she started going off. So she's always trying to watch out and stuff like that. Her exact words were like, "I'm just a little white girl." We were all like, well, I mean nobody's going to do anything. I mean, you have nothing to be afraid of or anything. I mean, nothing's going to happen unless you like do something, and she's just like, "I don't know, I just get nervous. I don't know why." She doesn't feel like comfortable in her own school, like that's not a good way to feel . . . I thought that was sad.

Victoria was saddened that black students, her friends, had the ability to instill fear in their white peers. However, she was not saddened that her black friends were so quickly made into perpetrators in the minds of their white classmates. She did not seem aware of the ways in which white students were negatively stereotyping black youth. She did not consider that black students were also victims of verbal racial bullying, jokes, slurs, biases, and prejudices about their violence and their badness or that there were almost never physical fights between students across or about race at Jefferson—that there was little for her white classmate to actually be afraid of. Instead, Victoria went along with the story that only white students were being mistreated in her school and spent significant time trying to reassure her white classmate.

[handwritten margin note: lack of awareness regarding black stereotyping]

BLACK-ON-BLACK VIOLENCE

The presumed physical prowess of black students helped maintain racial conventions in which, despite the palpable tensions between black and white students, they did not get into fights. Farrah (black) said that as a general rule, interracial fighting was unacceptable: "A black girl is not going to feel that it's fair to fight a white girl, because they think . . . [the] black girl's going to have more power." Madison (white) agreed: "I know a lot of people say white people can't fight, black people can fight." Because black people were presumed to be inherently more violent, students told me it would be dishonorable for a black student to actually engage in this way with a white student. And since so many white students told me they perceived their black classmates to be big, dangerous thugs and saw themselves as "tiny little white kids," they were unlikely to pick fights across race. This is one reason why the fight that opened this book was so significant. The clear lines of race kept a lid on what might have otherwise been explosive racial tensions at Jefferson and facilitated less dangerous forms of bullying and violence between students.

Unfortunately, although black students largely avoided physical altercations across race, the same could not be said of their interactions with each other. Black students were notorious for being likely to engage in, and eagerly witness, physical fights with other black youth. The sanctions against in-school fighting were strong enough to discourage most fights during the school day, but black students fought each other at a park nearby after school. These events were almost always pre-planned, with news spread by text message and word of mouth throughout the school day. Chelsea (black) explained, "They don't want to fight in school and get suspended, so it's like meet me at the park and everyone piles in cars [to] go watch the fight."

The park was the social center of black out-of-school life, where "all the [popular] black boys play basketball and the girls just sit around on tables and talk." According to Chelsea (black), there were no class divisions when it came to attendance at fights: "Middle, rich, poor, live in apartments, they will go." Young men and young women both engaged in fights at the park. In fact, the most notorious fight of my time at Jefferson was between two girls, Menna (black) and Crystal (black). Once fights were announced, students faced considerable social pressure to follow through. As Kaleem (black) explained, "If you make us go [to the park] for nothing some people are gonna take care of you . . . beat you up, you know." This phenomenon suggested to all students that black youth might be dangerous, but it also revealed that they were a bigger threat to each other than to any of their white classmates.

The spectators who showed up greatly outnumbered the students who actually ever fought. As Menna described, "the entire black school" was sometimes in attendance. Kiara (black) said students went to see the fights "so they can say they were there, and . . . like, you know, so that they can spread the word about what happened. See, sometimes I think people do consider it entertainment." They watched the fights as though they were the latest episode of a reality TV show, and treated them as no more significant. As Madison (white) described, black students fought because of "TV and stuff like that . . . 'Cause if you think—like in all videos you see black people, they're always fighting."

Unlike the black middle-class adults around them who understood that media depictions of blackness fail to capture the diversity of the black experience, students at Jefferson bought into the notion that in order to be black they had to look, act, dress, speak and behave like the black people they saw on TV—athletes, rappers, entertainers, and criminals,[1] as "'folk devil,' as Other, as Enemy."[2] The dominant narrative of black people as innately tougher, more ghetto, more gangster, and more violent, was reflected to black youth through the media and through school. Black youth frequently reported that they believed themselves to be all of these things and took opportunities to prove the point. And so, to many of them, fighting was simply what black kids did—an expression of racial identity.

take violence on as part of racial identity

Black students were well aware that their behavior was shocking. When asked why they fought, Dwayne (black) said, "I don't know. Black people just, I think they just turning crazy. I mean, I don't know. I don't know why they fight. I have no clue why they fight." When I asked some of the fighters why they had engaged in this behavior, they reported being "angry," feeling "disrespected," feeling the need to "prove they aren't scared," and the desire for "bragging rights," as reasons. Menna (black) was dismayed by the culture of black students at the school. Exasperated, she said, "It's always black people. It is. I mean, you'll see some of the white people get into it once or twice, but they handle it differently . . . But it's like the African Americans, black people, it's always like, 'Oh, well, you called me a name. Okay, well, I'm gonna fight you.'"

These explanations were particularly disturbing because they suggest that some middle-class, upwardly mobile black youth were struggling with identity to such a degree that they adopted behaviors that would be appalling to their parents, teachers, and even their peers. They were engaging in and eagerly witnessing physical violence not because this behavior was sanctioned in their homes or communities, but because being violent was at the core of their notions of what it was to be black.

In fact, their middle-class suburban lives may have facilitated their violence. As Mary Patillo has noted, "Black working-class and middle-class youth are not exempt from the thrill and excitement of . . . actual criminal behavior. For that matter, neither are young rich and middle-class whites. There is little glamour in being simply middle-class. In riches, there is showy extravagance, and poverty demands a noble struggle. To be middle-class . . . is to be blah."[3] Perhaps black students at Jefferson were bored by their middle-classness. Although not personally living it, they may have bought into the "noble struggle" of urban black poverty, which they viewed as a more authentic kind of blackness, and of which they believed violence was a manifestation. The economic and career success of their parents did not serve to challenge these ideas, nor did what they were learning in school.

validation

The ways in which some black students performed their identities were not harmless reflections of popular culture, but rather evidence of internalized racism in which black youth intimidated their white peers for fun—and out of rage that they struggled to name—and beat each other up for validation. When black students at Jefferson decided to, as Kaleem put it, "[make] fun of white people" in ways that straddled the line between the antagonistic and the humorous, it was seen as an attack that validated the biases of their peers. In contrast, white students could justify their own verbal bullying as joking. They were frequently allowed to express racist ideologies under the cloak of post-racial coolness without being subject to physical retaliation. This cycle of white racial prejudice and black racial performance created a hostile climate in which the hallways were a highly regulated battleground. Students could engage in racial bullying by making racial jokes, using racial slurs, and deliberately bumping into each other, but they could not fight across race.

These seemingly contradictory patterns of interaction reveal the strength of the taboo around race at Jefferson. Students were both fascinated by racial differences and fully invested in the narrative of their school as beyond race. They had developed a set of norms—implicit *norms* rules governing who could tell what kind of racial jokes, how communal spaces like the hallways and cafeterias were to be navigated, and how to be cool—that maintained the racial order of the school with virtually no guidance from adults.

Given the everyday conflicts around the N-word, racial jokes, and jostling in the hallway, the scarcity of cross-racial fights shows just how strong the norms functioning to prevent them were. However, the brawl in front of the school that opens this book showed how quickly those norms could break down and let the simmering racial tensions boil over. Notably, the principal participants—a group of freshman black boys and a recent immigrant still working to learn English—were not fully acculturated to "the Jefferson way."

The stories of how Jefferson students navigated race might lead some to write it off as an exceptionally racist place. But what was happening at Jefferson was not unique. If you walked the hallways and sat in classrooms on an average day, Jefferson looked like the model American high school. It was racially diverse and economically integrated, and on the surface, students from different racial backgrounds got along with each other in the ways we would hope. Students laughed, joked, forgot their homework, hugged their teachers, got into arguments, and claimed they hated and loved school. Moreover, the narrative students were most likely to tell about their high school suggested that they were a generation unwilling to perpetuate discrimination in the ways their parents and grandparents had. It was precisely Jefferson's ordinariness that made what was happening so significant.

What appeared on the surface to be a story of racial harmony was actually a much more complex system in which racial prejudice and hierarchies were being reinforced—a pattern that can be discovered at many integrated schools in the United States. This cycle was one in which the actions of white youth tended to be framed as acceptable—even progressive—while those of black youth were denigrated. Class mobility and integration did not challenge this hierarchical structure. As Stephanie, the only white student in the gospel choir, explained:

> I think a lot of people out here are taught, not necessarily . . . flat-out like, "Oh, you're a white kid. Listen, you don't hang out with black people," or "You're a black kid. You don't hang out with white people," I think it's just like underlying. Like parents will make little remarks, like the students do. Like just little hits of racism, and then it builds up, and then the next thing you know, you've raised a full-blown racist.

CHAPTER FOUR

"Full-Blown Racists"

Students often said that their hyperacial humor, racial stereotypes, and negative judgments of black people were about something other than race or racism. But closer investigation revealed that despite students' claims that they all got along, the majority of young people at Jefferson did not have significant relationships across race. At the end of the day, most white students, even the cool ones, went home to families, communities, and a larger society in which anti-black prejudice was not joking or post-racial, it was a reality that shaped their ideologies and relationships. The biases that many white students expressed in their discourse with and about their black classmates was not just ironic commentary. It was cultivated in communities in which the influx of black neighbors was not welcomed by many and in families where racist attitudes were too frequently expressed.

SEGREGATION

I think there's a social or a racial boundary between African Americans and whites here. Like a lot of students that go here don't really notice it . . . Just go into the lunchroom and you'll notice. You'll have the African American students stick to one section and then you have the whites that stick to their section, because you have the group thing. Like you're more friends with like your own race type deal. I've noticed that a lot here.

—Robyn, white student

There was a strong narrative among students of Jefferson as a place where "everyone got along." As Matt (white) described, "There's a lot of accepting people here. Like it doesn't matter if you're black or white. It doesn't matter really. As long as like you're not a prick, then people are okay with it." In some regards, he was right. In classrooms, black and white students sat next to each other, talked, laughed, and worked together in groups. In hallways, students from different racial backgrounds could be seen socializing and joking with each other. Some students, like Jasmine (black), also dated interracially. However, while students were "cool" across racial lines, for the most part they did not sit together at lunch, they did not hang out together in their neighborhoods, they did not go to each other's houses, and they did not join the same extracurricular activities. Jefferson was not the melting pot students imagined. Rather it was deeply divided along racial lines.

There were two cafeterias at Jefferson High School. The newest was a large "cafetorium," built when the school was renovated to accommodate the growing (black) population. It had twenty-foot ceilings and a stage at the front and was freshly painted. The older cafeteria—the original to the building—was smaller, with low ceilings and yellowed paint. Very early in my fieldwork, I learned that at lunchtime these rooms were highly segregated.

Before I had a firm sense of the racial demographics of Jefferson, I visited the two cafeterias. I had previously spent time only in the new cafeteria, a space that seemed to me to be diverse, albeit segregated by table. The white students, who were in the minority, sat gathered together at a few tables. Black students also gathered together in friend groups. Occasionally there was a white student sitting at a "black table," or vice versa.

I presumed the older cafeteria looked similar—black and white bodies, segregated by table and clique, a pattern that has long been discussed in popular culture and academic research. But I kept hearing whispers and comments from students, direct and indirect, about segregation as being more than table-specific. The words "new" and "old," "black" and "white" were casually tossed around in ways that sounded like a poorly kept secret.

I decided to see the extent of the segregation for myself. When I entered the old cafeteria, I was shocked. The room was full to the brim, and almost everyone was white, save three or four black students. There was not just a black table at Jefferson. There was an entire black cafeteria.

Pamela, a multiracial student from a middle-class family whose mother was black and father was white, described the cafeterias: "They're segregated. Like point-blank, they're segregated." She ate in the black one. Over the course of my time at Jefferson, students from all grade levels, socioeconomic positions, racial groups, and genders bluntly referred to the two spaces as the "white cafeteria" and the "black cafeteria." While the descriptors were not completely accurate, they did reflect students' understandings of who belonged in each. This pattern went back so far in Jefferson's history that no student was able to recall a time in which the lunchrooms rooms had not been segregated. Likely, lunchroom segregation and the construction of the additional cafeteria to accommodate the racially expanding district happened simultaneously.

shocking to me

Learning which cafeteria to eat in was one of the first racial lessons of a Jefferson student. Although their class schedules assigned them to a cafeteria, in practice students were free to choose where they ate. They most often chose to sort themselves into the existing racial order. Victoria (black), who had transferred from another district, talked about the process of "discovering" the black cafeteria:

> My first year coming here, my sophomore year, I didn't know there was two cafeterias. And I went to one, and I'm like, "Wow—am I the only black kid in this school?" I think it might have been like me and one other black person in there. And then after a while, I found out there was another one on the other side of the school, and I was like, "Oh, this is where all the black people are!"

Crystal (black), who was also newer to the district, had a similar story: "When I first got here . . . my schedule said you eat on the old side because that's where your class is." However, the black students she met "were like, 'Nah, come down here, eat at the new end' . . . They were like, 'You know the white people eat at [that] side.'"

While not all of the students were given this kind of explicit direction, most eventually figured out the social rules. Brandy (black) explained: "Freshman year, a lot of people I guess are confused; they don't catch on. It's like there's a lot of freshmen right now, white kids, they still eat . . . [in the black cafeteria], but I guarantee you, next year they will probably be [in the white one]." Brandy thought that the white students I had observed in the new cafeteria had not yet learned the social norms of the school.

Segregation was not only prominent within the cafeteria, the entire Jefferson community was segregated—neighborhoods, friend circles, and activities. The trailer parks in the district were almost all white and low-income, while the apartments in the district were almost all black and low-income, with very little crossover. Even within the subdivisions where middle-class black and white students lived next door to each other, it was not common for students from different racial backgrounds to hang out in any significant way. As Logan (white), admitted, "I honestly can say I've never hung out with a black person outside of school." He had once been inside of Trevor's (black) house for a party, but had not stayed long and had not been back since.

Extracurricular activities were also segregated. The swim team was almost all white. The step team was almost all black. Pamela (black and white) explained:

> I think people just gravitate toward their own race. It's kind of funny, and it reminds me of [the movie] *Freedom Writers* . . . It's like in the classroom everyone's cool with one another and usually in the hallway, but when it comes to like sitting down and talking, you know, and who you're gonna be seen with, people identify with their race.

Jasmine (black), who lived in a townhouse in one of the apartment complexes, agreed. She said that in Jefferson, "black people hang out together, white people hang out together, mixed people hang out together."

However, most students did not think of racial segregation as being particularly racial. According to Ed (white), "Usually people sit with their friends . . . it don't depend on the color." Other students, like Molly

[handwritten margin note: Whole community is segregated]

(white), acknowledged that friend groups often fell along lines of race but said, "I don't think it's segregation. We just *happen* to sit with our friends and the majority of some people's friends are one ethnicity." Gina (white) agreed, "Who you're comfortable with is who you hang out with." These students claimed it was natural that their friends tended to come from the same racial background—so natural in fact that they did not think the word *segregation*, which they felt implied something *intentional* and *negative*, was appropriate to capture what was happening. Instead, they believed, unlike generations past, their choices were not about prejudice or bias, but rather "comfort" and "commonality." The fact that their comfort was racialized was coincidental. Salim (Arab) explained this dichotomy, "Everybody gets along . . . that's true," he said, but there is also "an awkwardness" when it comes to the mixing of groups.

about "comfort" and not intentional

In the book *Why Are All the Black Kids Sitting Together in the Cafeteria?* Beverly Daniel Tatum notes that the overwhelming majority of integrated schools deal with racially segregated cafeterias in large part because young people are in the process of figuring out who they are, where they belong, and how their racial and ethnic identities matter. Building an *intra*racial community of individuals who have had similar racial experiences is an important part of social and personal development, especially for students of color whose identities are so often under attack.[1] However, while same-group relationships are important, they also reveal the salience of race. It is only because our society is fraught across racial lines that notions of belonging, identity, and race are so closely interwoven.

Some students were able to recognize the fissures, biases, and societal norms at the root of their segregation. Seth (white) revealed, "I've heard some . . . comments [from my classmates], which is really ignorant, which I won't repeat, but just . . . if a person of a different race would go sit near them then they move to a different table." Similarly, even as Matt (white) argued "It doesn't matter if you're black or white," he admitted, "Maybe subconsciously . . . we want to sit with like our own color." These students were aware that there were racial barriers at Jefferson that they were unable to overcome.

Brandy (black) was especially bothered by segregation. Although she ate in the black cafeteria, she also said, "It's unfortunate—because you don't learn anything new by sticking with the same crowd of people. Like if you went out of your way to talk to somebody else or meet somebody else you could learn a lot." She worried about the messages cafeteria segregation sent. She said, "it looks bad if a parent comes and he's taking a tour and it's noticeable that all the black kids are down there and all the white kids are . . . it just doesn't look good . . . I don't like my school looking . . . racist like that."

While Brandy was unsure whether or not her school actually *was* racist, she was very concerned that it might *look* that way to outsiders. Her concern mirrored that of many Jefferson students. They wanted to believe that everyone got along and that it did not matter if you were black or white. But it was clear that it mattered very much.

EXPLICIT RACISM

I guess you would say we all kind of grew up trained to be [racist]. I mean we all grew up with our own parents. Our parents all have their own personal biases and we grew up learning those biases and you just instinctively just kind of pick that stuff out.

—Ethan, white student

There are racist kids. I know that for a fact, because I know a lot of parents are racist and their kids go here, obviously; you know, that's where you live, that's your model. Just the words that they use, the way they talk to people like they think they are superior or . . . smarter or whatever . . . I don't really deal with those type of white kids I guess 'cause I don't want to be bothered with all that bull.

—Ahmed, black student

Although students tried very hard to sweep it under the rug, there was explicit racism at Jefferson. Even students like Winnie (black and white) who fervently insisted that race is "not really noticed" at Jefferson acknowledged, "There's definitely white kids who I've heard don't like black people . . . I know there's racism here." The most overtly racist students were not cool; they did not conceptualize the world or their school as a place in which "everyone got along" nor did they think everyone *should* get along. Instead, they wanted to maintain the racial status quo in ways that protected their social status. Some students reported hearing white peers publicly declare their racism. For example, Curtis (white), said he knew some of his peers did not like black people because, "they say it . . . There was this one kid . . . he went here last year, and he was in the cafeteria and he stood up and just said the N-word out loud and was like, 'I hate you,' and then he just got jumped by a bunch of black kids." According to Logan (white):

> There's certain kids that are like, "No black at all." When they're walking around they'll be like, "I hate black kids." I think it's [because] we're kind of out . . . in the boons. We're out in the middle of nowhere. 'Cause you look out this school and you see field, field, field . . . [So there's] more hicks.

Because the exurban community of Jefferson had been built on rural farmland, Logan assumed the white people from the area were likely to be racist. It was unclear whether or not the Jefferson community was any more racist than other places in which there had been a significant and rapid shift in racial demographics. Nonetheless, Jefferson's historical narrative provided ammunition for both racial humor and actual racism. Ed (white) reported that in 2008, there was a "gang at JHS called J Poodle that was all white boys, and they [were] trying to bring the KKK back and stuff." Although these students had graduated by the time this study began, their reputation lingered. Interestingly, when other students at Jefferson talked about "gangs" in the school, the white members of J Poodle were never mentioned.

While a number of racist white students were open about their disdain for their black peers, others admitted it only in racially homogenous spaces. This made it difficult for students, especially students of color, to accurately identify which of their peers were "real racists" and which were "cool white kids" just playing around. Some students, like Logan (white), said "The people that are serious [racists], you can see like anger in their face, like how much they really don't like black people." However, most recognized that the line between "real racists" and "cool whites" was nowhere near as clear, neat, or solid, as they wanted to believe.

Black students like Ahmed worried that they might be misinterpreting their peers' "joking" commentary. "That's the thing," he said, "They try to mask [their racism] as just like humor . . . so I really don't know if they mean it or not, cause it's meant to be humorous, but you never know, they might have like an alternative motive for it, so I don't know." Ahmed was wise to be cautious about discerning the sentiment behind white students' racial commentary. The experiences of three different students who had access to both black and white spaces illuminated the racism in the Jefferson community that was sometimes obscured.

LEARNING RACISM

Gina was a white student who had grown up with a black stepfather and half-black siblings, who were the targets of racist hostility from the white side of her family. Most of her friends were black, and she dressed "black"— often wearing clothing brands such as Rocawear, which she thought were more fun and had a wider range of expression than the simple T-shirts popular among white students. Having black friends, adopting stereotypically black styles, and being raised by a black man gave her a heightened awareness of contemporary racism and access to a world that black people could not enter. When asked about white students at the school, she said:

> Most of the other kids, like black kids, they don't know how many racist people that they talk to on a day-to-day basis, because they're not white. But I would say like 40 to 50 percent of the white kids that go here are racist . . . It's a lot of people . . . and you just know that they're racist . . . They'll be like, "Stupid 'N,'" and they'll be just like, "See, that's why black people don't get this." And you just know right away like they're racist. And that's in all the classes.

Many of her black friends laughed off the racist comments of their white counterparts as jokes. Similarly, many white students justified their racism by arguing that it was not about race but about cultural performance. Gina's observations challenged both narratives.

Brielle, whose mother was white and father was black, had a very similar experience. She had close relationships with white people both within and outside of school, and in some situations, when her hair was straight, she said she could pass for white. She had experienced being both the target of white racism and privy to racist conversations about black people among whites. Like Gina, Brielle believed there were significantly more racist white students at Jefferson than black students were aware of:

> There's a lot of people that are racist but they don't come out about it because there's a lot of crazy black boys here that will fight people if you say the N-word or whatever. But there definitely is a lot of old-fashion rednecks and stuff in this school. A lot of them lie about it, because they don't want people to know. 'Cause like I think that it's embarrassing to them, but that's how they were raised so that's all they know. People don't just come out of the womb thinking, "Oh, I don't like certain people," it's something that you've been taught, so I think they're embarrassed maybe that their parents are stuck back in the old times when this is 2009—it's supposed to be diverse, you know.

Brielle suggested that white students who held racist beliefs had enough self-awareness to know their ideologies were no longer socially acceptable and so went to great lengths to hide the most egregious aspects of their biases. She told the following story:

> I have a (white) best friend who goes here, and she has this ex-boyfriend . . . they went together for like a year and she wasn't allowed to walk with me in the hallway or else he would get mad. She wasn't allowed to talk to me when they were together. I was like sleeping over at her house and he would call, she would have to lie 'cause she would get in trouble because he didn't like me 'cause I was black. And he's made it clear to me before. Like in person, like I'd be walking with her, he'd go, "You can't walk with her, you're black," and he like calls people the N-word and stuff. Everyone thought he was kidding, but now that they know [he's not]. They're like, "Wow, I would have never known that he was really like that!" But then like if you meet his dad, [he] will like broadcast it to you like, "Oh, I don't like black people, can't have them in my house, can't have no girlfriend that's black, don't bring them home to me."

Many students did not believe this young man was racist because the cloak of humor at JHS was so thick it was hard to see the reality underneath—especially for students who had been socialized to ignore, dismiss, and justify racist humor as post-racial. In contrast, because Gina and Brielle lived on the fringes of racial groups, the picture they painted of race relations at Jefferson was rooted in an understanding of both the surface interactions happening between students and the racism that permeated white communities. It was distinctly different than the one white students presented publicly.

Brielle's story revealed that many white students were navigating racism in their homes and communities. Students who were not overtly racist themselves reported having friends, family members, or neighbors who were. Arguably, white people in the United States commonly experience this; they are not only dealing with racism and race relations when in the presence of people of color, they are also negotiating race every day in all-white spaces.[2]

Madison's experiences present a particularly poignant illustration of the struggles many white students faced in navigating the complex racial politics of their school and homes. She lived with a low-income single mother and younger sister. In addition, she had a number of siblings who were more than a decade older and had long moved out. Madison was friends with white students as well as popular black students. At the time of this study, her two best friends, Brielle and Victoria, were both black. Nonetheless, in her broader life, she regularly had to make decisions about how to address white racism:

> A couple of my [white] guy friends, they actually are very, very, very racist . . . I think it's just mainly people's opinion and how their parents raised them. [My friends] were in the car one day and . . . there was a black guy, he ran a red light or a stop sign or whatever and [my white male friend] said the N-word, he's just like going off like and I was just kind of sitting there just like, "Oh, don't say that word around me like, like I don't like that word at all."

While Madison was disturbed by the racism she witnessed, she could not simply avoid racist white people or limit her interactions to the bus ride home like her black peers could. They were her friends and family members. Madison described the presence of racism in her home life:

> My mother actually raised my older sisters, not racist in a way, but to like not really be best friends with them [black people], never date them or nothing like that. Now, all she works with is black people, and so her opinion has changed. Like I think maybe 'cause it was back then like twenty years ago, it was different and now more and more people are together. 'Cause like actually for a while since I was in eighth grade, all I've dated was black boys. I have never dated a white boy since seventh grade. So like it's definitely changed, 'cause like they've all came over. And like they actually sit on the couch and have conversations with my mom. They actually talk to my mom more than me . . . My mom's boyfriend, he's actually very racist also and so he gets—he will drink on occasions and he will say the N-word quite a bit—and so I either go in my bedroom and listen to music just really loud so I don't have to listen to it or I just like go outside and go for a walk . . . 'cause I don't like it. I don't look at how people act in a way, like I don't judge a book by its cover. I read the pages and look at what's on the inside. 'Cause like, I think it's my mom's mom's dad, he was actually a slave owner, so that kind of gets to me quite a bit—just knowing like, how could actually one of my family members put somebody through that? Like that's just, that's horrible.

Madison viewed herself as accepting and nonjudgmental. Her personal friendships were a testament to her ability to build relationships across race. However, she came from a family just starting to break the cycle of racism. While her mother was becoming more open-minded as a result of her work experience and her daughter's social networks, she still had a racist boyfriend who spent significant time in her home, influencing her children who were in the process of trying to figure out their own racial identities.

Many white students at Jefferson shared aspects of Madison's experience. The precarious class position of a lot of white families in times of economic crisis can make racist sentiments even more salient.[3] As Lillian Rubin found in her study of working-class families, "minority gains seem particularly threatening to white working-class families . . . partly because we have so little concept of class resentment and conflict in America, this anger [is] not directed so much at those above as at those below. And when whites at or near the bottom of the ladder look down in this nation, they generally see blacks and other minorities."[4] The economic success of the black families in the district, combined with the scarcity of resources in the state and country at the time of this study, likely heightened racial tensions and increased white families' negative sentiments about their black neighbors.

It was therefore unsurprising that white students were struggling to navigate race. Society was telling them they lived in a post-racial world, as evidenced by the newly elected black president, and that they were supposed to be color-blind, but at home many white students heard racist comments and stereotypes about their black neighbors. They knew their parents, grandparents, aunts, and uncles were raised in a time where racism was commonplace; and for an overwhelming number of them, this history was present in their daily lives. Their sense that their black classmates where ghetto, loud, obnoxious, sources of humor was developed not only in a context of racial progress, but also one of lingering racial prejudice.

During my time at Jefferson, a white student confessed that her father was a KKK member who had forbidden her from playing with her black neighbors as a child. Another white student said her parents would kick her out of the house if they knew she had black friends at school. Black students told me they saw racist slurs written on the bathroom walls. A handful of white students wore confederate flag necklaces, T-shirts, and fingernail polish, and there was a swastika permanently etched in the desk of a classroom I regularly observed.

Jefferson students were not beyond race as so many claimed. Instead, they were *hyperracial*—so concerned with race that it limited their friendships, shaped their interactions, and dominated their discourse. These young people thought about, talked about, and made stereotypical judgments about race, frequently. They lived in a community and went to a school where there was an ongoing series of "racial hits" that adults seemed all too willing to ignore. As a result, likely without even knowing it, parents, teachers, and administrators were at risk of raising "full-blown racists" who would enter their adult lives with biases, prejudices, and beliefs about blackness that they had, for many years, assumed were just jokes. According to Stephanie (white), intervening in this hyperracial culture "would take years and years of like deprogramming. Like some of these people are set in their ways so much that you'd have to definitely like go back and re-teach them a lot of stuff." Unfortunately, most Jefferson teachers and administrators did not have the awareness, knowledge, skill, or confidence to do this.

PART II

Teachers

CHAPTER FIVE

See No Evil, Hear No Evil, Speak No Evil

On a Tuesday afternoon in November, I was sitting alone in my office at Jefferson High School, a small windowless storage room with a desk, a collection of empty file cabinets, and a stack of chairs. The Jefferson administrators had kindly given me a key to the room, where I often interviewed students and wrote up my field notes. As I was typing away during sixth hour with my shoes off and my feet curled under me, I heard a commotion in the hallway. A group of students was yelling what sounded like "SENIOR!" in long, drawn-out syllables.

I listened again. It was not "Senior" I was hearing, it was "NIGGER!" I stood up so quickly I almost fell and ran barefoot to the door just in time to see a group of four white and one multiracial male students walk by giggling. "NIIGGGEERR," they called out again loudly. Seven times in a row, down two long hallways, past numerous classrooms, the boys shouted the N-word at the top of their lungs. No one stopped them or came to see what was happening. Soon after they faded into the distance, the teacher in the classroom next door stepped into the hallway and gave me a knowing look. When I asked if she had heard the boys, she said she had not.

While shocking, this incident was not unique. Frequently, I would be sitting in my office and a hyperracial exchange—like "cool" white students shouting the N-word while walking beside their half-black classmate—would take place right in front of my door. This time, though, I was not focused on the behavior of the students. I was more concerned with the responses of the teachers whose classrooms the young men passed. Though tempted to interrupt them, I decided to wait and see how Jefferson educators would intervene in such an incident. What I witnessed confirmed that white teachers at Jefferson, who made up over 90 percent of the teaching staff, went to great lengths to avoid anything to do with race. They claimed not see or hear racial problems, and so they were unlikely to intervene.

TEACHERS' AVOIDANCE OF RACE

Some of the times they'll be like, "Come on guys, that's enough." Some of the times they'll not notice or sometimes . . . sometimes I think they pretend not to know . . . Maybe they know we're just playing around . . . Like sometimes I'll see the teachers ignoring a lot of things people do or say . . . just to avoid conflict, I guess.

—Salim, Arab student

Nope . . . we never talk about race . . . Maybe teachers are uncomfortable.

—Farrah, black student

A number of researchers have documented the phenomenon of teachers avoiding issues related to race. Mica Pollock's *Colormute* finds that educators use a number of mechanisms to silence conversations about race.[1] In *Black American Students in an Affluent Suburb*, John Ogbu discusses this tendency among educators as the "code of silence."[2] Similarly, Douglass Foley argues in *Learning Capitalist Culture* that "many teachers [in his study] felt like they were 'walking on eggshells' to avoid racial issues."[3] At Jefferson, racial silence among teachers was especially pronounced.

Although students at Jefferson regularly made racial jokes, used racial slurs, engaged in physical racial intimidation in hallways, ate in segregated cafeterias, and admitted holding biases that reinscribed notions of black inferiority, the majority of white teachers claimed to have no awareness of this hyperracial student culture. When I asked them directly about the racial tension between students, most said our conversation was the first they had heard of these issues. For example, when I asked teachers about racial jokes and slurs, some of the responses I got were:.

Ms. Kennedy (white): You know, I don't hear it [the N-word]. I hear [gay slurs] far more.

Ms. Ladig (white): I mean, I haven't heard any kids . . . call each other you know, racial derogatory . . . . but my room is pretty well integrated.

Ms. Valenzuela (white): In my class, I haven't heard it.

Ms. Meguschar (white): I have not heard them . . . I've never heard like racial jokes for the most part.

Ms. Ladig (white): No, never heard, no.

Ms. Dunlap (white): Not in my classroom. I don't hear black jokes, I don't hear gay jokes . . .

Ms. Wenzell (white): I don't see a lot of racial hatred or anything like that. I think that this is, it's . . . in my opinion, very healthy around here . . .

Some white teachers conceded that although they personally had not heard the jokes, it was possible that students were engaging in this sort of behavior elsewhere:

Ms. Mayes (white): I have never heard that once. That doesn't mean it's not occurring . . . maybe they're smart enough not to do it around me?

Mr. Edwards (white): Is there [racial joking]? I haven't heard it . . . but I think they're smart enough not to say it right in front of a teacher.

Ms. Guthrie (white): Oh, no—if they're joking about it out in the hall, I don't hear it.

A few teachers admitted occasionally hearing a racially tinged joke. For example, Ms. Davis (white) said, "I'll hear them crack little jokes. Fried chicken, you know, things that are typically Southern black. You know, grits, sweet potato pie, those kinds of things." However, these teachers did not seem to think the comments were a big deal. As Ms. Kennedy (white) explained:

> [I]t is truly kind of a joke here . . . Thinking of my fifth hour again because you had Asad (Arab) and Josh (white) and Kurt (black) and so they would just, you know—Asad and Josh would make jokes about black people and Kurt would make jokes about terrorists, you know, meaning Asad. And so . . . a couple of times I told them, I said one joke may be funny but more than that's picking on someone, you know, but it worked for them.

supports culture of school

Ms. Kennedy was not oblivious to these exchanges, as so many of her colleagues were. In fact, she pointed out that making such comments repeatedly was closer to bullying than joking. However, even she ultimately determined that this sort of interaction "worked for them."

In some ways it was clear that these exchanges did "work" for students. They laughed along and came back to class the next day ready to do it all over again. However, as noted in chapter 1, students had little recourse for dodging attacks couched as humor. Moreover, the unidirectional nature of the jokes made them more problematic. The acceptance that black jokes and terrorist jokes, without any corresponding white jokes, "worked" indicated a certain level of denial on the part of teachers about the dominant racial hierarchies that these interactions were reinforcing.

Other teachers, like Ms. Knadler (white), said they heard these comments and were bothered by them but were struggling to navigate a world they perceived to be very different from that of their own adolescence:

> Well, you know how it's easier for us as adults . . . to pursue something as, quote, "really serious or problematic" when the kids will say, "Well no, we're just playing around . . . "And I can't tell. It's enigmatic to me. Sometimes it's puzzling. Like I'm not certain, and then I end up looking really, "square, old fashion . . ." just because I don't know if they're really being sarcastic, facetious, or if they are actually insulting one another. So I'm sure you've overhead loads of exchanges here. Like, I can't tell sometimes . . . . I have heard again some racial jokes, which I always find really upsetting, but they act like they're just kidding around.

Ms. Kennedy and Ms. Knadler believed racial humor and racial tension could not coexist. If students claimed to be joking after saying something racist, teachers reported that they generally believed them. As Michael Billig writes, they "downgrad[ed] the possible links between humor and prejudice, as if what is to be celebrated should be kept distinct from that which is to be criticized."[4] Because most teachers ignored or downgraded hyperracial exchanges, they consciously or unconsciously let everyday racial jokes slide.

For example, I was standing in the hallway during passing period one day with Ms. Meguschar (white) and a group of white students who had congregated in front of her classroom. One of the students, Logan (white), had a purple bandana tied around his head under his chin covering his ears. He declared, "Yeah, I'm Arab today!" Instead of explaining why it might be offensive to jokingly appropriate the cultural styles of marginalized groups, Ms. Meguschar smiled at his joke while a few students chuckled.

When exchanges between students were highly offensive and public, some teachers attempted to interrupt them. In these cases, teachers would say something like "Stop," "Knock it off," or "Hey, unnecessary," without further discussion. When I asked Harrison (white) what teachers did when they heard students making racial jokes or using racial slurs, he said, "just ignore it and let [students] do what they want for the most part. I mean, if it's *really* offensive I think a teacher will like jump in and say 'No, don't do that.'" Riley (white) agreed: "In the hallway . . . I've never heard a teacher say anything . . . And then in the classroom, some teachers will just ignore it and be totally oblivious to things going on. And other teachers will say, 'Hey stop, that's not right. Get back to work.'"

Other students said that teachers sometimes threatened punishment when students made such comments. For example, Alena (black) said she had heard teachers say, "Chill out, don't do that anymore, you want a referral or something like that?" Willie (black) also said that teachers "either tell you to stop, or they might even write you up or they might threaten to write you up . . ." However, Trevor (black) contended that while teachers sometimes made these threats, they were largely empty: "I've never seen a teacher actually like write anybody up or do anything to anybody just 'cause somebody said somebody was racist."

None of the responses noted above provided students with opportunities for reflection and growth. Jefferson's culture was one in which teachers did not engage students in critical discussions about race, racism, or their own cross-racial interactions.

When I asked students if they ever talked about race, stereotypes, segregation, diversity, or bullying in their classes, they definitively said, "No":

Shayla: Do teachers ever say, "Hey, y'all seem interested in race. This is a diverse school. Let's talk about race?".
Brielle (black and white): No.
Shayla: Let's talk about stereotypes, let's talk about segregation . . .
Brielle: No.
Shayla: . . . let's talk about bullying?
Brielle: No, we've never talked about that in any class I've ever had. It's all strictly whatever the class is for, that's what you go for.

Shayla: Do teachers talk about race in class?
Trevor (black): No.
Shayla: Do they say like, "Oh, it seems like you all are interested in this subject?"
Trevor: No. They just go on with their initial learning plan.

Students repeatedly said they never talked about race with teachers. And yet, all students at Jefferson read *Huckleberry Finn*, *To Kill a Mockingbird*, *Of Mice and Men*, or *A Raisin in the Sun*—American classics that deal with U.S. race relations. Moreover, the civil rights movement was a part of the standard ninth-grade social studies curriculum. Their reports reflected two things that my observations confirmed. First, mention of race was restricted to course units that dealt explicitly with a particular book or content area (generally U.S. history). As Shannon (black and white) described, "It's usually when we do the slavery chapters." Similarly, Sarah (white) said race only came up, "like if we're reading a book and there's something in it." Teachers like Ms. Kennedy (white) agreed:

I do talk about it in class . . . We will when we get to that. I don't know if it's the next unit or the unit after. It's the Civil War unit, where some of that African, the old Negro spirituals come up, and then we get into . . . *Of Mice and Men*, which is 1930s, so that section we do talk about it.

Second, even in instances in which teachers presented content on race in their classes, they almost never engaged students in any kind of meaningful dialogue. As Shannon explained, even when they were doing the slavery chapters, "we never really get into diversity and that kind of stuff." Harrison (white) said race was sometimes brought up, "maybe as like a journal entry, but that's not talking about it . . . we just write in our journal and go on with the day." In other words, teachers treated race like a static, historical phenomenon, relevant only between slavery and the civil rights movement. It was not discussed as a dynamic, contemporary reality that the Jefferson community, and the rest of the nation, was dealing with every day.

THE POWER OF FEAR

Although the majority of white teachers claimed they were not aware of the hyperracial exchanges happening between students, many students believed teachers only *pretended* not to notice racial bullying. Shannon (black and white) explained, "Maybe [teachers] just want to pretend like they don't hear it, or something . . . they ignore it, like it never happened . . . because [they are worried] . . . there will be drama or something." Similarly, Robyn (white) said, "I'm sure the teachers see it, but they don't say anything."

A number of white teachers admitted that their reluctance to engage students in conversations about race was rooted in fear—as many students had guessed. This was true even among teachers who had spent their careers teaching race-related content. They were afraid these conversations would be viewed as outside of the scope of their content or that, as Salim (Arab) suggested in the quote that opened the previous section, talking about it would lead to student conflict. They were afraid that parents would get upset, that they might be perceived as racists, and of what their colleagues might think.

Fear of Standards

Some teachers thought that engaging students in conversations about race would be a worthwhile endeavor. However, they did not feel they had permission to do so given the objectives for their particular courses. Ms. Mc-Williams (white) explained this dilemma:

> Can I justify going there when . . . it's nowhere in my curriculum? . . . If I could find a way to link that conversation back to [something] that's in the list of what I'm supposed to cover, I would really enjoy engaging in that conversation . . . . because it's about being a human being. There's more to it than just the academics . . . kids are people. But they're people who I'm supposed to teach how to problem-solve inside the content that I've been hired to teach. So I struggle to figure out how I'm going to justify that.

A number of teachers argued that the reason students were not taught to think critically about, interact around, or build relationships across race was because the entities at the district, state, and national levels responsible for deciding what students would learn had not made this a priority. These teachers felt that taking time out of their schedule to talk about race was not aligned with the standards by which teaching and learning were measured. However, even in instances in which teachers had obvious opportunities to have these conversations within the confines of their content, they struggled to do so in ways that pushed students to challenge their biases and behaviors.

Fear of Student Conflict

Ms. Stovall (white) was a social studies teacher who taught the civil rights movement every semester. She had a multiracial family, was the daughter of civil rights activists, was well informed about U.S. racial history, and kept up with contemporary racial issues in the news. Nonetheless, she did not feel comfortable having conversations about race with her students. She admitted that when she overheard students make racial comments, she did little to interrupt them. She explained:

I don't stop the whole class and say, "Let's talk about it." And I think some-times that may be a good idea to address these issues—but again, opening a can of worms. I don't want it to explode . . . I'm more fearful that it'll turn racist than the other way. And I don't want that to happen. So I avoid it.

Rather than seeing what was happening between students as already racist and conflictual, Ms. Stovall worried that talking about these ex-changes would be the source of tension. She was particularly concerned about making issues of race worse because she felt she did not have the skill to facilitate such conversations:.

I'm not a counselor . . . It's just too much for me to handle. But racism, or those kinds of things are very hurtful, and I would love to be able to do some-thing. I hesitate, I've always hesitated . . . I think a lot of teachers—and I'm guilty of it—you avoid issues that are hard to deal with. And I really would love to do that, but I feel like, one, I don't have a lot of time in my curriculum, two, I want it to be done well and I don't have the training . . . How do you allow the kids to open up and really deal with these issues and not explode inappropriately? That's really hard to do, and I feel like you have to have some training.

Because Ms. Stovall had not been given any instruction or support in how to engage students in conversations about race, she mostly avoided such discussions. Yet, despite her concerns, Ms. Stovall wanted to do more. During one interview, she asked me to weigh in on how she could approach discussing lynching with her students:.

When I do the civil rights unit, and I should ask your opinion about this . . . These people were brave . . . And I think that people don't realize how vi-cious racism was and that's why we can't joke about it . . . I tried to bring that up, but it was hard because I think it didn't go over well with some white students . . . But I don't know, what do you think about that? . . . 'Cause I'm worried. What goes through my mind is that there's some kooky [white] guy in here that's going to do something kooky. Or as an African American male, how does that feel to hear this?

The remainder of this interview was a conversation about how Ms. Stovall might prepare herself to effectively broach this topic with students.

Ms. Stovall's story illuminates the deep concern white teachers had for how they would manage student conflict during conversations about race. Many teachers at Jefferson avoided these conversations because they had had previous experiences in which race discussions had gone poorly with students. Years before this study began, another social studies teacher had tried to engage students in a conversation about stereotypes that had not been well received. Brandy (black) explained:

> [Students] had to . . . take turns going out on the board, and they had to write down a whole bunch of, um, racist stereotypes. And then they discussed them, and I guess it became like a huge debate and huge conflict. Like they don't do it anymore because it became such a problem. Like it went home to parents, and parents [began] e-mailing [and] complaining.

Mr. McPhee (white) had had a similar experience:

> It's happened to me in the past when we were reading *A Raisin in the Sun* . . . when the white guy comes in and he's clearly being racist . . . so we have conversations about that portion. And there's been this heated debate back and forth between the students. It was like four years ago . . . but I think I was just like, enough, we have to stop. Lets move on, 'cause it wasn't very productive anymore.

In these instances, teachers often found they lacked the facilitation skills, personal knowledge, and efficacy to successfully talk to students about racism. Their schools of education had not prepared them to do so, most of them had few experiences with this conversation in their own lives, their professional development did not address these issues, and the mandated curriculum left little room for the development of these skills. As a result, when opportunities to have these discussions arose, teachers like Mr. McPhee often opted to skip over them.

Teachers were in such need of support when it came to issues of race that many saw me as their only resource. Most of these teachers were very open in talking to me, were knowledgeable about issues of race related to their particular content area, and wanted to have these conversations with their students. However, their personal knowledge and commitment were not enough to give them the tools to actually facilitate conversations. Over the course of my study, four different white teachers, including Ms. Stovall, requested that I come to their classes to co-lead discussions about the N-word, stereotypes, and racism, which I did in twenty different classes.

Fear of Parents' Responses

The third major fear teachers harbored was of parents. Virtually all of the teachers who had to deal with race in their curriculum had received complaints from parents at some point in their career. According to Ms. Mitchell (white), when ". . . teaching something like *To Kill a Mockingbird* or *Of Mice and Men* where that word [the N-word] comes up and you have to offer the disclaimer . . . you know inevitably you'll get some phone calls from parents who just don't understand and don't trust the teacher to teach that word in context." She said this happened with both black and white parents who believed, ". . . that word shouldn't be even brought up in school . . . They're just uncomfortable with it. And I think that's part of it . . . We tend to . . . push it under the rug and hide from it rather than dealing with it face-on because we're afraid of the ramifications . . . and then that just creates more confusion."

Ms. Hill (white) had a similar experience. When reading *A Raisin in the Sun*, an African American mother "[told me] I must be okay with books that have the N-word in them." Ms. Scott (white) believed that when it came to race, "This system just breeds this crap." She said that when she attempted to diversify her reading list a few years back by adding *Black Boy* by Richard Wright, "a couple of [white] kids, the ones that really seemed like they could be members of the KKK . . . their family, they were like, 'Are we going to read any white literature?' And I was like, 'We did Shakespeare.'" She stopped teaching the book, despite the fact that her students ". . . loved it! They'd come in, 'Are we reading today? Are we listening to the tape [of *Black Boy*] today?' And if we were doing something else, they were just dying."

For many teachers, the possibility of backlash from parents was too much of a risk, especially at Jefferson, where teachers believed that, in the words of one, parents were "very pushy and . . . wield a lot of power." As a result, even English and social studies teachers did the bare minimum when it came to topics of race and diversity.

Fear of Being Perceived as Racist

Teachers were also concerned that by bringing up race they were at risk of being, as Ms. Davis (white) put it, "labeled a racist." Negative racial incidents in white teachers' lives had left many of them feeling, as Mica Pollock describes in *Colormute*, "emotionally scarred by experiences with unsuccessful race talk."[5] On multiple occasions, white teachers privately revealed their shame about failed race conversations. For example, in a previous job, Ms. Conger (white) had had a racially hostile interaction with an African American coworker. Since that time, over a decade prior to this study, she had been very reluctant to discuss race:

> I don't know what I did. And this woman hated me . . . I don't judge all black people by her . . . because . . . I've had enough positive experiences that that isn't the first thing that comes up . . . . But I am afraid to bring up race stuff because what did I do that was wrong? I don't know what I did that was wrong. Right now, talking to you, I don't know what I did that was wrong. So what [else] am I gonna say? What else might I say that's wrong, that's out of line, that's offensive? And how is [what happened] bad? . . . Can you answer that for me? I'm asking you. Is that a bad thing?

Ms. Conger repeatedly asked me if I thought she was racist in the situation she had revealed. This was not a rhetorical question, she was really asking me. She wanted confirmation that she was a good person—that she was not racist—and she wanted me, a black woman, to give it to her. Although she had significant enough relationships across race that she did not "judge all black people" by this experience, she continued to worry that she might say something wrong again, and so instead she said nothing.

In addition to a number of experiences of white teachers revealing past racial traumas, often in which they had been called racist, more than one teacher reported that our conversation was the first time they had talked substantially with a person of color about race. Ms. Guthrie (white) was an example:

Ms. Guthrie: I feel very comfortable talking to you, and it's probably 'cause you have been around white people enough that you know how to negotiate . . . and you, there's something about [you] I feel safe talking to you.

Shayla: I'm special and magical.

Ms. Guthrie: [Laughing] There are some people that I, that I couldn't . . .

Because many of the teachers did feel comfortable talking to me about race, they capitalized on the opportunity. An overwhelming number of the conversations I had with white teachers became confessionals in which they attempted to work out their deep-seated race issues, or opportunities for them to get feedback on their attempts to have conversations with students, or a chance for them to ask their burning questions about race. Mr. Sallee (white) believed this was because his white colleagues had few, if any, opportunities to do this in other areas of their life:

People are afraid to ask questions, because it sounds like you're either ignorant or you're being a racist if you ask, "Why did you do this or why did you do that?" 'Cause it does sound like, "Why did *you people* do that?" . . . There's this fear between us (white teachers), asking those questions or asking them wrong is going to make us look bad. So we just don't do it.

The conversations I had with teachers revealed a conundrum that many teachers face when it comes to issues of race: they were being asked to do something in their jobs that they had not done successfully in their own lives.

Educators at Jefferson needed to be able to engage students in conversations about race and racism, interrupt racial bullying, and intervene in racial segregation. And yet most of them knew little about issues of race; had not engaged in substantive conversations about or across race; did not have significant relationships with people from different racial backgrounds; and did not know much about the history and contemporary realities of race and racism in the United States. Moreover, many were shaped by histories of negative racial experiences that, unlike that of Ms. Conger, had not been counterbalanced by a lifetime of racially diverse friendships and interactions, nor did they have the ability to view their previous experiences as mistakes they could grow from. As a result, many white teachers reported feeling unequipped to talk race. Those feelings did not leave room for them to have these conversations with students or with each other.

Fear of Colleagues' Opinions

Teachers were not talking to students about race in part because they were not talking to each other about it. According to Ms. Hill (white), the Jefferson school culture was one of silence and fear that made such conversations virtually impossible. She lamented, "Kids want to talk about stuff, but there's no forum." Her own efforts to provide an outlet for dialogue had not been well received: "I noticed that when I first started here, I'm like, you know, there's . . . [racial] identity things going on . . . Could we start a support group or something? 'Well there's a lot of legality about support groups' [I was told]. Fear. Everything's fear."

Ms. Wenzell (white) believed most Jefferson teachers were uninterested in this conversation because of their own biases:

Ms. Wenzell: I don't think there's any point in having teachers in this school try to get together and talk about race. Flat out.

Shayla: Well, let me stop my research here. Thank you for your time. [Laughing]

Ms. Wenzell: There is NO POINT.

Shayla: Why do you say that?

Ms. Wenzell: Because . . . it is going to take the minds and hearts and souls of truly involved individuals who really do care about these students to become something else here. You're not going to teach old dogs new tricks, if you got a bunch of old white people that work here that are not interested. No black people work here. They probably figure, "Why do I need to talk about that?" They don't want to understand. They don't care. To them, they want to put it under the guise of, "Well, they're all just students" . . . I think they need to retire. I don't think you're going to get anything out of these teachers. I swear to God, girl. I'm not lying to you.

It was true that the larger school culture was one in which race was treated as a taboo and that many educators held deeply seated racial prejudices. However, there were a number of teachers in the building like Ms. Wenzell (white), Ms. Hill (white), Ms. Mitchell (white), Mr. Edwards (white), Mr. Sallee (white), and Ms. Stovall (white) who wanted to talk about issues of race and wanted to engage their students in these conversations. Unfortunately, because they never discussed it, most believed they were alone in this desire. As a result, they did not share creative ideas about how they might have these conversations more productively in their classrooms.

One reason why these teachers were not talking to each other about race was because they struggled to organize themselves in ways that created safe spaces for dialogue. Mr. Edwards (white) had tried to create a book study group in which he and his colleagues could discuss race:

> [Four years ago] we tried to do the . . . book *Why Do All the Black Kids Sit Together in the Cafeteria?* [by] Beverly Daniel Tatum. And nobody showed up . . . [except] the three people who wanted to . . . actually lead the discussion . . . nobody else came . . . So we talked about it for twenty minutes, and that was the end of that. But that was the discussion I think teachers should have, especially with each other.

It is unclear why other teachers did not attend the meeting. However, it was not necessarily lack of interest, as Mr. Edwards seemed to believe. It was likely that with a more structured organizing and recruiting strategy, including one-on-one conversations with colleagues, a number of the teachers I spoke to would have been interested. But this kind of deliberate organizing was not taking place within the school.

It is also worth noting that the three teachers who came to the book discussion did not manage to have a more substantial conversation among themselves. To them, like many teachers, the problem was those "other" teachers who were unwilling to engage in the conversation—who did not "get" race or who were "racist." They did not consider how the three of them might continue growing in their own development of racial consciousness, how they could support each other in having more successful conversations about race with students, or how they might build a coalition of leaders in their school who could make sustained change around issues of race. Instead of using this space to consider what the three of them *could* do, these teachers were discouraged that no one else participated and so had not met since that time.

The second reason why interested teachers were not having these conversations with each other was because, according to Ms. Rich (white), teachers in the building did not talk to each other much at all. "I don't know a lot of the teachers here," she said. "I feel like even though this is my third year of teaching, that I don't know people here. I think a piece of it is school climate." As a result, although, as Ms. Conger (white) said, "People are very curious and they want to have these conversations" there was great trepidation about doing so in a culture in which they did not know or trust their colleagues.

The hyperracial student culture at Jefferson flourished in part because teachers and other adults in the building were doing little to challenge these interactions. Students at Jefferson could make racial jokes, use racial slurs, and push each other around, and most of their teachers would ignore it. Nonetheless, there were many teachers like Ms. Davis (white) who believed that engaging students in conversations about difference was essential:

> Aren't we a place of education? . . . [I]f you can change the ideas and attitudes of some of these kids, then we might have less problems that exist [in the world] . . . The job is to educate students in the content, but . . . I think . . . teachers need to really tell them how to become good citizens . . . I know the state of the education system that we have right now. I don't know if they're really so worried about the social aspects or the humanistic aspects as they are about the academic aspects . . . [but] I think you need to have a complete package when you're walking out the door . . . This is the time where we should talk about race and to be aware of each other's cultures and so forth and to eliminate those myths so that we have a better understanding of, "Oh, hey, that person who sits next to me might be a six-foot-two black man that plays basketball here . . . but you know what? He puts his pants on the same way. His mom and dad work. They like nice things just like my parents. We

both want to have a decent education, get a decent job," and so on . . . I think we still, as much as we don't want discrimination of anything, it's so out there. It's so blatant . . . It's like, how do you stop it if you can't stop it with these kids?

Students also told me it was important to learn how to interrupt discrimination and inequality at school. Reflecting on the racial humor, Nathan (Asian and white) said he worried what would happen "if no one [ever] tells them that's not funny." Similarly, when I asked Alena (black) if issues like race and bullying ever came up in class she said:

> No. I wish it did, though. I would be the first person in that class. I like debate classes and I feel like sometimes we should debate on like race. Like not black against white, but we should just all sit down and have a conversation like— like we're doing now! . . . I guess, it's a good school . . . but it's just white . . . They worry about the dumb stuff, you know, worried about your pants sagging, but they don't worry about the fact that you just got into a fight with somebody over racial stuff.

CHAPTER SIX

The Cycle of Mutual Disrespect

A black person will say anybody's racist just . . . because they felt they
were done wrong so they'll be like, "Oh, that person's racist" . . . instead
of actually dealing with the problem . . . 'Cause most of the time they
know it wasn't [racist] and they're just mad. But sometimes they might
actually think that, depending on what happened.

—Trevor, black student

I bet like they're scared of like some students reporting to the office that
they were being racist. That gets thrown around so much in this school.

—Bethany, white student

Teachers' avoidance of race would not have been as surprising if hyperracial exchanges were happening primarily among students in hallways,
lunchrooms, and classroom corners where educators were not present or
not paying attention. However, teachers regularly had their own hyperracial exchanges with students in which young people casually tossed
around accusations of racism, sometimes framed as jokes or convenient
excuses for poor behavior. Like student jokes, just beneath the surface
were actual racial hostilities, tensions, and biases, particularly between
black students and white teachers. Although students' accusations were
sometimes a form of deliberate taunting, they were also a way of calling

out the inequality they witnessed in how students from different racial backgrounds were treated by teachers.

ACCUSATIONS OF RACISM

At Jefferson, students from all racial backgrounds frequently accused teachers of being racist in two ways. In the most common version, students would respond to the directions, requests, or actions of a teacher by saying something like, "You just did that because I'm white," or "You just said that because I'm black." Mr. Wade (white) explained:

> Whenever anything gets said to any kid about anything, it [is] automatically, "She's saying something because I'm black." "She's saying something because I'm white." . . . A [white teacher] said something to [a white girl] one day, and she walks up and goes, "This is 'cause I'm white." So is she [the teacher]! . . . I hear that from kids all the time . . . That's just the excuse du jour.

The "because I'm . . ." commentary was so prevalent at Jefferson that almost all the teachers I talked to mentioned that at some point such an accusation had been directed at them. Moreover, most students admitted they had made such accusations.

The second way in which racism was played by students was through explicit accusations that teachers were racist. In most instances, black students, who constituted 35 percent of the student body, and white teachers, who made up over 90 percent of the teaching staff, were at the center of these exchanges. Ms. Mendenhall (white) described her experience:

> I've had white kids say I'm racist too . . . just using the term because they hear it said, [but] it tends to be more, honestly [something] black students would say . . . I think we have that whole, you know, you go back . . . to slaves and of course, "Woe is me," and I'm like, "You know what? Everybody has a woe is me story in their life . . . so knock it off . . . Let's get past that."

Ms. Mendenhall thought these sorts of accusations might be more prevalent among black students because of the history of U.S. race relations. However, rather than acknowledging some of the ways in which racial inequities remained, she held tightly to the belief that racism was something students should "get past."

Both versions of accusations of racism were delivered in ways that straddled the line between the joking and the serious. Students made such comments in fits of anger, while overcome with laughter, and everything in between. Despite the range of context and delivery, teachers largely explained these comments as "jokes" at best and "excuses" at worst. According to Mr. Bozeman (white), students would say that he was racist or that he was doing something because of their race, "but then the kid is laughing at the same time." He told me that when students made these comments, "It's just totally a joke because it's not true at all and they know it's not true . . . I really think it is [a joke]. It doesn't sound like it should be something to joke over, but it is." Like many of their students, teachers told me that they also believed racism had become a laughing matter that, while odd, was not particularly concerning.

The commonness of these accusations was illustrated in an exchange I had with Brielle (black and white) about an incident I witnessed between a white teacher and a group of black students:

Shayla: Did you hear what just happened in the hallway when we were walking over here?

Brielle: I wasn't really listening.

Shayla: There were students hanging outside the door saying [a teacher] said that they were late three days in a row. Did you hear that? And then we walked by, they said . . .

Brielle: Probably they said, "Is it 'cause I'm black?" or something.

Shayla: They said, "It's 'cause I'm black," and they said, "Why did they let that dark gorilla guy, that black gorilla in? African booty scratcher."

Brielle: Wow! I don't know. It's like, I mean, I say that too, like me and my mom (who was white) joke around like and my mom tells me to empty the dishwasher then I was like, "Oh, is it 'cause I'm black?" like it's just like a joke, I guess . . . I don't know. I just say it 'cause like, I mean, in the society we live in, like rap songs and stuff, there's like a lot of stuff about race and stuff and that's just how people joke nowadays.

Accusations of racism were so prevalent that Brielle easily guessed what had taken place in the hallway. A group of black students standing outside the classroom of a white teacher had racial implications. Moreover, she very casually admitted that she did similar things in her own multiracial family. Many students, and their teachers, believed that joking about race in this manner was simply how people communicated in integrated settings.

Some teachers and students admitted that accusations of racism were not always joking. However, most presumed these charges were excuses made by students who were not performing in accepted ways rather than reflections of actual bias. Ed (white) explained:

> Some black kids . . . when they don't do their homework, they blame all the white teachers. They say they're racist . . . They just use it as an excuse . . . because they just don't feel like doing their work and they think it's just a game. They think high school's just a game and then they're gonna be the ones on the street either shooting somebody or robbing something. It's both the colors too . . . anyone who's not doing well in school.

Ed was a fairly low-achieving student who had failed many classes himself and had struggled with behavior throughout his educational career. Nonetheless, racist narratives allowed him to separate himself from his black peers. Although Ed eventually softened his remarks by saying "anyone" might accuse teachers of racism if they were not doing well, his first words strongly implied that he felt this to be a uniquely black excuse, and that he further believed these students were likely to grow up to be criminals.

Black students also believed that racism had become a problematic excuse for poor behavior—especially being loud and talkative. According to Jada (black), many black students would say things like, "This teacher is racist because I'm black and she kicks me out of class every day." She believed the question those students should be asking is, "What are you doing to get kicked out of class? . . . So did that make her racist when you deliberately did what she told you not to?"

Stella (black) said she thought students used racism "too loosely, you know . . . Like every little thing like, 'Oh that's racist.'" She believed that many students said it because "it's the first thing that comes to their mind . . . I don't think they really think about what they're saying, like the deeper meaning of it, you know. I think they see it as black and white. He's white, he's yelling at me. That's racist." Because many students felt "racism" was overused in the school, like the boy who cried wolf, they acted as if it held little weight.

While most teachers did not take accusations of racism particularly seriously, they did find them frustrating and struggled with how to respond. The majority simply ignored the students' comments just as they ignored most things related to race. Those teachers who were more comfortable talking about race would at times confront students, usually with witty, silencing comebacks. For example, when a student told Ms. McCandless (white) she was giving her homework because she was black, Ms. McCandless responded, "Yeah, that's right. Everybody is getting homework because you're black." Mr. Wade (white) similarly used dry wit to respond, "I'll walk up and I go, 'God, I hate white people' [or] I say, 'No man, I don't hate you because you're black. I hate all you kids.'" Ms. Wenzell (white) similarly "joked" back. She said she often confused students because she did not challenge their accusations. Instead she would just agree:

[I'd say], "Yeah, yeah, you can't do that because you're black." And people got quiet and looked . . . "Are you saying that to me? Like really?" You know, I'll throw it right back at you. I mean, white people can't be afraid . . . they can't walk on eggshells because they know they've always been wrong, and black people can't use that as an excuse to be hateful and not do what they need to do.

If accusations of racism were just jokes, the responses of these teachers might have been adequate. In instances in which students were being careless or trying to explain away their own misbehavior, these teachers challenged them. However, there was often more going on that teachers' responses did not address.

TEACHERS' RACIAL JOKES

We don't have a problem teaching white kids, but they have a problem teaching our kids.

—Black staff member

It was common for teachers and students to write off accusations of racism as jokes gone too far, problematic excuses, or offhand remarks. However, the students' comments also reflected something real. Black students *were* negatively judged by teachers; they *were* more likely to be disciplined for behaviors that white students got away with; and they *were* less likely to be thought of as smart or good. White teachers *did* struggle with racial biases, and some *were* unquestionably racist. So, when students called teachers racist, sometimes they were not joking or trying to distract from the fact that they had neglected their homework. Sometimes, they were engaging in critical commentary of the discrimination they witnessed and experienced in their school.

A number of teachers regularly made thoughtless and prejudiced remarks about race. One day, I was observing a racially diverse class with two mixed (black and white) girls, two black girls, one Arab boy, and a number of white students. When I entered the room, students were already in the midst of a conversation about race. I heard someone say that one of the white male students had "Aryan looks" because of his blue eyes. A white student then said that the Arab student "doesn't like white people or black people." The Arab student responded, "Shut up!"

One of the students then turned and asked if I was going to stay and observe. She said it would be interesting because, "There's always drama in this class!" Then one of the multiracial girls suggested that they play a game, "Duck, Duck, Hitler." Someone else then made a comment about Native American savages. Rather than stopping this conversation or directing it, the teacher ignored the students, who were supposed to be working independently. Later in the hour, the teacher began going over the answers to the quiz. She told them one of the answers was something that sounded Spanish, "You know, tortilla, burrito, taco bell," she laughed, then immediately said, "I'm sorry, that was inappropriate."

This class was interesting because it was evidence not only of the frequency with which students talked about race in interracial settings, but also of teachers' propensity to not only ignore it, but join in. Although she immediately realized what she had said reinforced stereotypes about Latinos, the teacher later admitted that she often put her foot in her mouth in this way. It was a struggle for her personally to avoid making inappropriate racial remarks.

Some students of color reported incidents in which white teachers made even more explicitly racist jokes. For example, Salim (Arab) told me that he was not only called a "terrorist" by his peers, one of his white female teachers also made jokes about him in class. While he mostly shrugged off these interactions, many of his peers revealed how horrified they were by this teacher's comments.

Kaleem (black) had very similar experiences. He told me that some of his teachers made fun of the fact that he was African. He particularly struggled with one teacher:

Kaleem: I mean, he made a lot of jokes about me, I didn't mind that but . . .

Shayla: Like what?

Kaleem: Like an illegal alien, things like that, but I didn't mind that, you know. Like one day I was absent, and he said, "He probably got deported back to Africa," and things like that. But I took it as a joke because I'm a person that can take a joke pretty hard. So I came back to him and I called him the king of the douchebags, and he took that really personal and then he started being mean.

Previously, Kaleem had said that many black students used racism as an excuse: "Even I've done that; I've done that with my coach." However, further conversation revealed that real bias on the part of his teacher had preceded Kaleem's counterattack: "I thought he [the coach] really never liked me and this was when I used to be bad . . . and then I would say he calls me out because I'm black and he would make racist jokes and things like that." Kaleem's experiences came full circle. While he had accused teachers of being racist to distract from his poor behavior, he also regularly experienced racism from teachers who made discriminatory comments about him and then treated him poorly when he responded in kind.

A number of students also told me that they had witnessed white teachers making jokes about black students being drug dealers. Brandy (black) told the following story:

> One of my friends, he was kind of, going like this (hand gesture) to a student, I think they were just playing around or whatever . . . And [the teacher] said, "What are you doing? Selling drugs?" And he was a black student and she was a white teacher. And, you know, he kind of then laughed at it, but then later on talked about it like, "I can't believe she said that!" . . . It just, it was rude. It was very rude . . . She's said something similar to that . . . a few times . . . Like I thought about reporting it to the administration, but I didn't want my name to get all in there. I didn't want to make a big deal.

Brandy's feelings were almost identical to those she expressed in previous chapters about the interactions occurring between students. She felt she should do something in this instance, but struggled to find an appropriate course of action. The power dynamics between students and teachers made this situation even more complex. Teachers were figures of authority who determined students' grades and how they would be disciplined. When they were the ones making racist jokes, students I talked with felt there was little they could do.

In part, teachers engaged with students in this way because they used racial joking in their own interactions across race. White teachers admitted they had friends who jokingly called them "honky" or "dumb blond." Others said their friends sometimes made derogatory jokes about people who were Polish or Italian. Because teachers' own relationships took this tone, it was not altogether surprising that they would engage with students in this way. Nonetheless, even with their friends, these jokes sometimes crossed the line. Mr. McPhee (white) explained, "It'll come out wrong. You intend to be joking, but it's too serious and that ends the conversation."

Many teachers were not navigating race in their lives any better than their students. Perhaps Danny (white) or Brittany (white) or Raymond (black) would one day pursue teaching careers. Without the opportunity to think about race, challenge their own behavior, or interrupt their penchant for bullying those from marginalized groups, it was unlikely that they would be able to guide and support their students any better than their own teachers were guiding them.

MUTUAL DISRESPECT

There's always those teachers that you just kind of wonder about. You know, like sometimes you notice they may pick on some kid who is of a certain race, like all the time.

—Pamela, black and white student

If you keep observing in the classrooms, you'll notice how some of the black students get treated a little differently . . . just keep observing.

—Hampton, black student

Sometimes I feel like teachers they think like the black kids are harder to work with . . . Sometimes teachers don't want to be dealing with the black kids or they don't want to see us.

—Shantel, black student

There was two Caucasian boys that acted up constantly—every day, every day, every day—and they did pretty good in her class, though. But it was like, us, I guess she always yelled at us and we ended up with bad grades.

—Brandy, black student

There was one teacher that was actually racist . . . I guess all the black kids in his class had like Cs and Ds and then all white people had As and Bs.

—Madison, white student

I think too, with black students, they can tell if you're harboring some sort of racis[m]. They can tell. They can tell if you're being fair with the whole group. You know all those things translate . . . to how they're gonna interact with you.

—Ms. Hill, white teacher

Teachers were not especially likely to discuss their prejudices about black students. However, many students and a number of the more racially conscious white teachers said that, in addition to making racial jokes, some teachers were hostile toward the styles and performances of black youth. Crystal (black) explained:

> I feel like [teachers] always perceive their image, like not necessarily black people, but certain black kids. Like if a boy comes in with the sagging pants and the shirts and the hats . . . I don't care what anybody says, you're automatically given the stereotype like, "Oh, he's this or he's that" . . . When class first starts in the beginning of the year, people walking in your classroom: "Oh, you know, she looks nice, she's going to be a good student." "Oh, he has the baggy pants and the hat and yo-yo." You know.

Crystal reported that teachers often made snap judgments about students based on how they looked. Because what looks "nice" is always filtered through one's own cultural lens, it was difficult for some teachers, the majority of whom were white, to see their black students positively.

Many black students believed that some white teachers treated them unfairly. Raymond (black) was a high-achieving student in advanced classes. He smiled often and gave me a hug every time I saw him. Some might describe him as overfriendly and a bit naïve. In other words, there was nothing ghetto, gangster or hard about him. Nonetheless, he felt teachers had judged him because of his race:

> I can tell you . . . right now that teachers do base how to teach a student, how to treat a student, how to look at a student by looking at their behavior, looking at . . . what they're wearing . . . It's a big thing . . . I dress like a black guy . . . and I can say that some teachers, not saying all of them or a majority of them, just some . . . of them will look at a student . . . like, "Oh, my God, another one of these kids who are not gonna focus and just gonna be hard for me to get my point across to them."

While Raymond talked about himself as dressing "like a black guy," he generally just wore polo shirts, jeans—not particularly baggy—and white tennis shoes. I never saw him in a hat and I never saw him sag his pants. Even during this conversation, I did not find him to be particularly stylish. In short, if Raymond, who was relatively conservative in his dress, was classed as "another one of these kids," then it seemed unlikely that *any* black boys could escape negative valuation.

Fallon (black) was not as well behaved, but she had similar experiences:

Fallon: How can I say it? Like . . . half of my black friends, they come in late and the teacher's like, "Oh, you lost your four points." But when other people come, "Oh you have a warning." But that's their third time being late. Okay, but then we talking in class, you tell us to be quiet, but you see the Caucasian people talking and you don't say nothing at all . . . I just think they just got favoritism on some students, some colors.

Shayla: Do you think that the teachers have negative opinions of the black students . . . when they walk in the classroom?

Fallon: Heck yeah! You can just tell by . . . the look on their face how they think—well, how they react with that student. Like my friend Nakita, she is so loud and obnoxious, ghetto, hood rat thing, teacher just look at her, like he puts his head down and just types on his computer . . . I know he's thinking like bad things about her in his head.

Shayla: Should the teachers do anything different?

Fallon: Yeah, they should do things different . . . Stop treating the white kids better than we are getting treated.

This scenario was one that highlighted the ways in which student/teacher interactions across race got caught in a negative cycle—black students witnessed teachers treating them unfairly and the behaviors of black students reinforced the negative stereotypes teachers already held about them. Salim (Arab) called this the cycle of "mutual disrespect":

Salim: Sometimes [teachers will] just like have an attitude with the . . . black kids . . . You know, there'll be like a mutual disrespect between each other, the teacher and the student.

Shayla: A mutual disrespect? . . . And what's this mutual disrespect look like?

Salim: Usually what will happen is the loud kid in the class or the kid that the teacher doesn't like, he'll get in trouble more often 'cause the teacher will put up less with him.

Shayla: And what is the student's response to that teacher?

Salim: Just keep disrespecting the teacher and then they'll talk about him later.

Shayla: So what do you think? As they say, the chicken or the egg?

Salim: Sometimes it's a big circle, you know.

Salim's observations were astute. There was a cycle of interaction, particularly between white teachers and their black students, in which the outcomes seemed to be very much shaped by race. This cycle was especially apparent in the school experiences of Dwayne (black) who believed his low grades in Ms. Mitchell's (white) class were connected to discrimination. He explained:

Dwayne: Last year, she gave me, well she gave me an E (a failing grade). I told my momma to get me out of the classroom. She didn't want to listen, and I'm trying to tell my momma because Ms. Mitchell to me is racist . . . But I was like, "If you pull me out of the classroom, I bet you I get a better grade." Once they pulled me out of the classroom, I had got in Ms. Gasper's [class] and I pulled an A in her classroom two times in a row.

Shayla: So what was it about Ms. Mitchell that you thought was racist?

Dwayne: She's a racist. She just kept picking on me, and I kept telling her about herself 'cause like I'm not going to let a teacher—I know you grown but you're not going to sit here and keep picking on me . . . Like she just kept, "Dwayne . . . move your stuff out the way, get your things out." I mean, like it's a classroom. You need to be telling the whole class, not just me.

Shayla: You feel like she specifically targeted you?

Dwayne: Yes.

Shayla: Because you were black?

Dwayne: Just like, yeah . . . She just kept giving me bad grades, so I got out of there. And once I got out of there, I got an A. So it had to be her.

Shayla: Do you think you were doing A work in her class?

Dwayne: Not A work, probably B or a C work.

Shayla: So how did you get an E?

Dwayne: I don't know—'cause I ain't care about her. I just wanted to get out of her classroom.

Similar to Angela Valenzuela's findings in *Subtractive Schooling*, Dwayne's comments highlight the importance of care and relationships in the academic success of marginalized students.[1] While Dwayne complained that Ms. Mitchell was "racist," it was his perception that she picked on him—that she did not care about him—that led him to stop caring for her and her class. As a result, Dwayne did not work as hard as he could have.

A number of black students who were highly motivated academically also believed that race negatively affected their grades. Chris (black) generally got along with adults and was held in fairly high esteem by many of his teachers. To my knowledge, he never had disciplinary issues. However, even he believed he had experienced racial discrimination by teachers:

> Like the teacher next door, I felt like she didn't like me and a group of other students. Her favorite students was a group of white kids, but I felt like she's always probably targeting the black males . . . Like, you know, just like giving them bad grades for no reason and just like not caring at all about them . . . It was one presentation that I worked so hard on last year . . . really hard. I dressed up and everything, you know, I made my point, you know, I read what I had to read very well and I got my point across. I got a C minus . . . I was like, "This is some bull crap" . . . The other students that didn't come dressed at all, you know, didn't make the same point as I did, didn't connect it to really any [course content], which we were supposed to do, they got like B pluses, and As! I went to talk to her about it and she gave me a B-S point . . . She was like, "You didn't make your point very well. You know, I just wasn't understanding." I was like, "If I would have made it any clearer, it would be invisible!"

Like Dwayne, Chris felt that his teacher preferred her white students, as demonstrated by the fact that they often hung out in her class during free time and they got better grades for what he perceived to be poorer work.

It is unclear whether Chris got a low grade because of cultural miscommunication between him and his teacher or because he simply had not done as well on the assignment as he thought. Arguably, the reason did not matter. The outcome was that for Chris, a black male student, this experience confirmed this belief that students like him had to work twice as hard to get half as far in the classes of teachers they perceived to be racially biased. This widely shared sentiment shaped many black students' educational experience.

According to Trevor, the negative feelings particularly between black male students and white teachers stemmed in part from black boys' broader distrust of figures of authority. This distrust was rooted in their visceral understandings of the structural racism they faced and the ways in which black males in general are unfairly criminalized in the United States. He described these dynamics:

Trevor: Well, for me, all the black males that I know that are my age don't really like teachers that much . . . A teacher is like a big contradiction . . . Teachers can be very rude . . . and make you feel like you're smaller than them just because they're a teacher and they're superior.

Shayla: And . . . why is it that you feel like in particular the black people?

Trevor: Um, because—this is gonna sound really funny, but—all the black people that I know . . . including myself . . . growing up, we were always taught not to like authority . . . just something you learned is, "You don't like authority, you don't like the police," quote, unquote . . . So as you get older, when you're in school, teachers are basically police . . . So especially for a black male, that's kind of a, that's just an unwritten rule.

I'm a good student. In terms of grades, I get As and Bs and stuff. But in terms of behavior . . . I don't know. I feel as if I only show respect to people who show respect to me . . . I don't like when teachers try to belittle me when I do something or try to make me feel as if, you know, they're better than me. So let's say if I ask a question and they say, "Oh, you should know that," I don't feel like you should say I should know that. You should just answer my question because obviously there's a reason I'm asking a question . . . I don't like feeling like I'm stupid.

Trevor's analysis of student-teacher interactions was highly insightful. He connected racism, racial socialization, and black male students' daily experiences in classrooms. His analysis spoke to the ways in which the criminalization of black men in America, noted by scholars like Michelle Alexander in her acclaimed book *The New Jim Crow*, has led to a distrust of authority, reinforced by events like young, unarmed, black men being killed by police officers.[2] When teachers engaged in biased behavior, they were, in the minds of some black male students, representing this larger system of injustice.

Trevor often found himself in verbal altercations with teachers whom he felt had disrespected him. Unlike many of his peers, though, he was a high-achieving student whose GPA was often a shock to teachers and peers who assumed he did not care about school. To the contrary, Trevor came from a highly educated family in which mother was getting a PhD and he had clearly thought deeply about his own racial experiences in school. Trevor was not unlike the successful young men in Jonathan Gayles's study who accepted the "utilitarian value of schooling" while also managing to maintain social and cultural connections. Their success was not rooted in a significant connection to teachers or in a rejection of blackness, but rather in an acknowledgment that doing well in school was necessary for other life goals.[3] However, most of Trevor's peers were not able to approach school in this way. Their failure to connect with teachers too often translated into a failure to do well academically.

I also observed teachers treating students in biased ways. It was not uncommon for middle- and upper-middle-class white students to talk back to teachers, sit on desks, and congregate in classroom corners. A few, like Logan, regularly skipped class. However, their behaviors were less likely to be seen as a challenge to teachers' authority or as evidence of students' deficiencies. Instead, teachers frequently assumed that these white, middle-class kids from "good" homes were being silly, witty, or bonding with them through banter that was all in good fun. In contrast, when black students displayed similar behavior, they were more likely to be disciplined.

Very few of the white teachers I spoke to admitted that they had racial biases. Those who did were often the most racially conscious teachers, who had reflected on the realities of racial prejudice and oppression. These teachers believed a number of their colleagues were prejudiced against black students, and in some cases feared them. For example, Ms. Hill (white) thought that her colleagues often made assumptions about students based on how they dressed. "Yeah, if your pants are sagging, there's an immediate assumption," she said. Ms. Russo (white) also noted the difficulty teachers had in overcoming racial stereotypes:

> I'm sure some teachers do discriminate. You hear people talk and . . . a lot of teachers, you get stereotypes in your mind and it's very, very difficult as a teacher to get those out of your mind . . . And as a teacher you . . . just get certain behaviors and sometimes you . . . just can't help but relate them to certain groups of people . . . And a lot of teachers can't let go of that.

Ms. Russo went on to say that the best part of her job was "being proved wrong" by students she assumed would be troublemakers but who "turned out to be like this bright light in my day." She acknowledged that some of her colleagues never got to this point.

Mr. Martin's (white) observations of his colleagues were even more direct:

> You know . . . we have suburban black kids and yet some of our teachers are terrified of these kids. It's like, "Oh, the black man," and I'm like, they're kids first off. They're from the frickin' suburbs, you know. It's not like they're gang-banging, pulling up in their . . . lowered Chevy . . . blasting shots out the window . . . Like they're talking right now, "Oh, they just had those black kids go and break in over [in a majority white district] and they were students here." I'm like, "Really? How about [the boy] who graduated two years ago and just got twenty-five to thirty years in prison? He's a white kid. I don't see you guys saying anything about him . . . " Yeah, I think they're scared of them.

Mr. Martin's picture of the true nature of teachers' feelings was even more extreme than I had observed. In his experience, not only were teachers profiling students of color based on their style, speech, and behavior, they genuinely feared their black male students, despite the fact that many were middle-class.

While some teachers rejected the idea that they were engaging in biased behavior, the disaggregated data on achievement and discipline, the reports of students from various racial backgrounds, and the stories of their colleagues suggested that such practices permeated Jefferson. Students were not simply navigating "joking" interactions with their teachers across race, they were regularly dealing with real racial discrimination from their educators.

Jefferson's hyperracial culture was not just upheld by students making sly comments in the shadows. Teachers also played a significant role in maintaining racial hierarchies through jokes and biases of their own. They were a part of daily exchanges with students in which racism was casually raised both as provocative distraction and as real political commentary. These remarks revealed racial tensions, especially between white teachers and black students, which mirrored the conflicts students had with each other.

Even if teachers were not aware of the hyperracial exchanges between students, every day they heard students accuse *them* of being racist or say *they* had done something because they were black. Nonetheless, many teachers repeatedly claimed that they did not see race problems at Jefferson. When juxtaposed against their own hyperracial experiences, these claims illuminated that many teachers were not only in denial about their students' racial experiences, they were in denial about their own.

Given the constant barrage of stereotypical racial images in the media, in the news, even in textbooks, it would have been nearly impossible for teachers to avoid holding some racial biases. The problem was that too few of them were pushing themselves to challenge their stereotypes. In her book *Other People's Children*, Lisa Delpit writes that schools often "look at other people's children [black and low-income students] and see damaged and dangerous caricatures of the vulnerable and impressionable beings before them."[4] At Jefferson, this meant that—as Mr. Wade (white) said point-blank—"There's a lot of prejudice here in this building." And while students were aware of it, too many of the teachers were not.

CHAPTER SEVEN

Reframing Race

We often assume that political activism requires an explanation, while inactivity is a normal state of affairs. But it can be as difficult to ignore a problem as to try to solve it.

—Nina Eliasoph, *Avoiding Politics*[1]

I have often said that white people will do *anything* not to talk about their race and to avoid our responsibilities to take apart these systems that keep us primary.

—Frances Kendall, *Understanding Whiteness*[2]

How was it that in a school where students and teachers were having highly racialized interactions, race was also silenced, avoided, and ignored by adults? What were the mechanisms through which this happened? One contributing factor was the desire of many teachers at Jefferson to think of themselves as "color-blind." Because these teachers claimed not to notice racial difference, it was easy for them to ignore racial discrimination. However, a considerable number of teachers were color-conscious—they understood that race was an important part of identity that shaped how individuals saw themselves and how they were seen by others. These teachers also played a role in maintaining the status quo of silence. They utilized similar frames when talking about racial differences, disparities, and discrimination to sidestep directly discussing race. In so doing, they allowed the problematic racial culture of Jefferson High School to flourish uninterrupted.

COLOR-BLIND

> First of all, one thing about me that I should tell you—honestly, when a kid walks in a room, I don't notice their color. I really don't. I don't pay attention to that, I don't pay attention to their clothes, I don't pay attention to how their hair looks . . . It doesn't matter to me. It really doesn't.
>
> —Ms. Mendenhall, white

About half of the teachers at Jefferson claimed, like Ms. Mendenhall, to be color-blind. They said when it came to their students, they did not *see* race and they did not believe students' racial backgrounds mattered for their teaching practice. Ms. Hogan (white) was one of these teachers. She had worked at Jefferson for decades during which the numbers of students of color had more than doubled, but did not think the demographic shifts mattered much:

> To me, kids are kids. You know . . . a fifteen-year-old is a fifteen-year-old is a fifteen-year-old, whether it's 1985 or 2009 . . . Doesn't matter what their physicality looks like . . . 'cause they can so surprise you . . . I've got a kid back there with all the piercings and every goofy-looking thing and he's one of my sharper kids, so you really can't judge a book by its cover . . . Now, behaviorally I can tell. The kids have these defense mechanisms and they have their way of avoiding doing work . . . After [this many] years, you can spot that after the first week of school. You know who's going to have a heck of a time.

While Ms. Hogan did not explicitly connect behavior to race, students of color were more likely to be thought of as poorly behaved by their peers and their teachers and were significantly more likely to be referred, suspended, and expelled. By adopting a color-blind stance, Ms. Hogan was overlooking the fact that those students seen as "having a heck of a time" were disproportionately black.

Color-blind teachers not only adopted this stance for themselves, they also wanted students to ignore race. While making copies in the teachers' lounge, Ms. Wilson (white) told me that she had covered for an absent colleague earlier that day. As she was letting students into the classroom so that they could wait for their substitute teacher, a black girl asked if the substitute was going to be African American. Ms. Wilson responded, "Why does that matter?" Shaking her head incredulously, she told me that the students at Jefferson clearly needed a lot of help moving beyond race.

The "race negative" approach taken by Ms. Wilson, in which any mention of race was perceived as a problem, was common among color-blind teachers. They worried that raising the subject in any way was racist, with no notion of the possibility of a healthy racial awareness.

Since over 90 percent of Jefferson's teachers were white, it was no surprise to me that a black student, who had likely never had a black teacher, wondered if she would see a face that looked more like hers standing in the front of the classroom that day. However, color-blind teachers did not recognize that this might matter for students. Instead, color-blindness created a narrative in which "those kids" who openly expressed noticing race were framed as the problem, rather than the lack of teachers of color.

Scholars like Gloria Ladson-Billings argue that color-blindness has been a real hindrance to creating a more equitable education system. As she writes, "The passion for equality in the American ethos has many teachers (and others) equating equality with sameness . . . The notion of equity as sameness only makes sense when all students *are* exactly the same . . . If teachers pretend not to see students' racial and ethnic differences, they really do not see the students at all and are limited in their ability to meet their educational needs."[3]

When teachers ignored race, they were often unknowingly contributing to a system in which racial disparities and discrimination could not be addressed and racial difference could not be celebrated.

COLOR-CONSCIOUS

We're not in a post-racial society . . . they're full of crap. They're full of crap if they say that, and they know they are.

—Mr. Martin, white teacher

It is impossible to be color-blind in a world as color-conscious
as ours.

—Lani Guinier and Gerald Torres, *The Miner's Canary*[4]

A significant number of teachers were highly critical of their colleagues' claims that it was possible to be oblivious to race. They thought of themselves as racially conscious and talked openly about concepts like racism and white privilege—the idea that white people have unearned social, economic, and political advantage in our society simply because of their race. Mr. Edwards (white) was one of these teachers:

> I don't think other teachers for the most part are aware of [white privilege]. 'Cause I always hear, "Oh well, I'm color-blind." But you know, maybe that's not such a good thing . . . because that's going to help you deal with students of color, and students who aren't straight, and students who aren't the same sex as you—understanding that this [country] is not . . . a meritocracy. We pay lip service to it, but no, it is strictly race- and class-based. If that should be broken, this is the perfect place to do it, school.

Mr. Sallee (white) was similarly critical of his color-blind colleagues. While he ideally envisioned a world in which, "like Haile Selassie's comment, you know, the color of a man's skin is of no more importance than the color of a man's eyes," he did not believe color-blindness was a useful ideological position, given the present reality. "Saying, 'Oh, race doesn't matter,' that's just plain ignorant . . ." he said. "Are you blind? . . . Yeah, that's foolish."

Color-conscious teachers knew that fighting against deeply ingrained racial bias was a constant internal battle. "I think everybody has [racism] in them somehow," Ms. Kennedy (white) said. "And it's not necessarily against a whole race, but I think everybody has it in them to a certain degree 'cause it's been for hundreds of years in our society . . . Somebody has a relative that's overtly racist. Sometimes something is happening and you just have that thought. Everybody's got it, and it's just a matter of . . . you don't act on it. You don't make ignorant comments." She believed it was disingenuous for teachers to deny having preconceived notions about race, if for no other reason than they were a part of the fabric of hundreds of years of history in which race and racism have been so prevalent.

Like Ms. Kennedy, Ms. Gorski (white) also knew that it took active and conscious work to interrupt one's own racial biases. Her experience growing up in a segregated racist community in which she was ostracized because of her ethnic identity had led her toward racial consciousness. She noted that a number of her peers would say things like:

> "Oh I'm not racist, or something," you know. And like I said . . . it's an effort to not be racist . . . The racism is so strong in this country. I mean, they did everything but call Obama the N-word . . . I don't watch TV, but I do scan every once in a while . . . So I go on the country music channel, okay? Well, there's a black artist on there . . . so, you know, all the images of the music videos are just images, right? But here they go. They have to have the Confederate flag in the background with a bunch of Asian kids. And its like, "What are you doing. What are you saying here?"

Ms. Gorski was able to apply her critical racial lens not only to music videos, but also to her work at Jefferson High. She was especially concerned about how race influenced which students were diagnosed with learning disabilities and placed in special education. Many studies have found that African American students are overrepresented in special education.[5] Ms. Gorski believed this trend was also true at Jefferson:

Ms. Gorski: They're definitely more black [students in special education]. Yeah.

Shayla: Why do you think that is?

Ms. Gorski: Because they're racist.

Shayla: Really? And on whose part?

Ms. Gorski: Well, it's racism on the part of the testing and stuff. I mean, I had a student in the back of my cognitively impaired class, they were twins—a black girl and her brother. She was in the back of the classroom reading a paperback book . . . and I'm going, "cognitively impaired" really precludes your ability to read, especially a paperback book . . . She graduated actually with a 3.5. And the whole time I'm thinking, why was she in there? . . . It was almost as if she was there to take care of her brother . . . Since her brother was labeled as special ed, then . . . she is. And then, so why did that happen? . . . But then I even went further and said, well, was her brother even cognitively impaired? And, no . . . I think it's [discriminatory placement in special education] allowed.

Although Ms. Gorski was open with me about her observations, she had not engaged in this conversation with her colleagues. Nor did she do anything to advocate for these two students and others like them. She kept her thoughts to herself, convinced that Jefferson was a place in which these issues could not be safely raised.

Perhaps not surprisingly, many of the color-conscious teachers had had significant personal exposure to racial diversity through familial relations, close friendships, world travel, and personal reflection. Nonetheless, when it came to discussing issues of race with students or other educators, they were just as likely to sidestep the conversation as their color-blind colleagues.

COLOR-CONFUSED

Racial ideology at Jefferson was messy. The lines between the color-blind and color-conscious were not always so clear. Many teachers were confused about what they were supposed to hear, see, think, and say when it came to issues of race. Ms. Wenzell (white) was a good example. She had grown up in a racially diverse community and connected well with black students. Nonetheless, she was sometimes at a loss:

I think that there's a little too much stress on, is it color-blindness? Or should . . . no . . . people talk about "You shouldn't be color-blind, you should be color-conscious" . . . I think it's another PC bunch of crap. If you say you're color-blind, that you'd like people to understand you don't . . . judge people . . . then you're wrong because you shouldn't be color-blind . . . can I win please, somewhere?

Ms. Wenzell's feeling that, when it came to race, the rules were always changing was not inaccurate. Making sense of race is a complex and often contradictory endeavor. Teachers at Jefferson had grown up in a post–civil rights era during which most white Americans were taught that color-blindness was the next step in racial progress. As a result, many believed they were supposed to pretend not to see race, even as they noticed the ways in which race mattered in educational outcomes.

Ms. Stinnett's (white) experience was an illuminating example of the internal battle many teachers faced:

Ms. Stinnet: Like color wasn't an issue in my family. We helped a [black] family move . . . who lived with us . . . My grandparents marched in Washington. We have really liberal values. I mean, my parents said there is nobody that I could bring home that would shock them except a Republican . . . I was educated in a way that we weren't supposed to see color . . . you know—everybody's supposed to be treated the same way.

Shayla: Would you describe yourself as color-blind?

Ms. Stinnett: I would not describe myself as color-blind. I wish I was in a lot of ways . . .

Shayla: Would you describe yourself as color-conscious?

Ms. Stinnett: I think that's my issue. I'm color-conscious and I don't know if that's a good thing or a bad thing . . . I would never say, if I was de-scribing a person across the room that I wanted you to notice—I would tell you what their hair color was. I would tell you what they're wearing. I would tell you what they were doing, all before my last thing that I would tell you is what color they are . . . For me to point out what color somebody was . . . I think it is an issue. I don't think my friends would ever, they would be like, "Why are you telling me they're black?" And I would be like, "I'm just trying to point them out to you." They would be shocked . . . It's considered unacceptable.

Shayla: Do you think it's good that it's unacceptable?

Ms. Stinnett: I don't know. I think it's unacceptable because I would never tell you, if I was describing a person and they were the same color as I was . . . I would never say, "that white person over there."

Rather than considering the possibility that white people *should* have more racial consciousness, that by consistently failing to name whiteness she was contributing to an inequitable system in which white was treated as the norm, and that perhaps she *should* say "that white person over there," just as one might say "that man over there," Ms. Stinnett believed she should not mention anyone's race.

COLOR-BLIND FRAMES

Racism for whites has been like a crazy uncle who has been locked away for generations in the hidden attic of our collective social reality. This old relative has been part of the family for a long time. Everyone knows he's living with us, because we bring him food and water occasionally, but nobody wants to take him out in public.

—Gary Howard, *We Can't Teach What We Don't Know*[6]

Despite the variation in teachers' racial ideologies, few were able to discuss race with colleagues, incorporate content about race in their curriculum, or effectively interrupt problematic student interactions across race. Instead, almost all of the teachers at Jefferson—those who were intellectually committed to racial justice and those who were not—adopted color-blind frames when making sense of their day-to-day experiences.

In *Racism without Racists*, Eduardo Bonilla-Silva writes that ". . . whites with differing levels of sympathy toward minorities resort to the *same* frames when constructing their accounts of racial matters."[7] In particular, Bonilla-Silva notes four frames that make up the ideology of color-blindness or what he calls "racism lite"—abstract liberalism, naturalization, cultural racism, and minimization. These four frames perpetuate racial inequality through seemingly nonracial mechanisms.

Abstract liberalism is when white people espouse support for "equality," "diversity," or "education for all" without enacting any policies or practices that would achieve such goals. As Bonilla-Silva writes, ". . . whites can appear 'reasonable' and even 'moral' while opposing almost all practical approaches to dealing with de facto racial inequality."[8] For example, using the frame of abstract liberalism, teachers and administrators could say that they supported diversity while failing to hire a more diverse staff or create a more multicultural curriculum.

Cultural racism is a rebirth of the "culture of poverty" thesis, in which the continuation of racial inequality is blamed on the cultural and behavioral deficiencies of people of color—for example, style, language, or family structure.[9] Rather than addressing the fact that students of color are likely to be disciplined more harshly than white students for the same infractions, educators displaying cultural racism might say that discipline disparities stem from the failure of some families to teach their children how to behave appropriately. The students in part I often used this frame to justify their biases.

The frame of *naturalization* argues that racial division is not rooted in discrimination, but rather is a part of the natural order. By claiming things like segregation were "natural," teachers, administrators, and students who used this frame were able to ignore the ways in which Jefferson was perpetuating racial tensions, discrimination, and inequality.

Finally, the frame of *minimization* is the belief that race is no longer an issue because race relations have significantly improved since the days of slavery. Bonilla-Silva argues that because white people perceive race relations to be better than they used to be, as evidenced by things like the election of an African American president, claims about continuing legacies of racism by people of color can be written off as overstatements, or "playing the race card."

There was a similar usage of color-blind frames among teachers at Jefferson. Along with cultural racism, naturalization, and minimization, I noticed two other common constructs through which faculty avoided directly confronting race: *willful ignorance*—rooted in a kind of abstract liberalism in which they actively avoided thinking about race so as not to have to do anything about racial inequality—and *class conflation*—in which class, not culture, was used as the proxy for racial bias. Combined, these frames allowed many white teachers to let themselves off the hook for addressing issues of race, even many of those who thought of themselves as racially conscious.

Willful Ignorance

While teachers at Jefferson varied in how much they claimed to notice race, most said they did not notice racial *problems*. For example, most teachers said they did not know about cafeteria segregation. As Ms. Scott (white) said, "I don't even pay attention 'cause I just don't register stuff like that." While it was true that teachers did not spend much time in the lunchrooms, students regularly talked about the "white" and "black" cafeterias. Virtually every student I talked to mentioned them. Moreover, the year before this study began, there had been efforts at the administrative level to integrate the cafeterias by assigning students to lunchrooms—efforts that were announced to teachers in staff meetings and that *they* ultimately had to explain to their students. In other words, teachers had multiple opportunities to know what was happening at lunchtime. Unfortunately, most ignored it.

Most teachers also ignored how race mattered in student outcomes. Black students underperformed on all standardized test areas, were underrepresented in AP courses, and were almost entirely absent from the National Honor Society. The majority of teachers claimed to have little knowledge of these trends. When I asked whether or not there was an achievement gap at Jefferson, a few offered to "go get their grade books" during our conversation, or quickly began scanning their students to answer the question more accurately, but said they had not thought about it previously. As Ms. Palmer (white) put it, "I don't know . . . I like don't even pay attention to that . . . I would probably have to sit there and look at like individual kids and really think about that." In part, the problem was "nobody comes to us and says, 'So here's your [class]. It's disadvantaged in this sense or you're getting more of this population' . . . and I mean maybe I should, maybe some people pay attention to it . . . I just look at these kids, and I'm like, all right, so what do they need?"

It was true that administrators did not adequately share school-level disaggregated data (see chapter 9). However, teachers did not track racial trends in achievement and discipline within their own classrooms, nor did the federal mandates of NCLB motivate them to do so.

Some teachers admitted they purposely avoided seeking information about racial disparities because they worried it might *increase* their biases. Mr. Garner (white) observed:

> Maybe I'm intentionally oblivious because I don't care. I mean, I don't care who walks through the door . . . They're all unique. I hate to make sweeping generalizations . . . I don't want to sound . . . oblivious, you know—somebody that doesn't care—but like I said, I haven't really thought about it that much because I don't want to have those like preconceptions. I'd rather just deal with people.

For Mr. Garner, noticing racial differences and treating people equally could not coexist. He wanted to believe that all students at Jefferson had equal opportunities to succeed. However, the data and the experiences of students suggested otherwise. Mr. Garner called on his desire to "just deal with people," to let himself off the hook for having to address the unique needs of marginalized students.

Other teachers had looked at their disaggregated data, but they did so with great caution. For example, Mr. Sallee (white) had thought a lot about issues of race. He had family members of color and had independently tracked achievement in this classroom because, as he explained, "I was curious if there was [an achievement gap] . . ." However, he worried about the implications of his investigation:

> You know, I mean, if you're a black teacher and you ask that question, but if you're a white teacher and you say, "Gee, are blacks not doing as well?" then automatically there's some suspicion and you're being racist . . . So then you go, "We don't notice any difference. No, they're all the same."

Other teachers said they avoided this information because they could not see what good would come from it. When asked if there was an achievement gap, Ms. Mendenhall (white) said:

> I really don't, I don't know . . . I probably do want to know, but I guess I don't want to know because it doesn't matter to me. My job's not going to change any whether or not there is one. I'm not going to do anything different because I don't look at that when I'm teaching.

Many teachers shared this sentiment, believing that they were already providing opportunities for young people to learn and grow to the best of their abilities. If the data suggested that their efforts were not effective with some groups of students, this would only make them feel bad. They could not conceptualize a way in which seeking information and increasing their awareness about racial disparities might actually improve their practice.

Class Conflation

> We use euphemisms, code words: "welfare problem," "poverty problem," "crime problem," assuming these mean something other than what they are—a backhanded way of talking about what we believe is a "race problem."
>
> —Julie Landsman, *A White Teacher Talks about Race*[10]

> These white teachers think just because these kids are black, they're poor! And they're not! Look at their clothes! Somebody is taking *good* care of them. They aren't poor. But to these teachers, they all look the same.
>
> —Black staff member

> I've had squirrely kids of every description. That's my favorite word. Like you know, I have so many squirrels in this class and so many squirrels in that class. If there was a link to race, I would . . . I think I would be looking one step further and see if that's actually more socioeconomic status.
>
> —Ms. Ellis, white teacher

Many teachers denied the possibility that race was a relevant factor when considering achievement, behavior, and segregation. Instead, they argued that the issues students faced were really about class. For example, when asked about racial disparities in academic outcomes, Ms. Meguschar (white) said, "I see an achievement gap more so between SES [socioeconomic status] than I do race, across the board. I see my higher SES whether they're white, black, Asian, mixed . . . doing better for the most part than my lower SES. I see that as a bigger achievement gap than the race." To some extent, Ms. Meguschar's assessment was correct. There was an economic achievement gap at the school. However, there was also a very significant racial one, even when class was controlled for. Rather than recognizing that both existed, she used the economic gap to avoid discussing the racial one.

Ms. Hill (white), a racially conscious teacher, also fell into this trap of identity picking to explain differential achievement:

> I really think socioeconomics in a lot of ways can supersede the race issue. I think the socioeconomic is really what we should be focused on as a school, as a community, as a nation . . . The media or whoever wants you to focus on the race, but really it's . . . the rich are getting richer and the poor are getting poorer and the middle class are going away. And if we don't have any of that, we're all the same, man. We're all poor.

Ms. Hill's comments indicated an awareness of the political and economic climate in which the ramifications of failing to develop class-consciousness in the United States were becoming more and more apparent. However, she did not acknowledge that being black and poor was qualitatively different from being white and poor,[11] especially at schools like Jefferson, where test scores, course tracking, and disciplinary trends could not be explained by class alone.

Ms. Dunlap (white) also thought of herself as racially conscious. She talked openly about her family's involvement in the civil rights movement and her own desire for a more equitable world. However, she did not think race mattered in education:

> I think the biggest problem is the economic . . . You know a young black man whose father and mother are MDs or PhDs . . . he may [have] some problems if he's at the mall or . . . when he's driving, but achievement-wise . . . you're not going to be able to detect color from his test scores or his performances in a classroom.

Ms. Dunlap could acknowledge that "out there" in the world, people were discriminatory. However, she was unwilling to accept the ways in which middle-class black students have been repeatedly shown to underperform when compared with middle-class white students in class-rooms like hers.[12]

Some Jefferson teachers also used class to explain racial segregation among students. For example, Mr. McPhee (white) said:

> The deep root of [segregation] is socioeconomic, where people live. 'Cause you have your group or clique, if you will, from the trailer park . . . versus your small subdivisions, and they're not in close proximity that much . . . So you have people of lower income, middle income, and higher income kind of hanging out together . . . I think that is the bigger issue to address than color.

It was true that class facilitated social divisions between students, but as was seen in chapter 4, race was perhaps a more significant divider. Unfortunately, the large majority of teachers were not aware of how federal and state policies—such as Jim Crow laws, redlining, which barred families of color form moving into white neighborhoods, and more recently discriminatory subprime mortgages—created a racially unjust housing system in the United States.

Many teachers depended on economic inequality to explain disparities because they believed all of the black students in the school were poor. Ms. Stinnett (white) was a good example of teachers' struggles to separate race and class:

Ms. Stinnett: I have found that it's more socioeconomic. I think we have a larger black population that is socioeconomically low than we do a white population.

Shayla: The rumor I had heard about this school was a lot of the poor kids are rural white kids and a lot of the black kids are middle-class.

Ms. Stinnett: I don't know if I really believe that now, especially since we are a school of choice [a school that allows students living outside of the district to enroll] . . . [So] I don't really think that's true. I think it used to be true. I think that used to be true for sure. I don't think it has been in the last four years or so.

Shayla: When did the school of choice thing start?

Ms. Stinnett: Two years ago . . . But we definitely had people moving into this district or saying, "I live with Aunt so-and-so" to go this school.

It is unclear whether large numbers of black students at JHS were actually living in poor communities outside of Jefferson, as Ms. Stinnett suggested. However, in the years before and after Jefferson became a school of choice, the population of black students did not change significantly. Even if it had been the case that students were coming to Jefferson from other districts, their parents were those who were invested enough in their children's education to move them to a district they perceived to be better. As shown in the introduction, they were not the most disadvantaged black families, as many teachers' comments suggested.

Another reason teachers focused on class was because they were more comfortable talking about economic inequality than racial inequality. Ms. McWilliams (white) was a good example. She knew nationally there was a racial achievement gap and even acknowledged that Jefferson followed this trend. However, she simply could not bring herself to discuss it at any length:

> Every time we're shown our schoolwide statistics, yes, that is true, [we have a racial achievement gap]. And when I look at what happens inside my classroom, I haven't . . . looked at the racial breakdown. I just look at—okay, I know how hard you work, and I know what grade . . . and it never really is anything that I have sorted out. But if I had to guess, let me think about this for my classes . . . I have a lot of kids who are in special ed, who come from poor families, black and white. And then I have kids coming from single parents, poorer families who are absent a lot, black and white. And those are the kids that struggle. And it isn't so much about the color of their skin. But I would guess that probably we fit into the national average.

Ms. McWilliams knew intellectually that Jefferson students fit into "the national average" when it came to race and achievement, yet she talked about special education, single-parent homes, and poor families, which she disconnected from race by continually saying that it applied to students "black and white," as the real issues. While she perhaps gave some insight into the economic achievement gap, she ultimately failed to explain the racial one.

Why Teachers Rely on Class

Ironically, although many teachers claimed class was the real determinant in how well students did in school, they also claimed to be class-blind. When asked directly about class or when pushed to explore which students were low achievers because of their socioeconomic status, teachers almost unanimously said they did not know the economic backgrounds of their students. As Ms. Mitchell (white) described it:

> Honestly, how would we know students who are [poor]? Only when it's brought to our attention through a social worker or somebody else. We don't know the class of the student. I don't know where they live unless they tell me. You can't base it on how they dress because the most affluent students go to [the thrift store] for their clothes because they're cool. There is absolutely no way, unless they stink and look dirty, to know, and even then they just might have poor hygiene, you know . . . I don't think they know at all. I know I don't.

As Ms. Mitchell pointed out, class was often harder to see on students than race. While class was also a cultural identity that was performed and sometimes visible, teachers were not necessarily accurate in their efforts to identify class, and many knew this. Nonetheless, they frequently pointed to class as the major cause of the achievement gap.

Teachers may have emphasized the role of class in educational disparities because the lowest-income students did the worst academically. However, class was not merely called on because teachers thought it to be more pressing—they were not addressing economic inequality either—instead, it was an identity that was less risky to discuss.

In the United States, race and racism have been politicized and made taboo in ways that class has not.[13] Unlike many European countries where there have been widespread social movements around economic inequality,[14] U.S. popular discourse around class remains rooted in the belief that if you have not attained economic success, it is because you have not worked hard enough. Although researchers have long noted how class status is also reproduced and maintained through unfair policies and biased practices, most people believe in the myth of the American Dream: if you

work hard, you can be anything you want to be.[15] In fact, racial divisions
in the United States have often hindered class solidarity.[16] As Frances Fox
Piven and Richard Coward write, the history of the United States is one of:

> failed efforts to [produce] multiracial, class-based protest movements. And so,
> when massive socioeconomic and political changes finally made an independent black struggle possible, black eruptions provoked the violent opposition
> of southern white working-class people and later the opposition of northern
> working-class people as well, [widening working class racial divisions].[17]

Because class "has not been a source of pride, critique, or collective consciousness" in the United States, it has not received the kind of heightened
scrutiny or critical reflection that race has.[18]

In order to acknowledge that race was a factor in achievement and discipline, JHS teachers would have had to accept that schools were biased
against students based on race—an immutable identity—or worse, that
they themselves were. In contrast, if poverty were the issue, they could
blame marginalized students, parents, and communities for not working
hard enough or not caring enough about education. Unfortunately, its
lack of politicization allowed class to be made invisible and co-opted as a
safe retreat, and allowed teachers to not only ignore racial inequality, but
also subvert real discussions about disparities that fell along lines of class.[19]

Cultural Racism

A number of teachers talked more about culture than class when explaining disparities in achievement and discipline. Not unlike many of their
white students, these teachers claimed it was not blackness that was problematic, or even poverty, it was "those kids" who were loud, used slang,
sagged their pants, and congested the hallways. Ms. Kennedy (white)
explained:

> I know they did that study that African Americans make up—what?—90 percent of the discipline referrals generally in schools . . . but I also find that
> they're generally the kids that don't stop talking when you ask them to and,
> "You can't disrespect me," and that sort of thing, which I think is a culture
> thing, not necessarily a [racial] targeting.

Ms. Kennedy was aware that there were differences in discipline, but she did not think specific *racial* groups were being targeted. Instead, she believed it was somewhat coincidental that the students teachers viewed as consistently behaving inappropriately were predominantly black.

Many white teachers, even those who were racially conscious, simply found black students confounding. Mr. Wade (white) explained:

> I've got white kids that are dumbasses too . . . I think it's a cultural thing. And you can answer this better than me, 'cause black people are louder in general . . . They're just louder. I'm not used to it. So . . . is that a problem? No. I just wish you'd tone it down a little bit 'cause it hurts my ears. Does it bother me? No . . . you are what you is . . . [But] I can see some people struggle with it. I can see other people struggle with that.

While Mr. Wade was able to make a claim for cultural relativism—the notion that cultures are neither better nor worse, just different—those students from cultures that were "naturally" louder were also more bothersome to most teachers. As a result, they tended to get into more trouble.[20] By making an argument about natural differences between cultures, teachers like Mr. Wade did not have to make one about race.

Some teachers were also very disturbed by the ways black students spoke and viewed it as evidence that black students were not as committed to education as their white counterparts. For example, Mr. McPhee (white) knew black students often had to code-switch from the linguistic traditions of their homes to those of the school in order to be successful:

> The black students, in my experience, is much lower than the white families . . . How much they read, how much they write. It's just the way that they present themselves in speaking to others. The language that dictates our nation is based on the white male . . . And I'm not saying that black students have to conform to that and just be that way or assimilate . . . I think it's important to have a voice, and it's almost a bilingual voice. But knowing when it's appropriate to speak, you know, without all the slang Ebonics . . . black vernacular with their friends or their family . . . They don't see that, where the line is.

Mr. McPhee's observation that black students often needed to be "bilingual" was very much aligned with theories of culturally relevant pedagogy and culturally responsive teaching.[21] However, he struggled to identify his own role in this kind of education. He did not challenge the white-male-dominated structure in his own classroom, nor did he believe it was his responsibility as an educator to teach his black students how to code-switch in the ways he expected them to. Instead, he was frustrated that black students did not come to school already knowing "when it's appropriate to speak without all the slang Ebonics." While Mr. McPhee was color-conscious—able to discuss racial differences, the privilege of whiteness, and the inequality that resulted—and was even aware of what some solutions might be—teach students to be bilingual—he was not able to translate this knowledge into classroom practices that created opportunities for black student success.

In *Notes from the Back of the Room*, Karolyn Tyson asks what would happen if schools made "explicit to black students the goals of cultural socialization and the necessity for competence in their own as well as in the dominant, culture . . ."[22] Similarly, Lisa Delpit posits, "If you are not already a participant in the culture of power, being told explicitly the rules of that culture makes acquiring power easier."[23] Unfortunately, the majority of educators at Jefferson were failing to teach students of color the "culture of power" while punishing them for the culture they came to school with.

In the conversations noted above, teachers used some aspect of cultural performance to highlight their challenges with black students. Rather than thinking about how schools might allow for a broader range of cultural performance, how to scaffold students of color into the expected behavior, how classroom discipline consistently fails black students, or how their own biases shape their perceptions of misbehavior, many teachers saw black youth as "an intrinsically 'problematic' population."[24]

Naturalization

Some teachers used the frame of naturalization when discussing racial segregation in the cafeterias and other school spaces. This was a particularly appealing frame because it also allowed teachers to feel better about their own racially segregated lives. Most Americans, particularly white

Americans, do not have significant cross-racial friendships.[25] This includes teachers. Ms. Guthrie (white) explained:

> Adults are no different than kids . . . Kids segregate by color because that's where their friends are. And I didn't even realize that 'til someone told me . . . I had to go look for myself . . . I don't see it as a problem . . . It's like people associate with people they feel comfortable with . . . People that you don't have to worry about if you say something that it's going to be misinterpreted, and that's what people do . . . So it's no different than if I go have lunch with three other women who are my age.

Ms. Mitchell (white) agreed. As she put it:

> We all hang around with people we have things in common with and we have things in common with people of our same gender, our same race . . . And so I think the same thing goes [for students] . . . I think it would be naive to think that you could break that up and that you could force them to be friends with and hang around people of different, you know, colors.

As both of these teachers observed, people often have common life experiences and shared understandings of the world with those from their own racial groups. However, racial divisions are not immutable, as they suggest. Instead, segregation is often more about nurture than nature, created over generations through inequality, discrimination, and fear. The fact that so many students struggled to find connections across race, and that some teachers did not think they could, was more a reflection of their own racial discomfort than of fact. Nonetheless, those teachers who thought segregation was natural and inherent tended to take few steps to provide students with opportunities to build relationships across difference.

Some teachers *did* think it was their job to challenge and interrupt student segregation. As Ms. Dunlap (white) put it:

> I know that I prefer being with women during my lunch, I know that. But my thing is that our job isn't to provide the kids comfort . . . Part of our job is to . . . test their comfort levels. And I agree . . . that we do have an obligation because our society needs it. I did not work in the civil rights movement so that we can have segregated classrooms or segregated lunchrooms. That's not what I had in mind.

Mr. Edwards (white) also believed that "part of school is to introduce you to things that you don't know, things that you are not familiar with. And you know, that means a tablemate that looks different than you. Beautiful. That's a form of learning."

Nonetheless, the majority of teachers did little to provide students with such opportunities.

Minimization

Finally, some white teachers minimized hostile racial interactions between racial groups. As Ms. McWilliams (white) put it, "We don't have race wars here. [M]ore often than not the two kids fighting are the same . . . race and the same socioeconomic [status]." Because there were so few fights across race, many teachers presumed race was not a point of conflict for students. They did not recognize racial jokes, slurs, and other forms of bullying as manifestations of conflict.

Other teachers minimized the racial issues between students because they perceived the adults in the building to be so much worse in comparison. Ms. Wenzell (white) explained:

> What I've come to realize last year is that really it's the adults that need to talk . . . I don't think we even need to talk with students about racism because you can't imagine, people can't imagine . . . how much change will happen from this generation to this generation . . . I don't think it's as big of an issue as everyone makes it out to be. We want to heal somebody, but we're trying to heal something that's not broke, making me uncomfortable . . . I think we are moving into "It's a lovely world." I think it's moving into a direction like that.

Teachers who came from a generation or community in which racism seemed to be especially prominent often looked at the young people at Jefferson and saw progress and hope. However, in so doing, they tended to be overly confident about the state of race relations at the school. Like so many of their students, many teachers thought "everyone got along" and so made little effort to help young people navigate racial difference or conflict.

A number of researchers and practitioners have suggested that one way to improve white teachers' effectiveness with students of color is to increase their racial consciousness. However, the experiences of teachers at Jefferson reveal that consciousness is not necessarily enough to change practice. Although some teachers claimed not to see race, a significant number understood racial inequality and rejected the color-blind approach. Yet in practice, both groups struggled to take productive action around issues of race.

When it came to explaining racial disparities in their school or applying their knowledge to their content and pedagogy, even those teachers who were intellectually committed to racial justice ignored racial inequality and conflict; conflated race, class, and culture; and naturalized and minimized the continuing legacies of racism. Why, besides fear, did these racially conscious teachers so easily fall back on color-blind frames? One major obstacle was that in spite of national racial disparities in educational outcomes, they were teaching in an era in which their administrators and the many school reform initiatives under way in the district, state, and nation, did not support deep reflection, discussion, or action around race.

PART III

Administrators

CHAPTER EIGHT

"No One at the Table"

What school administrators do interests me not only because their behavior affects what happens in the whole complex of formal education,
but also because that behavior . . . reflects both the education subculture
and the American value system . . . It is ironic and even paradoxical that
school administrators have been so touted in recent years as "agents
of change." I believe that their contribution in education is quite the op-
posite . . . School principals serve their institutions and their society as
monitors for continuity.

—Harry Wolcott, The Man in the Principal's Office[1]

The simultaneously hyperracial and colormute culture of Jefferson's students and teachers was a reflection of a broader district culture that priori-
tized maintaining the racial status quo. Jefferson's school board, administration, and teaching staff were overwhelmingly white. The few black
employees, most of whom had been in the district for over a decade, were
consistently overlooked for promotion and wielded little power, even when
they were in administrative positions. Nonetheless, when problems arose
around race, staff of color, particularly the former black principal, were
framed by their white colleagues as responsible for both creating them and
solely responsible for fixing them.

These personnel practices created a leadership structure that limited
perspectives on diversity and equity being heard in the district. There was

"no one at the table," as one black staff person put it, to hold the district accountable for dealing with deeply seated racial biases in the community or considering how Jefferson might more effectively educate students of color.

WHITE TEACHERS

Although the Jefferson student population was only 60 percent white, like most schools in the country, the educational staff was over 90 percent white (figure 8.1).[2] As one white administrator put it, "The district has not taken a proactive approach to hiring black teachers or diverse teachers at all. There are obviously qualified teachers coming out of schools [of education], but the district does not reach out to them." Unfortunately, as seen in chapter 5, the majority of the white educators hired to teach in Jefferson were unable or unwilling to proactively address issues of race in the classroom.

While these numbers were not unique to Jefferson, they were nonetheless disappointing to some employees I spoke with because the director of

Figure 8.1   Staff by race, Jefferson School District, 2009–10

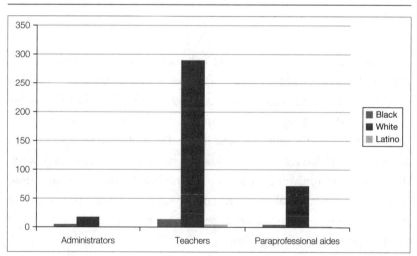

Source: State Department of Education.

Human Resources was an African American man, who many expected would make more efforts to diversify the staff. Instead, they thought that Jefferson had done a particularly poor job of recruiting, hiring, and retaining black teachers under his watch. I learned that one frustrated black staff member had personally tried to recruit more black teachers, with little success:

> I would send black folks, Jefferson grads, to [the HR director] for jobs, to teach. Good people! Great people! I would tell him, "They are great, great teachers!" And they would never even get called for an interview. [He] would say, "Well, that's up to the building principals"—always passing the ball. I said to him, "Someone at the top needs to say it! If people at the top don't change, then it won't happen. You have to step outside of their comfort zone. You have to say, 'I want this person because they're black and it matters for our diversity and our community.'" But no one here will say that. [He] wouldn't. He was too busy trying not to stir the pot . . . He was black, but he didn't want to put himself out for anyone else . . . He didn't see this as a social justice project.

Despite frequent administrative turnover and almost annual new teacher hires, no new educators of color were hired during this HR director's tenure. His presence revealed that having a black person in a position of power does not have broader impact if that person does not feel responsible for providing opportunities to other candidates of color. As a result, some in the community described him as an "Uncle Tom"—willing to overlook other African Americans so as not to risk his own position.

Nonetheless, it was not the fault of the HR director alone that there were so few staff of color, nor should it have been his sole responsibility to consider diversity in hiring. *All* of the decision makers in the district, white and black, should have been committed to creating a diverse staff that reflected the Jefferson community. Unfortunately, the trend of not hiring black teachers existed long before the HR director's arrival and lingered long after he left. As one black staff member described:

> No, there aren't black teachers in the school still. I talked to [the former superintendent] when he hired nineteen new staff and no black staff. Then the next year, they hired eighteen or nineteen more, no black. But there's

nothing wrong with that. It's just the norm, right? Where we are with the absence of affirmative action, we don't have to. We don't have to hire black teachers.

This employee felt that without a mandate, the district would never address staff diversity because to them there was "nothing wrong."

HANDPICKED HIRES

[White administrators believe] they're deserving. They earned it. They're favored. They aren't even thinking about the fact that [the black female administrator] wasn't even considered, wasn't asked, wasn't interviewed, nothing. They aren't even thinking about that she's been here thirty years. They aren't even thinking about that.

—Black staff member

The ways in which district leaders were appointed in Jefferson maintained a white hierarchy. The district tended to seek out administrators with "strong Jefferson ties" in ways that systematically overlooked candidates of color. For example, in 2008, Ms. Linwood (white), who had worked in the district for fifteen years, was hired by the Jefferson board to be the superintendent of the district. The year before, she had been moved from principal of the high school to superintendent on an interim basis. Because she was the only candidate interviewed for the position, many in the school saw her appointment as evidence that white insiders who had shown a willingness to abide by the wishes of the board were rewarded in Jefferson.[3]

The practice of filling top-level administrative positions by appointing handpicked internal candidates on an interim basis and then making their appointments permanent, was the norm. Ms. Linwood appointed Mr. Jackman, a white male teacher who had worked in the district for decades and was, as teachers described, "an insider" and a "good ol' boy" to replace her as interim principal. In fall 2009, he was permanently given the position, which he kept until January 2011, when he was then tapped to be acting superintendent when Ms. Linwood retired. The following year, Mr. Jackman was given the permanent position of assistant superintendent.

The white male assistant principal, Mr. Janz, who had been in the position fewer than three years, was appointed to replace Mr. Jackman as interim principal of the high school for the remainder of the 2011 year—a decision that was not discussed with Ms. West or Ms. Billingslea, the two black female assistant principals who had worked in the district for decades.

In his early forties, Mr. Janz was a former athlete and coach. He had a booming voice and towered above most of the staff and students. Because he had grown up in the area, he knew many students' families and was able to connect easily with young people from a range of backgrounds, including black and low-income students. Most of the staff found him to be competent and innovative and believed he was being groomed to be the next school leader. Nonetheless, employees from custodians to administrators were upset by the clandestine process through which he was given the position—one that again failed to provide opportunities for black promotion. As one white teacher put it, "Everyone on the school [board] is for the status quo . . . Ms. Billingslea, like I said, has ten times more experience than he does, but she was never considered!" Six months after his appointment, Mr. Janz was hired as the full-time high school principal.

By fall 2011, there were five new administrators in the high school and middle school—all white, all appointed through nontransparent processes. Some of those chosen were even known among students and staff to struggle connecting with African American youth. A black staff member reflected:

> Black folks have to apply for stuff, they're put through hoops, and they still aren't hired. White folks just get appointed . . . They give them favor . . . [The black female assistant principals], the time they've been here, they should be running this school. But that's not how it works here. They don't interview, they don't hire. They appoint. And they are not giving favor to black people . . . There's no democratic process . . . Now there are no black people on the school board. When [a black man] was on the school board, it was a great day!

A great day! A lot of the things they used to do, they couldn't do anymore. Just his presence there made a huge difference. He could ask. But now there's no one at the table . . .

Mr. Martin (white) agreed, "Ms. Billingslea and Ms. West, they've been here all six years I've been here, and I can't say enough good things about them. Like I said, I do find it kind of offensive neither one of them has ever gotten a shot at being principal."

In a district with a top-heavy power structure, in which school board members, in collaboration with the superintendent, regularly appointed insiders for promotion, even racially conscious administrators were unable to challenge the status quo.

Mr. Janz and Mr. Jackman were both very open about the need for more diversity in hiring. They believed it was important that all students have adult role models who looked like them, they thought young people needed connections with adults from diverse racial backgrounds, and they felt having the perspectives of educators of color was important for their school's success. Mr. Janz in particular also expressed awareness that racial bias and small-town politics had played a role in his own promotion. However, he felt he had little power to challenge this trend. Even when it came to hiring, he said that by the time potential candidates got to his desk—a process he says he was not involved in—they were already all white.

Promoting from within could have been an innovative way to tap the resources, knowledge, and skill already present in the district. However, when a primarily white institution relies solely on this method of advancement, it is almost impossible to diversify leadership.[4] It is likely that the superintendent, school board, and other staff on the hiring committees throughout the years did not consider themselves to be deliberately denying opportunities to people of color when they promoted internal candidates they liked without posting the positions. They probably did not think much about race at all when making these decisions. And that was the problem.

By continuing to use a hiring process in which race was ignored as a point of consideration and having a personal connection with decision makers seemed to be a primary qualification, the district shut black staff, who were significantly less likely to have relationships with district leaders, out of higher-level positions. Moreover, administrators created a structure in which inexperienced and often underqualified white staff were continually moved up the ladder with little opportunity to develop knowledge and skill along the way or to think seriously about issues of race.[5] One teacher told me that in the twenty years he had been in the district, he had worked for seventeen different principals. The number was eighteen by the time my research concluded.[6] Even Mr. Janz, for whom so many had great hopes, was gone from the district within two years of being appointed principal. His replacement was a white woman, internally promoted and rumored to be handpicked by the board.

THE ROLE OF BLACK STAFF

Although the overwhelming majority of Jefferson educators were white, there were a number of African Americans in administrative positions in the district. In addition to the director of HR, two of the three assistant principals at the high school, Ms. West and Ms. Billingslea, and a former high school principal, Mr. Williams, were black. Some in the building felt this was no accident. They believed these individuals had been hired because they were considered capable of "dealing with" black students and their families, whom the white leadership perceived as more likely to cause trouble. As one staff member put it, "Those women were given those jobs to handle black kids and their parents, because these white folks don't know what to do with them."

As in most public schools, black students at Jefferson were disproportionately suspended and expelled (figure 8.2).[7] During the 2006–07 school year, black students made up only 32 percent of the high school but constituted 47 percent of suspensions. That year, 51 percent of black students at the school had been suspended at some point in their high school career, compared to only 27 percent of white students. Moreover, of the thirty-seven long-term suspensions and expulsions from 2005–08, 54 percent were black students.

Figure 8.2   Suspensions by race, Jefferson School District, 2006–07

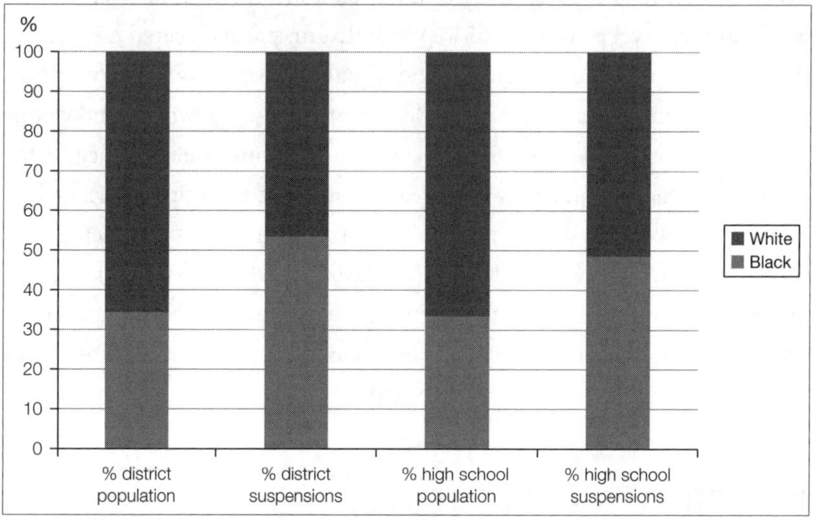

Source: State Department of Education.

Some staff believed black students were more likely to be suspended and expelled because they were more poorly behaved than their white counterparts. However, disciplinary trends in the school were as much about perception as they were about behavior. As theorist Michele Foucault notes in *Discipline and Punish*, ". . . it is society that defines, in its own interests, what must be regarded as crime: it is not, therefore natural."[8] Previous chapters have illuminated the ways in which black students' performances of self and expressions of community—like being loud and congregating in large groups—were often criminalized in the minds of their white teachers who had the power to define misbehavior. Moreover, when black and white students engaged in similar undesirable behaviors, black students were often more likely to get in trouble.

These trends were true not only in Jefferson but also across the nation. In 2014, the U.S. Department of Education's Office for Civil Rights released a report based on data from every public school in the country that found that black students are three times as likely as white students to be suspended or expelled. The report suggested that biased discipline policies were responsible for these disturbing trends, which appear as early as preschool.[9] In his book *We Can't Teach What We Don't Know*, Gary Howard notes that racial disparities in school discipline are often not about student behaviors; instead, he argues, "the solution to . . . 'discipline problems' may, in fact, have more to do with [educators'] own growth and development rather than any perceived behavioral deficiencies they were projecting onto their Black . . . students."[10] Rather than working to change the assumptions and practices of staff across the district, when it came to discipline, many believed JHS had hired black adults to deal with black students so others would not have to.

In addition to the two black assistant principals, the two community assistants who dealt primarily with discipline in the hallways, and the three long-term in-school suspension (ISS) substitutes, were all African American. Combined, these employees were the face of discipline in the school. A black staff member asserted:

> It's no accident that the ISS folks, the community folks, are black. They're not educators, they're here to control. To be the heavy. ISS, we want to keep a black person there . . . That's our bouncer, our school bully . . . They always want to make the black person in charge of the kids they can't control.

This tendency, the staff member continued, went back two decades in Jefferson's history, when there was a black male assistant principal:

> In thirteen years, they never let him advance. They brought in the elementary school principal to be principal of the high school [when the principal left], someone who had never even been in a high school. This district was actively looking for bass—[black] assistant principals to deal with discipline—but they never let them advance. I told him, "You can't just be a bouncer or a bully. You have to discipline with love." He was the bully in this school, and eventually it took a toll on his health. It really affected him physically.

Although no longer acting as "bullies," almost all of the black staff, from custodians to administrators, felt the weight of working in such a place. One staff member said the black employees called themselves the "Little Rock 9"—referencing the first African American students to integrate public schools in the 1950s. Six decades later, they were still fighting to be heard and to create an integrated school in which black children and staff were treated fairly.

Their low numbers also put black staff in very high demand by African American students and families. Black custodians could be seen giving counsel and encouragement to black students throughout the day, the classroom of the only black female teacher was always full of black students looking for an adult they could connect with during lunch, and black educators were often tasked with mentoring the black students of their white colleagues about their easy usage of the N-word. Even I was sought out by black students who interrogated me in hallways, lunchrooms, and classrooms if I missed a day of school.

Feeling such responsibility to Jefferson's African American students and families at the same time as they felt powerless to make the changes they thought necessary proved detrimental to most black staff, who generally did not last long in this environment. Those who stayed said they did so because they genuinely worried what would happen to the black students if they left. One demoralized staff member who had been in the district for many years felt "shame" at not having done more to change the racial culture of Jefferson. When I asked what had hindered such action, the staff member replied: "There was only so much time in a day. I am stretched so thin with (black) students coming to me, with (black) parents coming to me, with them needing to be around me, needing to see my face, there was not enough time to do more."

During my time at the school, I heard of black teachers filing lawsuits against the district, black teachers being fired for unsubstantiated accusations, and black teachers quitting at the first opportunity to work in another district. While the details remained vague, it was clear that there were tense relationships between the district and its black employees, a number of whom called Jefferson a "racially hostile place."

LEADING WHILE BLACK

He'd have kids miss their fourth-hour class, black males, so he could have lunch with them. It's like you want to alienate some more white women, take [students] out of your class.

—Ms. Guthrie, white teacher

In 2006, several years before this study began, Jefferson High School hired a black male principal. Mr. Williams was an "outsider" recruited from a small urban district. His hire suggested that Jefferson was willing to put black people in positions of power. In retrospect, however, Mr. Williams— who stood a stocky six-foot-two—believed the district thought they were "getting a big black man to come scare the black kids," when they hired him. "They wanted me to come out here and put the black kids in their place." For years after he left, Mr. Williams's name remained synonymous with Jefferson's race problems in the minds of many white teachers.

When I started my work at Jefferson, there were two distinct narratives surrounding Mr. Williams's time at the school. A smaller group of teachers, newer to the district when he arrived, thought he had "all these great ideas" to move Jefferson forward, as Mr. Edwards (white) put it. They thought his efforts had been derailed by an "old guard" of "saboteurs." This other group felt that Jefferson had never had race problems until Mr. Williams created them. Mr. Edwards explained the perspective of his colleagues, "I don't know if it's because he was black . . . I hope that's not the case, but I think he was expecting teachers to do more, expecting teachers to stand up to the plate, and they grieved him every step of the way."

Some of the resistance Mr. Williams faced was due to high administrative turnover. Almost annually, teachers had dealt with the bright new visions of idealistic leaders who never stayed more than two years.[11] Many felt that Mr. Williams was doing too much too soon, without first taking time to understand the unique needs of the school and the history of the area. Moreover, some suspected that he was secretly plotting with a posse of newer, more pliable teachers—all of whom were white—to make covert changes to the school. More progressive teachers believed their colleagues scapegoated him. As one white teacher put it:

> You know, again it's power and control. I mean, we had a black principal for two years . . . He wanted to change the climate and culture. He wanted to break down the old guard—this sort of status quo of "Well, we really don't need coordinated curriculum. Well, we really don't need deadlines. Well, we really don't need higher expectations . . . " He tried to use younger, you know, ideas . . . but, you know, those negatives are like . . . they're like pit bulls . . . They ran him out big time.

When I asked them directly, the "old guard" teachers claimed their issues with Mr. Williams were not his blackness. Yet almost every conversation about him ultimately came back to race. They accused the principal of giving preferential treatment to black staff, they said he allowed black students to "walk right into his office and talk to him," they believed he punished white students more harshly than black students, and they said he worsened race relations in the school. Ms. Guthrie (white) explained:

> It wasn't racial. It was young . . . And it was, uh, people who supported him and he had them as his little, you know—they had his back kind of a thing—and he said some bizarre things. He said things like he didn't know how to deal with old white women—and he says, "That's what this staff is." He goes, "You all are too powerful." And I said, "You know what? That'd be the last thing I'd say out loud if I was a principal to a group of white women, that you are all too powerful . . . You're the principal of a multicultural diverse high school; what did you think you were getting into?" . . . So he started off on the wrong foot . . . If you're trying to change the culture of a high school, the first thing that you don't want to do is alienate half . . . the white women . . . And then the other thing that happened while he was the principal was he and [the black female assistant principals] and [the black male counselor] and [the only black female teacher] started having lunch together. Now that to me is no big deal . . . but some of the counselors felt left out.

Although Ms. Guthrie initially said the issues with Mr. Williams were not racial, the things for which she criticized him—his strained relationship with white women in the building and his racially homogenous lunch group—were. I regularly witnessed white staff eating lunch together all over the building. They made few, if any, efforts to welcome their colleagues of color to these spaces. Yet they did not perceive their own lunch groups to be exclusionary.

Ms. Conger (white) a teacher who personally "never had a bad experience" with Mr. Williams, explained the feeling of some of her colleagues. Like Ms. Guthrie, she claimed race was not an issue, while making race the center of her analysis: "I don't think anybody had a problem with him being a black man. I think there were other things about him that they did have problems with . . . [and] maybe they jumped on the racist thing. That he was racist against them."

The notion of Mr. Williams engaging in "reverse racism" was prevalent in the district and was compounded by the fact that he was seen as an outsider who was challenging the status quo. As Mr. Martin (white) put it, "It's like they think like everybody has to pay dues around here before they can do something." Ms. Hogan's (white) perceptions of Mr. Williams suggested that Mr. Martin was right:

Shayla: I find . . . people really felt [Mr. Williams] . . . was divisive.
Ms. Hogan: Very much so! . . . And Mr. Jackman (the current white principal), I don't know if it's because he came from within the district or . . . just a different personality or a different approach. Things seem to have kind of mellowed out amongst everyone. They will tell you, our fights and our number of fights and conflicts have lessened. I don't know if that's their spin on it, but I think there is fewer conflict amongst the kids these last few years . . . [Mr. Williams], he had a different kind of agenda. He—I personally didn't have any problems with the guy. I kind of liked him—but he was just, I don't know, created some divisiveness amongst the staff . . . I thought some of his ideas were good, but morale just was not good. He just wasn't good . . . He had a lot of different ideas, which some [were] a little far . . . you . . . think, "Oh God, that's not going to work."
Shayla: So what were some of the ideas?
Ms. Hogan: You know, I can't think of some the specific things, it's been two or three years now. I can't even think of specific stuff . . .

This narrative was common. Many teachers could not name anything in particular that they did not like about Mr. Williams but they were sure there was more conflict when he was principal and regularly named race as a point of concern. Interestingly, low teacher morale was one of the biggest challenges faced by the school during my time there. There seemed to be no evidence that the new insider administration had created a healthier climate.

According to Mr. Wade (white), race very much played into how teachers viewed Mr. Williams. He said that while he "liked what [Mr. Williams] was trying to do, I understand there was a lot of controversy, and there was a perception, a very heavy perception in this school—now I don't know if it's true or not—that he favored the black kids." Ms. Meguschar (white) believed he did:

Ms. Meguschar: [Race] has always been this like, you know, hot item that you just don't talk about. And a few years ago, it did become more of a hot issue because there was definitely some higher-up authority that was making it quite obvious that there was a division between races.

Shayla: Among the teachers or among the students?

Ms. Meguschar: Both teachers and students, and that was nothing of the students' doing, and it was nothing of our doing, it was more [Mr. Williams's doing] . . . He basically made that the issue . . . And I think some of the things we're still seeing in the halls and the way some of the students are acting, it's still the trickle-down effect from that.

Shayla: And so what was it, I mean, 'cause I've heard something along these lines in kind of like vague references. Like what exactly did he do?

Ms. Meguschar: He made it very clear when he came that he wanted to be a positive male influence on, you know, not just black youth but any of them. Great. Wonderful. We're so happy you're here. We need you. You're young, great. Then as things started to happen and our more thuggy, gangster kids started having fights, skipping school, cussing out teachers, it was always, "Okay, well, just come to Mr. William's office" . . . and he would buy them lunch, and we're thinking, "Okay, mentor them, get them to do the right thing." No, it became, "It's the teachers' fault. You're not understanding them correctly," and that sector of our kids started to feel very protected and able to do whatever they wanted . . . The girls could fight and cut each other with razors and, "Okay, we'll just talk about it—it's okay." And it was always that group . . . And he made it very clear that he didn't know a lot of the white kids' names. He only really hung out with the African American students 'cause, you know, you've heard we have two different lunchrooms and one is primarily black, one is white. I don't know, I never even looked. He always hung out with one and he had a very odd relationship with the black girls. They always went to his office and it was always the ones that liked to get in fights. So it was just . . . it was as if he was telling them, "You're black, they're white, they're out to get you." And that's when you started to feel . . . And we didn't even do anything. We, you know, we did what we were supposed to . . . You know, you tell them to take off your hat, you're racist . . . And so you were hearing things that you hadn't heard before.

Ms. Meguschar's analysis of Mr. Williams was revealing in a number of ways. She was a relatively young teacher who thought of herself as a racial progressive and as someone who maintained friendly relationships with African Americans, particularly her students. While she claimed that she was not interested enough in race relations to investigate things like whether the cafeterias were racially segregated, though she clearly knew they were, she believed Mr. Williams showed preferential treatment to black students and thought him to be the source of racial segregation, racial tensions, and even violence between black students—all of which she thought had not existed before his arrival. As it happens, there were no official reports of any fights in which girls "cut each other with razors" during Mr. Williams's tenure.

Interestingly, during the years that white teachers claimed Mr. Williams was letting black students off the hook for violence, a report by the American Civil Liberties Union (ACLU) on racial disparities in discipline found that black students were disproportionately targeted for suspension and expulsion at Jefferson. In other words, white teachers' perceptions of "reverse racism" and "preferential treatment" by Mr. Williams were not supported by the data. Many white teachers could not connect how histories of discrimination, structures of inequality, and even their own prejudices were negatively affecting black students and coloring their perception of their black administrator. These teachers did not see themselves as bearing any responsibility or as being a part of the problem. To them, the issue was Mr. Williams and the black students they believed he protected.

Ms. Meguschar was not the only teacher to make such sweeping claims about the negative impact Mr. Williams had on race relations. Ms. Mayes (white) suggested that the segregation among students in the cafeteria was his fault:

Shayla: I heard that the cafeterias are really segregated.

Ms. Mayes: That was a couple of years ago, they were but that . . . we had a, we had a . . .

Shayla: Principal.

Ms. Mayes: Yeah, who tended to somehow . . . I can't say what he was doing and why I blame him. I don't really blame him but . . . it seemed to be characteristic of his regime, so to speak, but it got really black/white in the cafeterias. Now you would not see that in the classrooms or in the hallways . . . Granted, we've got a core—yeah, once in a while you get somebody that thinks, you know, that plays the white card or the black card . . . So I was seeing it more . . .

Shayla: So do you actually feel like that kind of cafeteria segregation stems from that . . . regime . . . ?

Ms. Mayes: I . . . you know . . . I mean, it can rear its ugly head every once in a while, but I never saw it as blatant as when that principal was here. I mean, all of a sudden we got kids with gang symbols and this crap and you know . . .

Shayla: So . . . do you think it was something in particular that he was doing?

Ms. Mayes: Well . . . I don't know . . . I've had different kids, different color, different sizes, different thing all my life and like I said, you know, the main thing for me is who you are.

There was also no documented evidence of increased gang activity or cafeteria segregation during the Mr. Williams administration. And yet, Ms. Mayes believed he was responsible for both, though she could not identify a reason why she blamed him. She then asserted a personal color-blindness to validate her observations. She was not the one who had the issues with race, she seemed to be suggesting—Mr. Williams was. Stories like these revealed that like driving while black, leading a school while black made Mr. Williams inherently suspect in the minds of many white educators.

NAMING THE ELEPHANT IN THE ROOM

Mr. Williams rejected the suggestion that he had shown black students preferential treatment, though he admitted that he had heard the rumors: "People said I would go up to kids and say, 'What up, dawg?' 'What up, homeboy?' That's just not true." In fact, he said:

> [I] felt more appreciated by white parents. I felt like I acknowledged *all* kids. I think they'd be hard pressed to provide evidence otherwise. I went to the front door and greeted every child who came in the building. I acknowledged their existence! Kids feel invisible because the adults ignore them. I told teachers on hallway duty to establish relationships with students.

He said that before he was hired, "they were expelling kids for no reason because these parents had no advocacy. The [district] trumped up charges and the parents didn't know." He believed that much of the resistance he faced was due to the fact that he brought issues of race and class to the forefront—that he dared to "address the elephant in the room."

His supporters also fervently defended him. Ms. Stovall (white) suggested that many of Mr. Williams's "bad" ideas were well received two years later when presented by Mr. Jackman.

"Some of . . . the exact same things that Mr. Williams wanted, that Mr. Jackman has tried to implement or Mr. Janz has tried to implement [are] going along now." She believed it was not the message the teachers ultimately had a problem with but the messenger.

When I asked about the rumors of preferential treatment swirling around Mr. Williams, another white teacher responded:

> You know what? I think that's so much total crap. I was a Williams guy all the way. I thought he was dynamic . . . I thought he was a guy that was trying to push through changes. I think he ran into some trouble . . . some teachers that like are wary of him and look at him funny. I think he screwed up in that he counted on everybody's professionalism that we'd all want to make change together . . . Some of the teachers who have been here the longest, I think some of them would like their small country school back that's all monochromatic and looks exactly the same and I don't think that's ever coming back, so lots of luck with that, champ! . . . They're *still* bitter. I'm like, "It's been two years, dude, give it up. You're still going to blame him? You know what? The economy's his fault now too, you know [laughter]! It's been two years. Let it go, let it go."

As this teacher suggested, among a certain segment of white staff, Williams was the scapegoat for all that was wrong with the school, especially when it came to talking about race –a challenge to the "the Jefferson way."

Ultimately, Mr. Williams says he left the district because of "fit." He wanted to address many of the issues Jefferson faced and he believed the Jefferson power structure demonized him for it. Whether he was a great principal remains unclear. However, what is striking is that, for so many white teachers, Mr. Williams remained the embodiment of "the race problem" so long after his departure.

Because honest conversations about race were not taking place in Jefferson, many educators I spoke with believed it was an issue only when black people made it one. This required assuming that white educators were naturally unbiased, that they had not done anything wrong, and that they and the school had no room for improvement. However, Jefferson's achievement and disciplinary data, the stories related by students and adults, and a study by the American Civil Liberties Union all suggested that race was not just the problem of black students and families, but also of white teachers and administrators who had for many years disciplined students of color more harshly, failed to protect them from racial assaults in hallways and classrooms, and struggled to provide relevant and engaging content and pedagogy. That so many white educators were able to ignore these trends and shift responsibility away from themselves and the school to black students and leaders revealed a deep disconnect from the realities of their own racial privilege and from the oppression faced by African Americans in the district and in the country more broadly.

In Jefferson, white privilege meant administrators could put forth no effort to diversify staff. It meant that insiders could be promoted to principal or superintendent with few qualifications and through processes that were not transparent or democratic. It meant that long after he was gone, staff could invoke the name of a black principal who served only two years as the source of the race problems the district currently faced. It meant that unsubstantiated suggestions that this principal encouraged violence, gangs, and segregation could be made with impunity. It meant that the district could get away with having "no one at the table" advocating for black students, staff, and families. And it meant that in a district in which students of color made up 35 percent of the student body and underperformed on every area of the state standardized test, it was acceptable to say there were no race problems, save the ones black people brought on themselves. This avoidance, bias, and privileging of whiteness, according to a number of teachers critical of Jefferson's racial culture, was "the Jefferson way."

CHAPTER NINE

"The Jefferson Way"

> In my opinion, this district is very . . . afraid . . . It's all about conceal-
> ment and about managing. And so then we don't ever talk about any-
> thing . . . but I think if you don't stir up things it bubbles up and rises and
> tensions and misconceptions and all those things keep getting perpetu-
> ated . . . We call it "the Jefferson way." It's always been that way.
>
> —Ms. Hill, white teacher

Race was a taboo subject in Jefferson when it came to student interactions, teacher relationships, hiring, and promotion. However, there was
much discussion about the changing racial demographics of the district.
Between 1990 and 2010, many black families had moved to Jefferson. Simultaneously, statewide school choice policies enacted in the early 1990s
began allowing students to attend schools outside of their neighborhoods.
These policies created competition between public schools for student
bodies, to which state funding was directly attached. They also created an
inaccurate statewide narrative that "those kids"—students perceived to be
poor and black—were coming in from other districts and ruining "our"
majority-white, suburban schools. In Jefferson, this narrative incited fear
in many long-term white residents, who worried that their way of life—
"the Jefferson way" as it was called by its critics, built on racially homogenous, small-town politics—was slipping away.

A white teacher explained the climate: "They always talk about the 'good old days' and when everybody knew each other's names, and we were in a cornfield, and we were all white . . . that's the subtext . . . The joke has always been, the Jefferson way . . . means know your role, don't do too much." Racially conscious teachers defined the Jefferson way as an attitude resistant to progress, particularly around issues of diversity. As another white teacher described it:

> I think the biggest problem facing this school is the attitude [that] . . . we're a little dusty farm school . . . For seventy years, this school worked. In fact, when I started here, all of that over there was cornfields. Because of the cheap land about five or six years ago, we had this huge influx of expensive houses and a bunch of new students. But still we had teachers who've been here since the '60s and the '70s. We had a teacher here who bragged about using the same lesson plan that he wrote in '79. You can't do that. You cannot do that . . . Again it goes down to the dusty school in cornfield. It's always been a very homogeneous school, and I think the institutional memory [is] that it has always been all white.

Many racially conscious teachers believed the pervasive nostalgia for the Jefferson way was linked to racial prejudice among those in the most powerful positions. In particular, they saw the all-white board of education as the linchpin of the Jefferson way.

Citing members' educational backgrounds, career choices, and political leanings, some teachers said they thought the board, made up primarily of long-time Jefferson residents, was underqualified to run a rapidly changing, racially diverse district. As one white teacher sarcastically put it:

> Don't even get me started on the school board. The school board is designed to make sure there is civilian control so that teachers don't get uppity with their "evolution" and their "book learnin'." Come on! You've got somebody who's never read a book of education, who has no idea how to guide you or how to run a multimillion-dollar operation. They're signing the checks of our bosses. Come on! They're just there to make sure the school reflects the "community standards."

Teachers worried that these community standards were those of, as one white teacher put it, "a very conservative, almost like a Southern faction of farmers who are, were, very, you know, racist back in the establishment of the community . . . almost a Confederate mentality."

There were many stories circulating in the district about the racial biases of the board and its allies in the broader community. These widespread perceptions of board members' attitudes solidified the belief among building-level administrators, teachers, and community members that the subject of race had to be obscured and suppressed in the district. And so when racial conflicts happened, like the fight that opened this book, the Jefferson way was for administrators to quickly brainstorm "what else" they could call it to make such events more palatable.

A significant number of students, racially conscious staff, and parents of color expressed little faith in the district's interest in or ability to work in the best interest of black youth. Although many black families viewed Jefferson as "the good school"—a perception that came from the fact that "we're more white . . . and we have, you know, higher socioeconomic status" than other schools in the area—a number had also become disheartened. Jasmine (black) explained:

> Jefferson has a reputation for being racist . . . Like a lot of the black students feel like the white students and the white administrators and teachers just treat them differently because they're black . . . Like some of my mom's [black] friends live in Jefferson School District, but they drive their kids to school in a different district because they don't want them going to Jefferson.

The dual narrative of Jefferson as both a good school and a racist one illuminated the complexities of assessing quality education in integrated settings. While test scores and shiny new buildings often lead to positive perceptions of schools, when it comes to the education of black students, these markers are not enough to inform parents about the educational experience their children might have there.

Administrators in Jefferson did not effectively navigate this duality. Instead, they neglected to utilize data in ways that supported pedagogical practice; they failed to celebrate multiculturalism and diversity; and they did not engage teachers in professional development opportunities that would have helped them think through racial bias and inequality.

THE DATA DILEMMA

In 2001, the federal No Child Left Behind Act (NCLB) mandated that schools begin disaggregating standardized test score data by subgroup, including race and economic status. Despite these new reporting standards, most teachers and administrators at Jefferson had limited access to accurate demographic, achievement, disciplinary, and enrollment data. Early in my research, I asked various school leaders how I could get access to such data to support my qualitative and ethnographic research. My inquiries were repeatedly met with resigned amusement. One staff member said, "There is no access to data here. It *is not* disseminated." She joked, "They might give it to you if you sacrifice your first-born child!" There was a strong sense among many JHS staff that this was no accident. Instead, they viewed the limited reporting as part of the Jefferson way, in which truths that were seen as unfavorable were suppressed—especially those related to race and class.

During an all-day professional development (PD) workshop run by an out-of-state consultant, Jefferson's failure to collect or disseminate data became especially obvious. The PD focused on how schools could engage in evidence-based practice by using data to develop plans of action. The consultant asked for a number of reports to use as baseline data for the workshop, but the school administrators were unable to provide them, a fact that was particularly upsetting to Mr. Janz and Ms. Billingslea:

Mr. Janz (white): I'm embarrassed, because [the consultant] keeps asking, "Do you do this?" "Do you do that?" and I'm like, "No."
Ms. Billingslea (black): Don't be embarrassed. It's the truth. We cannot hide from the truth.

This conversation revealed that upper-level district administrators did not give building principals pertinent data about their school, nor did building-level administrators take initiative to identify and disaggregate this data themselves. Although the information was available on the State Department of Education website, it was raw and disaggregated and took hours to calculate and analyze by hand, so it was unlikely that educators would have done this on their own.

The failure to disseminate data not only affected the success of a one-day PD, it also affected the school's ability to address the needs of students of color and low-income students. For example, during 2007–08 and 2008–09, fewer than 10 percent of JHS students were reported economically disadvantaged to the State Department of Education. In September 2009, the first year of this study, Jefferson administrators gave me a printout that said 31 percent of students at the high school qualified for free or reduced lunch. This discrepancy was further complicated a year later when the state reported that students qualifying for free or reduced lunch had grown to 38 percent (table 9.1). It was never quite clear who was responsible for these data discrepancies, or which numbers were accurate. However, many saw it as indicative of a larger effort in the district to sweep the increasing numbers of low-income students under the rug—a practice that made it difficult to provide them with adequate resources and support.

In many ways, Jefferson's reluctance to be perceived as a low-income school reflected fallout from the larger reform agenda in the state and the nation rooted in the assumption that schools should be run more like businesses and that increasing choice is the core solution to academic failure, particularly for marginalized students in underperforming schools. This market-based approach treats education like a product to be sold to consumers—in this case, students and their families.

For twenty years, the state in which Jefferson is located has had fairly liberal school of choice and open enrollment policies that allow students to attend schools outside their district. At the same time, changes to the school finance structure now link school funding to pupil enrollment, rather than local property taxes. These two policies have created a cycle in which schools are forced to compete for students for financial stability. Across the state, as one district—call it District A—becomes a school of choice, it starts siphoning off students from District B, a lesser performing, likely lower-income, and more African American district. District B

Table 9.1

Free and reduced lunch by year, Jefferson High School

Year	Black	White	Total
1995	—	—	18%
1996	—	—	18%
1997	—	—	17%
1998	—	—	21%
1999	—	—	18%
2000	—	—	20%
2001	—	—	21%
2002	—	—	25%
2003	—	—	25%
2004	—	—	27%
2005	—	—	29%
2006	—	—	26%
2007	—	—	9%[1]
2008	—	—	10%
2009	—	—	38%
2010	47%	36%	41%
2011	55%	39%	46%

Source: State Department of Education.
[1]The 2007 and 2008 data was likely misreported.

then has to become a choice district to attract students from District C, an even poorer, blacker, lower-achieving district, to replace the funds lost from the students who moved to District A. This cycle is hierarchical, with districts perceived to be "better," "whiter," and "richer," continually attracting students away from those perceived to be "worse," "blacker," and "poorer."

In the early 2000s, this competition became even stronger due to the passage of NCLB, which began harshly sanctioning schools with low test scores. In particular, NCLB mandated that failing schools provide school choice opportunities to students so that they could attend higher-achieving public and charter schools nearby. Since that time, the number of charter schools has rapidly grown in the state. In 2011, the Republican-dominated legislature voted to revoke the cap on charter schools, further expanding their numbers, which have grown at astonishing rates. These schools have created even more competition in the market, not only between traditional public school districts, but also between public schools and charter schools, the majority of which are managed by for-profit companies. The fear of being punished by the federal government, or of losing students and funding, made many districts like Jefferson nervous that being honest about their data—talking too openly about race and class—would lead to a detrimental loss of students and state funding.

fear of gov repercussions

Unfortunately, because Jefferson educators did not have accurate data, it was easy for them to create a false narrative of black youth and their families. In 2008, the year before this study began, Jefferson High School became a school of choice. Despite the fact that its "ACT scores were not all that great," as one teacher put it, "there is the perception that we're the best . . . Now, I don't know if that perception is because we have the most white kids, you know." As a result, a number of families from surrounding districts chose to send their children to Jefferson schools.

During the 2009–10 school year, around 2 percent of students in the Jefferson School District were school of choice enrollees who resided in other districts. In contrast, over five times that number of students who lived in Jefferson chose to attend schools outside of the district. In other words, there were significantly more students leaving Jefferson for other districts than coming in (figure 9.1).

Nonetheless, many JHS teachers inaccurately believed the black students in the district—who made up over 30 percent of the population—were there because of choice policies. Moreover, they thought these students were coming from poorer, lower-performing districts. Not only was this impossible numerically, but racially the number of black students in the district grew by only 1 percent from 2007, the year before choice, to 2008, the year after choice. In other words, the racial shifts they were witnessing were more likely the result of black families moving into newly constructed homes in the Jefferson subdivisions and apartment complexes.

Figure 9.1   School of choice enrollment, Jefferson School District

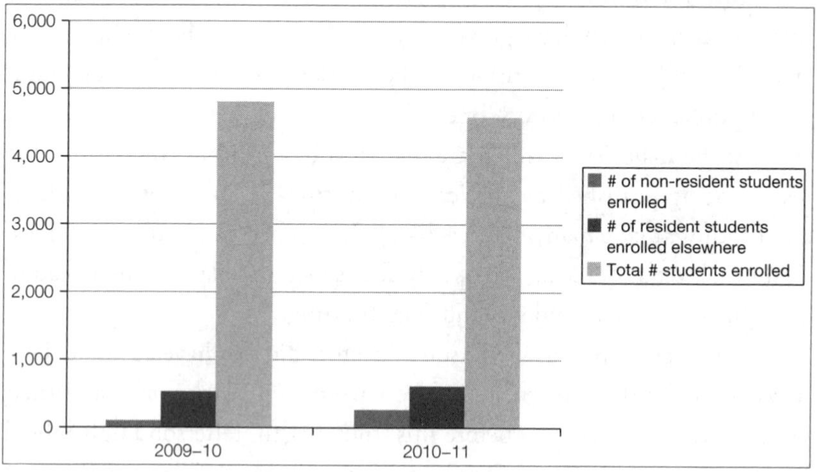

Source: State Department of Education.

And yet, when educators were asked about disparities in the school, many fell back on this dominant narrative, which allowed them to conceal issues of race behind notions of "us" and "them," "outsiders" and "insiders," the white students who they believed belonged in the district and the black students they thought did not. Ironically, many of the young people who lived in Jefferson were "those kids"—outsiders, choice students—in other districts, a fact that teachers never recognized.

Having limited access to data also made it easy for educators to avoid addressing racial disparities in academic and disciplinary outcomes. Teachers like Ms. McWilliams (white) were particularly frustrated by how easy it was to ignore such problems when there was no data available to make them visible:

> We don't talk about race here. We don't talk about how much money people have here. It's not a general topic of conversation . . . [We] pay somebody to come here and pretend to talk to us about our data that we don't have, which makes me crazy . . . I don't need you to come in here and take up my whole day to tell me how to work the numbers if someone will finally give them to me . . . This happens every time . . . year after year . . . I think that really, to have

these conversations without numbers is dangerous. Because it's just about our personal beliefs . . . It's much easier to get people to change their viewpoint if you can show them why they are wrong. Okay, so we don't have that problem here at Jefferson, then why is it that our failure rate for black students is blah blah blah, and our failure for white students is blah blah blah? Then I can live in my own little fantasyland that . . . that's not really the problem.

Ms. McWilliams believed strongly that because the district ignored data, discussing race was not only dangerous, it was likely to be unproductive. If teachers did not have to contend with the reality that there was an achievement gap at JHS or that black students were punished more harshly for similar offenses, she found it unlikely they would admit that these problems existed. Instead, they could ascribe larger school failures to "demographic shifts" without having to consider what they might need to do to better serve their student population.

CELEBRATING MULTICULTURALISM AND THE BURDEN ON BLACK STAFF

When I first met with the principal and assistant principal of Jefferson High School, they openly espoused a multicultural position. Both told me that diversity was both their biggest asset and their biggest challenge. They acknowledged that the school was changing rapidly and felt the shift could be a wonderful learning opportunity for students that would prepare them to be successful in a globalizing economy. They also knew racial tensions had caused a lot of conflict in the district and that they did not have the skills or efficacy to intervene. They told me that issues of "culture" were more problematic in the school than physical altercations. Nonetheless, in practice, their efforts to address "culture" boiled down to a one-liner: "Diversity is our strength."

In his seminal ethnography, *The Man in the Principal's Office*, Harry Wolcott writes, "Since their positions require them simultaneously to present the appearance of change and to provide the stabilizing effects of continuity, [the response of administrators] has been to become agents of the rhetoric of change rather than agents of change itself."[1] More than three decades later, a 2010 study found that when school administrators did not have clear direction and support from upper-level administrators about how to implement diversity plans, they often "did not know how to move forward." Principals struggled to define "diversity," were unsure of how addressing diversity might reduce inequities between racial groups, and failed to convince teachers of the importance and relevance of diversity to their school. As a result, "principals could only give 'lip service' to the concept. This lack of communication from the district level indicated not only to the principals but also to teachers that diversity efforts were not important."[2]

JHS administrators were very much struggling with how to make their rhetoric of change a reality. During this study, the district did not do anything in particular to address diversity, even in a celebratory way. There was never a district- or schoolwide celebration, convocation, announcement, or acknowledgment of Martin Luther King, Jr. Day, Black History Month, Latino Heritage Month, Women's History Month, or any diverse heroes or holidays. Despite administrators' desire for Jefferson's diversity to be a real asset, it quickly became apparent that they were struggling to acknowledge diversity at even the most basic level. When attempts were made to celebrate multiculturalism, it was almost always because of the initiative of faculty of color.

Ms. Billingslea and Ms. West, the school's two black administrators, were very interested in issues of race and culture. My shared racial identity and interests made both feel particularly comfortable discussing their ideas and frustrations with me. They regularly pulled me aside to explain the ways in which race worked in the district, share their insight regarding what students at the school needed, or note the ways in which they felt black students and staff were marginalized. Ms. Billingslea gave me copies of *Teaching Tolerance*—a diversity-focused educational magazine published by the Southern Poverty Law Center—and showed me other relevant source materials that were aligned with the kinds of interests she knew we shared. During these interactions, she often said, "This is the kind of stuff we need to be doing here," or "This will be good for your work." Nonetheless, at the time, the extent of her intervention was passing the information on to me—a researcher and afterschool programmer who was not employed by the school in any official capacity. Years of negative reception to race had made her feel that she could not raise these issues at Jefferson.

Ms. West took a more active role in addressing diversity. The year before I came to the school, she had been a part of a small movement known as the Cultural Committee. The group, which included the one black female teacher, the one Indian teacher, a Latina teacher who taught at the middle school, and one white female teacher who had grown up in primarily black neighborhoods, tried to organize a cultural fair in which students would make various foods from their cultural backgrounds and share them. However, this event never materialized. One of the committee members described the reaction when they presented the idea at a staff meeting:

> There were a couple of us, and when we presented [at] the faculty meeting, people were not even accepting. Like we were talking about this is the committee . . . "We are about to have a celebration . . . so that everybody can come together" . . . and nobody asked questions about it. They said, "Okay." So we [said] to them, "Anybody [who] wants to come to the meeting can join us."

No one took them up on their offer. This teacher said "being on that committee" was when she realized how taboo race was in the district—even in the context of a celebration. "People don't want to talk about it," she said. "Sometimes people get offended . . . it's negative. So maybe they try to avoid the confrontation. They don't want to talk about it . . . but I think they should so they understand each other [better]." While the group continued meeting throughout the year, they ultimately decided it would be too difficult to hold the event without more support from other staff. By the time I started working at the school, the Cultural Committee had all but dissolved.

It was clear that the committee failed for a number of reasons. First, it was primarily the initiative of faculty of color. Unfortunately, in many schools across the country, white teachers do not see diversity as *their* issue. This may have been especially true when it came to the Cultural

Committee, which was presented at the staff meeting by the few teachers of color.

The second challenge was that the committee members struggled with what exactly they should *do*. They started out wanting to critically engage issues of inequality, bias, and cultural misunderstandings. They were concerned with the dynamics they had witnessed in the school and district and they wanted to more effectively address the diversity of their student population. However, the complexities of this effort eventually led them to decide to take a more celebratory approach to multiculturalism in which they simply displayed the different cultures present in the school through a food festival—a much lower-risk project. But even this fizzled out. Although no one overtly dissuaded the committee from continuing, the nature of the topic combined with their limited organizing skills effectively silenced the group.

In addition to Ms. West and Ms. Billingslea, Ms. Gayles, the only black female teacher in the building, also took a lead role in diversity initiatives. Ms. Gayles was in her early sixties and had lived through the civil rights movement. She was passionate about racial justice and often committed time to teaching students the history of race in the United States. Perhaps not surprisingly, in collaboration with the black administrators, she had organized almost every event celebrating Martin Luther King, Jr., Day or Black History Month that had taken place in the school's recent history. However, by the time I arrived, she had reduced her efforts due to resistance from a number of the white teachers.

The year before the research for this study began, Ms. Gayles organized a convocation for Black History Month. She invited a black speaker who often did presentations in schools about race. A number of white teachers refused to take their classes to the convocation. One white female teacher said that she went to preview the presentation during her prep hour, and left feeling "completely attacked." She felt like slavery was blamed on her and her family and was particularly upset because her family had fought in the Civil War to end slavery. As she put it, "My family never owned slaves!" Her reaction, one often cited by white people struggling with issues of race, indicated both her own internal guilt—her sense that by hearing the connection between whiteness and slavery she was somehow *personal* *guilt ?* being *personally* blamed—and her lack of awareness of the ways in which *lack of* white privilege works—not through whether or not one's family owned *awareness* slaves or even were slaves, but rather through the continued privileges accrued to all white people and denied to all black people as a result of a historical institution of which no one currently living, black or white, was a part.[3]

The discomfort around race, racism, and white privilege was so strong at Jefferson that Ms. Gayles decided she was not interested in single-handedly organizing schoolwide celebrations. As a result, these events no longer occurred. A white teacher explained:

Teacher: I guarantee you, none of those administrators even asked about MLK. . . . because in the past she had done something for Black History Month, but she told me, she's like, "I will never do anything here again." So she feels shut down, cut off, unsupported . . . It should be a school thing. It should be an administrative [initiative].
Shayla: So if she doesn't do it, it doesn't get done?
Teacher: Right . . . Right, right . . . Nothing ever happens [here]. Nothing ever happens.

The fact that no one picked up the ball when Ms. Gayles stopped organizing these celebrations, even those white teachers who thought of themselves as racially conscious, represented another failure of the district to acknowledge and engage race.

OPTING OUT OF BARACK OBAMA

When white administrators in Jefferson did take initiative around issues of race, they usually did so in reactive, fear-based ways that hindered, rather than helped, racial progress. For example, at the beginning of the 2009 school year, newly elected President Barack Obama gave a back-to-school speech that a number of schools across the country either refused to air or allowed students and teachers to opt out of viewing.[4] Jefferson was one of these schools.

Media outlets reported that there had never been this kind of national resistance to allowing students to listen to their president and cited Obama's racial background as the reason. According to a number of teachers, some conservative white parents in the district had complained about their children watching the speech. As one teacher described, the response of the district was ". . . reactive, reactive, reactive . . . Very scared . . . They're afraid of parents." Jefferson made the decision to send the following permission slip home with students allowing their parents to opt them out of the screening:

> The Jefferson Schools will be airing the September 8th speech by President Barak [sic] Obama on Monday, September 14, 2009. The high school will be showing the speech during homeroom.
>
> If you prefer that your child not participate, please complete and sign the form at the bottom of this letter and *have your student return it to their homeroom teacher by Friday, September 11, 2009.* The school administration will honor your request once it has been received.
>
> Thank you for your cooperation in this matter.
>
> Sincerely,
>
> Jefferson High School Principal

> I do not want my son/daughter _____ to view the speech that will be aired during homeroom on Monday, September 14.

Although the permission slip was signed by the high school principal, two white administrators revealed that they did not support the decision and saw it as an absurd way to appease the board and accommodate racially biased families in the district. However, they were unable or unwilling to do anything to stop the decision. Many teachers were also upset. One white teacher had a particularly negative reaction:

> I think they really need to listen to the president when they put him on the TV . . . I thought . . . that was a travesty. I thought that was un-American, what we did. I mean, honestly, that they delayed it [the timing of the speech]

so they can watch it and then they cut him off. They started it too late and the bell rang. He wasn't even done and what he was saying was basically stay in school . . . I think that was, that was terrible, and they went along with . . . I mean, it's the president of the United States. If George Bush wanted to go on TV, no matter what I think of him . . . I mean, and I'm not a big fan of George Bush, but it's the president of the United States. He's not asking you to do something immoral . . . I think they were going along with a lot of the tenor, but personally I think . . . all the objections of him [were] racially motivated.

Another white teacher called the decision "right-wing bull!"

When Obama was elected, there were reports of significant conflicts across race between JHS students that were reinforced when the district allowed them to opt out of the speech. Some white students, like Bethany, felt that their black peers' responses to the election of the first black president were "ridiculous! So many people were screaming ignorant things. They were screaming like 'Black power!' 'We rule this!' and just like things that were unneeded. When a white president gets elected, we aren't like, 'We rule this!' White power!' It was just annoying." Similarly, many black students, like Jada, felt that:

[T]he whole election, it kind of seemed divided because you really saw people's views on what they wanted. And you could tell that some people's families were like really all for, you know, John McCain [the white Republican candidate] and they're like, "We're just strict believers and we just got to have a white president," and the black president came in office. And so like . . . that whole week after the election, after Barack Obama became president, it seemed kind of divided . . . [White] people would make comments like, "We got this black dude in office, he not gonna do nothing," "We just *had* to have a black president," "You know all the black people voted for him." And this became this big deal. So it just kind of divided us, like divided the school.

While many students thought that the election "divided the school," JHS, the district, and the broader Jefferson community were already very much divided racially. Rather than using Obama's speech as a moment to have critical conversations that might have unified students, teachers, administrators, and community members, it became another incident that solidified racial resentment.

The day of the screening, I was not aware of any particular students who left their classrooms to avoid seeing the president. However, some teachers did not bother to turn the TV on at all. The following year, the district once again allowed students to opt out of viewing the speech.

THE RUBY PAYNE INITIATIVE

The one instance in which an administrator attempted to engage educators in professional development around issues of race and class was not successful. During Mr. Williams's administration, teachers at Jefferson were given Ruby Payne's popular book *A Framework for Understanding Poverty.*[5] At the time, Payne's work was the most well-known resource on diversity and inequality in schools across the country. Although Mr. Williams's effort to engage in a schoolwide conversation about race was admirable, the book he chose served to reinforce stereotypes about black and low-income students. Based on a reworking of the "culture of poverty" thesis popular among social scientists in the 1960s and '70s,[6] Payne argues that differential achievement between students is largely the result of the cultural deficiencies of low-income, black families and communities.[7]

After reading the book, some teachers who had had limited exposure to racial and economic difference believed, as one white teacher sarcastically put it, "Now they're experts in poverty. That's your basis of the entire black race." This newfound "expertise" validated teachers' tendency to inaccurately attach the struggles of their racially marginalized students to class and culture. The fact that it was given to majority white teachers by a black man lent the book even more credibility.

Many teachers referenced the Payne book when talking to me, some without even realizing the source of their information. Ms. Russo (white) was a particularly good example. She had only recently accepted the possibility that some people have more privilege than others by nature of their birth. Describing her transformation, she said:

> I had never believed until I started teaching that environment played a role in who you are . . . I thought that . . . if you want to be something . . . you're

going to . . . I mean, that's how I was raised. You work hard. Now I was also brought up in a very fortunate situation . . . So I guess it's easy for me to say that because I didn't have one without the other . . . But I realized over the years that it is a lot more difficult to bring yourself up out of the situation, you know, when nobody else in your house emphasizes education. A lot of people are sitting around, drinking, smoking weed, you know, smoking cigarettes.

Although Ms. Russo was more aware of the ways in which structural inequality affected life outcomes, she still relied on very stereotypical and extreme depictions of marginalized students to justify their academic struggles. She presumed that many poor students came from families that did not value education and in which the adults were substance abusers. Her wide leaps, made at the same time as she was trying to acknowledge how privilege had facilitated her own success, revealed disturbing biases about students who came from different backgrounds than her own.

She described what she learned from the Payne book, which reinforced these ideas:

> This book points out, it's saying a lot of the [black] students can't help it because these are the type of households they're raised in, and they're just louder households, you know, and they go into the whole thing that TVs are on . . . more of the time compared to white households, so they have to talk louder, you know, they go into that whole thing. They also talked about how you know a lot of the black students don't perform as well in school because louder households tend to, you know, affect brain development and—I mean, it was a great book.

What Ms. Russo took away from the book was focused almost entirely on cultural deficiency—the idea that there is something inherently wrong with poor black families. Moreover, she connected this perceived difference to brain development with seemingly no awareness of how her comments closely resembled notions that black people were biologically inferior, debunked by scientists decades ago. Finally, her analyses of the struggles faced by her black students treated race, class, and culture as the same categories. By nature of being black, she mistakenly believed, her students lived in environments in which they were also poor. By the same token, she wrongly presumed white students' families were not poor, were not addicted to substances, and were not avid TV watchers. In Jefferson in particular, this assumption simply was not true. One of the black staff members was particularly upset by the implications of the book because, "these black kids are not poor! Why are we reading a book about black poverty when that is not the population we serve?"

Ironically, Ms. Russo also admitted, "I mean, in the same respect, I was raised in a very loud household. I have a very loud voice." Nonetheless, she did not find that this had hindered her achievement or brain development. Ultimately, Ms. Russo's observations, supported by Ruby Payne, led her to conclude that white people, whom she presumed to be middle-class, could get away with behaviors (poor) black people could not.

For educators at Jefferson, the Ruby Payne book, which was not followed up with any discussion or critical analysis, did not help teachers understand poverty or race. Instead, it validated and reinforced problematic stereotypes they already held and further marginalized black students in the minds of their educators.

"The Jefferson way" was about nostalgia for a community long gone and perhaps never real; the continued privileging of whiteness; the marginalization of black staff, students, and families; the failure to utilize data related to race and class to inform practice; the struggle to celebrate difference and diversity at even the most basic levels; and the reinforcement of stereotypes about black students and families.

Although many staff thought of these tendencies as unique to Jefferson, the Jefferson way is more often than not the American way. In too many school districts, administrators are uncomfortable having critical conversations about race and inequality. They struggle to balance their desire for a diverse, equitable, and unified school with their fear of the tensions, biases, hostilities, and miscommunications that can accompany cross-racial interactions. They fail to provide their staff with accurate data about the populations they serve, in part due to the current reform climate that has put school leaders in precarious positions in which their schools and jobs are on the line. As a result, state and federal mandated reporting of disaggregated data seems useful only insofar as it tells the government and researchers something about schools. It has not been a tool for improving the practice of most educators working on the ground.

When integrated schools do attempt to bring issues of diversity and justice to the forefront, these efforts all too often rely on the easiest, most obvious, and lowest-risk initiatives rather than those that would effectively address the many challenges they face. Instead of mandating that all staff celebrate Black History Month with their students in critical and engaging ways, in many schools black staff are made the "diversity workers"—allowing white teachers and administrators to avoid thinking or talking about race. Rather than allocating resources to professional development opportunities that would specifically address the kinds of challenges integrated schools face around race—like racial bullying, teacher bias, and inequitable discipline—many schools rely on the trendiest, most popular diversity initiatives without thinking critically about whether they will be useful for their particular situation or how they might reinforce stereotypes about marginalized students and families. What the Jefferson way reveals is that, in most integrated schools in the United States, there are no structured, systematic processes for creating an inclusive community, responding to the needs of a diverse student body, or ensuring equity and justice for all.

PART IV

Intervention

CHAPTER TEN

Learning Not to Be Racist

[Educators] cannot reasonably approach issues of the achievement gap without significantly enhancing their own awareness and effectiveness in cross-racial, cross-cultural interactions . . . If we don't grow in this way, nothing else will significantly shift.

—Gary Howard, *We Can't Teach What We Don't Know*[1]

On April 28, 2011, seven white teachers sat nervously in a circle of blue plastic chairs. They were voluntary participants in Race in the Classroom, a five-session, ten-hour professional development (PD) series I was co-facilitating with my colleague Naomi Warren (white) in the second year of the study. The walls of the classroom were bare except for the handwritten list of Guidelines for Dialogue the teachers had collaboratively developed during our first session. For weeks now, we had been meeting to discuss how they could better address race in their classrooms and they were eager to engage in this week's conversation with students from the Intergroup program—a twenty-week afterschool program that took place over three consecutive year—who would be joining us.[2]

"So how are you feeling going into this conversation with students?" Naomi asked.

Ms. Stovall (white): I'm excited. I feel disconnected from student culture, so I'm looking forward to hearing what they have to say.

Ms. Gorski (white): I don't think we're ready . . . to hear the unknown. To hear what they think. We understand things differently than they do.

Ms. McCandless (white): I told my students I was going to be talking with some of their classmates this afternoon about race, and I asked them how they were feeling about the conversations we've been having in our class about race as it relates to the book we're reading. I thought it was going okay, but my question unearthed a lot of feelings from the students that I was not prepared for . . . Students started using derogatory language. I was so uncomfortable.

Naomi: I think the fact that they shared so much with you means that there must be some level of safety and comfort.

Next door, I was talking to a group of students from the Intergroup program who had volunteered to participate in the session. I reminded them of the questions Naomi and I had posed the week before in our afterschool session in preparation for the dialogue:

A. How do students from different racial groups get along at this school? How does that make you feel?
B. How does race influence how students get along with teachers?
C. If you could tell teachers one thing about race at this school, what would it be?

After taking a few last questions, I led the students, three white, four black, one Arab, and one mixed (black and white), to the room where the teachers were waiting and asked them to sit in the empty chairs dispersed throughout the circle.

The conversation began. Teachers listened as students shared their experiences with race at Jefferson, much of which reflected the kinds of issues presented in previous chapters. The students of color were most vocal:

Jasmine (black): A lot of punishment . . . is unequal at this school. I feel in general black students get punished more harshly than white students or any other race . . . I see it so much, and it bothers me . . . [T]here's such a big difference in the way students from different races are treated.

Khalif (Arab): The racism is a big deal, and I feel like no one really acknowledges it. They just let it happen . . . I can tell you from personal experience I've been sitting in class and somebody will just think it's funny to shout out a random slur like, "Terrorist!" and everybody will just break out laughing. And I know a teacher will hear it, but they just won't acknowledge it. And when you don't acknowledge it, it sets the precedent that it's okay, and things just keep happening like that . . . Most of the time, it just looks like we're just smiling and just playing around . . . but even though I was fine on the outside, sometimes I just don't know how to handle the situation, so I just like laugh along.

Natasha (black): I hear a lot of racial slurs . . . and believe it or not, I think some teachers even laugh at it . . . Like you can go around and you'll hear . . . a different ethnicity than black . . . say the N-word—and, you know, teachers walk right by them. So I really just think they are scared to approach the situation . . . A lot of people . . . think teachers see these differences but don't do anything about it . . . At the same time, I feel like maybe on the other end for the teachers, maybe you guys don't know how to do something about it. Like maybe that wasn't taught in teacher school.

Nicole (black): The cafeterias at this school are very segregated. The black people think it's cool to eat at the new end and they think that the white people who eat at the old end are "lames" . . . But like they're segregated because no one acknowledged it. Nobody said anything . . . I know we're assigned . . . cafeterias but they don't follow those rules. They are not enforced.

Shannon (black and white): I would just like for the teachers to at least think about everything we've said. Like don't just hear us, actually *listen*. I want you to like be more observant. I know you can't exactly do everything, like you can't save the world, and I know you may not exactly know what to do about certain situations, but just like be more aware of what's going on in the hallways and in your classrooms and stuff.

Teachers responded with comments and questions of their own, some that challenged and pushed the students. They wondered if they should feel responsible for the ways in which students engaged with each other across race; they asked why students felt that young people from different backgrounds were disciplined differently; and they wanted to know how to make their school a place in which all youth felt welcomed and supported.

After the session, the students were excited that their teachers had asked them questions, shared their own perspectives, and listened seriously to their concerns. Many students wanted to come back the following week to continue the conversation. Teachers were similarly energized, but also disturbed by what they had heard:

Ms. McCandless (white): I'm glad it's over . . . I was upset inside because of the students' perception about inequitable discipline [by race]. It was good to have Shayla's reminder: "This is reality. The data backs it up." I have such a hard time believing that it's true.

Ms. Mitchell (white): I thought about my own discipline in class, and I betcha I write up more black than white. Not intentionally, but the infractions I am supposed to report are more often violated by those students. It's a vicious circle, and I don't know what to do. I feel like my hands are tied. I don't have control over punishments beyond my referrals, but I take the blame.

Ms. Flournoy (white): I was totally blown away by the lunchroom [segregation]. Why assign students if it's not enforced? This conversation really opened my eyes. It needs to be more widespread. I'm going to see things differently now and make changes in my classroom. I'm going to challenge the things I ignored in the past. The kids were so strong. It was really, really good.

Ms. Stovall (white): It was a great start. I think it would be great to do more and make this ongoing. I would like more dialogue. If the perception is that things aren't dealt with, I would like to change that. I will make more of an effort, will be more aware, and will get to know students better.

Ms. Gorski (white): I'm queasy about trying to make a change here in this school environment. But we, as educators, need to step up to the plate more.

This conversation, which took almost two years to organize, was one of the highlights of my time at Jefferson. Students and teachers came together on equal ground to learn from each other and consider how they might work together toward racial justice. Although the conversation was difficult and at times uncomfortable, it moved those who participated toward greater understanding in ways that Jefferson needed. Unfortunately, dialogues like this almost never happen in schools.

In my time at Jefferson, I came to see that by avoiding conversations about race and failing to consider how race shapes student outcomes, teacher practice, and broader school policies and procedures, the school community was creating and maintaining a culture that reinforced, rather than interrupted, racial inequality. This experience underscores my belief that in order to successfully educate all students, schools must discuss race; administrators must share data and ask how and why race plays a part in student outcomes; teachers must have the space to reflect on how bias shapes their interactions with student; superintendents must consider how their hiring practices encourage diversity and how they could more effectively celebrate and empower staff of color; and curricula must be rich with opportunities for students to meaningfully engage issues of racial difference and inequality. Yet in so many schools, this kind of "race talk" seems impossible.

What, then, am I recommending when I suggest that schools talk about race? How has this worked at Jefferson and other schools? And what might students and educators gain from such conversations?

STARTING THE CONVERSATION

Professional development for K–12 teachers on issues of diversity, multi-culturalism, and social justice has traditionally consisted of eight-hour "sit-and-get" lecture-style workshops, often led by nationally recognized experts flown in for the day. Similarly, most of the initiatives adopted by K–12 schools that seek to engage young people in discussions about race and other identities focus on celebratory approaches that honor the deliciousness of culturally diverse foods and multicultural holidays, rather than the insidiousness of racial inequality and discrimination.

These popular approaches are not aligned with how people learn, nor have they had much success in addressing the racial hierarchies and disparate outcomes that permeate our schools. In too many instances, our traditional approaches to diversity education have served to solidify students' beliefs that they are living in a post-racial world and reinforce the resistance and anger of teachers in denial about the continuing significance of race in education.

Since 2005, I have worked as a facilitator of student dialogue groups and teacher PD workshops that have addressed issues of race, class, and socially just education in more innovative ways, with varying degrees of success. I have focused on trying to figure out how to begin moving teachers and students, particularly those who see themselves as racially liberal, toward action that would improve the educational experiences and outcomes of marginalized students. My approach has been rooted in theories of intergroup dialogue,[3] Freirean pedagogy,[4] and critical race theory.[5] Through trial and error, research and observation, I have found that race work in schools is more likely to be successfully when it:

1. Is supported by upper-level administrators and the broader institution;
2. Flows from a systematic and authentic analysis of the school;
3. Is longitudinal and sustained over time, during which participants are asked to try out new strategies and come back to the group to get feedback on their efforts;
4. Is built on trusting relationships in which participants feel a sense of community and are safe to make mistakes;
5. Starts with the personal experiences of participants and allows them to contend with their own histories, biases, privileges, and racial identities rather than focusing on learning about the differences (or deficits) of others; and
6. Provides information, data, perspectives, and theories that are both specific to the particular school and relevant to broader social trends.

From 2009 to 2012, I piloted such a model at Jefferson through Intergroup and the Race in the Classroom PD workshop series. Different groups of diverse students participated in Intergroup each year. The findings in this chapter focus on the 2009 cohort, who participated in pre- and post-surveys and interviews about their experience.

The seven teachers who participated in Race in the Classroom series were all white. There were two reasons for this. Most importantly, over 90 percent of the teachers at Jefferson were white. Of these, fewer than 10 percent volunteered to participate in the PD. In contrast, there were only three black teachers and one Indian teacher in the school. In short, it simply is not possible to have equitable, cross-racial conversations between educators in schools in which there is not a critical mass of teachers and administrators of color.

The second reason the group was all white was because in many ways the workshop was designed to address the challenges white teachers reported facing in the school. Teachers of color were generally supportive of the PD but relieved that someone else would be taking on the burden of educating their white colleagues about how to better interact with black students.

Naomi and I took a Freireian approach to our work. We believed "the facilitator's role is to provide structure and ask questions until participants begin asking questions of themselves and of each other, to generate the data for critical thinking." We saw ourselves not as experts but as "co-learners and co-facilitators" with our participants.[6] Rather than lecturing participants about their shortcomings, bad behavior, or the continuation of racial inequality, we accepted participants where they were and built on their experiences in the learning process.

Because we thought of ourselves as both teachers and learners,[7] we did not request something of the students or teachers that we were not willing to do ourselves. Whenever possible, we participated in the activities we led. As Menna (black) described, " . . . like you guys are just adults and you give us things to do, but you guys do it too . . . I think it's just cool . . . cause like . . . you really don't get to interact with adults like that."

We were also flexible. Although we had designed curricula and agendas to guide our sessions, the teachers and students often led us in a different direction. For example, one day we spent twenty minutes talking about "politically correct" racial terminology after teachers revealed that some of their hesitation in talking about race stemmed from the fact that they did not know which terms to use when referring to students from different racial backgrounds. "Is it African American or black?" one teacher asked, confused and exasperated. Rather than giving a quick response or ignoring the question, we dedicated significant time to talking about racial terminology, the ever-changing nature of language, and the reality of personal preference. We then asked teachers to practice using various racial terms like *black* and *African American* in their own lives as "homework."

Finally, as facilitators, we admitted when we did not know things or when the answer was more complex than even we could wrap our heads around. We were open about the fact that when it comes to issues of race, we sometimes have more questions than answers. Because we worked hard to create a safe space for co-learning and to acknowledge multiple perspectives, teachers and students shared deeply about their own struggles and biases and received real feedback from us and from one another.

The remainder of this chapter presents some of the outcomes of the Intergroup afterschool program and the Race in the Classroom professional development series. It is based on my observations and participation in both groups, as well as post-interviews conducted with the participants. These outcomes support my belief that dialogue—small-group, facilitated, sustained, face-to-face conversation across difference—has the potential to provide young people and their teachers with opportunities to think critically about the maintenance of hierarchical race relations in schools and to plan how to interrupt these inequities.[8]

THE PROMISE OF DIALOGUE FOR STUDENTS

It's really fascinating how we're talking about all these topics that you—like you encounter them every day but you really don't talk deeply about them . . . I feel like if we had that . . . it would change a lot in our school . . . A lot of people would think differently . . . on how we treat each other.

—Kwesi, black student

The 2009–10 Intergroup participants came from racially, economically, and academically diverse backgrounds (table 10.1). As Whitney, a multiracial student, described, "Our group isn't full of the kids that are like goody-goody students." Raymond (black) agreed: "We're just ordinary students. Everybody is pretty ordinary." A few, like Maria (black), Bethany (white), and Raymond (black), were relatively high-achieving students. Others, like Willie (black), Shannon (black and white), Hailey (white), Ed (white), and Kwesi (black) struggled in some way. For example, both Willie and Ed had failed a number of courses. Hailey, Kwesi, and Shannon did not graduate with their classes due to missing credits. Yet in Intergroup, even the lowest-achieving students showed themselves to be keen observers of the world around them, able to speak honestly and thoughtfully about their experiences and to listen appreciatively and genuinely to their peers.

For most of the students, Intergroup was the first time they had participated in any structured, facilitated conversations about race and racism in an integrated setting while in the presence of adults. They responded well to this environment. Willie (black) described himself as "more serious in dialogue [than in class] 'cause, you know, we are talking about serious subjects so you. . . . have to be mature to talk about these things." Ed (white) also said that in Intergroup "I was serious, because I took it seriously." In

Table 10.1

Intergroup participants by race and gender, Jefferson High School, 2009–10

Race	Female	Male	Total
White/Caucasian	4	3	7
Black/African American	4	5	9
Multiracial (Asian and white)	1	1	2
Multiracial (black and white)	2	0	2
Total	11	9	20

contrast, he noted, in class, "I can get my work done and joke around." Students talked a lot about the importance of being "mature" and "serious" to participate in dialogue, not because they thought of themselves as different from their peers, but because they rose to meet the expectations placed on them in this particular setting. Raymond (black) explained, "It's not the students; again, it's not the students. It's the teaching." According to him, the biggest problem when it came to discussing race at school was that teachers "don't think we can handle it." When given the opportunity to engage in these conversations, students not only proved they were able to handle it, they were transformed in the process.

For many students, Intergroup challenged some of the stereotypes they held about their peers. For example, Ed (white) had once categorized black students in his school as generally ignorant. Intergroup changed his perspective:

Ed: Anyone could act ignorant and anyone could be a good student . . . Like I used to have Rottweilers, and they have a bad image because people used to abuse them and they would attack them, you know. And if you get a bad enough reputation, then people are obviously gonna look at you like look at the Rottweiler and say, "Oh that's a bad dog. It's gonna eat you," or something. That's how I always used to look at things.

Shayla: And do you feel like there are certain groups of kids at this school that have that kind of reputation?

Ed: I think that any black person has it . . . Like, you know, like I thought that black kids . . . thought different like 'cause you see like on TV, they broadcast like blacks are always thinking about killing and all that, when they're really not. They're just . . . like I thought about it, and it's really just skin color. I mean, I could be black, you could be white . . . you didn't get . . . to choose . . . I used to think that black girls were just loud and I just didn't like them.

Shayla: So what changed your perspective?

Ed: Just black girls in my classes and stuff. Like, that girl . . . Jasmine (black) from our Intergroup session, she's all quiet. It's honestly just the personality of the person . . . Some girl I hung out with over the weekend was loud and annoying and she's white . . . I mean Intergroup just helped me . . . just opened my eyes that were . . . halfway open.

Getting to spend time every week with Jasmine—a young woman who challenged what he thought he knew about black girls—helped Ed see his own biases more clearly and gave him the opportunity to begin overcoming them.

Hailey (white) also built connections in Intergroup that allowed her to learn from the experiences of others. "I've never really had to deal with [racism]," she said, "because I am white . . . But like listening to other people, like you always read it in like American History and stuff, but like seeing it and listening to it from other people who have actually experienced it . . . like the differences that they had to go through because they weren't white or they were a certain race . . . I would feel like, 'Wow, I can actually relate to this person.'" Hailey was coming to understand how race shaped what students in her school were experiencing every day.

After Intergroup, students were also less tolerant of racial humor. Willie (black) said he no longer participated in racial joking because:

> Like no one likes to be made fun of because of their race . . . I mean, I already knew that but I learned that . . . even though you might be joking, somebody might take it offensively. So I've learned just to watch what I say . . . Since we talked about it, it's always on my mind. Like I'm always thinking about it. So it's like easy . . . like, "Oh, I shouldn't say this." So I just don't say it.

In part, he no longer participated in this humor because he realized how he had personally been affected by it, "It's like you have feelings just like everybody else. Like . . . if you just sitting there dogging out black people and then you just like, 'I meant it to be funny!' . . . you know, really it hurts you deep inside 'cause he's like, Man, he's talking about me.'" Willie had been a target of and participant in these exchanges, not because he was malicious, but because he was going along with the racial culture of the school. Once he was given the opportunity to challenge these norms and think about them more critically, he was able to change his behavior.

Matt (white), a student who had told me a particularly disturbing racial joke in the fall of 2009, admitted that before Intergroup he assumed there were no racial tensions at the school. "Like when I hear stuff about that . . . like my first thought is like I'm never around . . . like I'm never around to hear that," he said. "But like at the same time I think like maybe I am around, I just don't notice it." It became clear over the course of the year that Matt had not noticed racial jokes because he was often the perpetrator—something he was reflecting on quite seriously:

Shayla: Tell me if I'm wrong, but I'm pretty sure that you told me the joke, "How do you stop five black guys from raping a white girl? Throw them a basketball."
Matt: Yeah, I did tell you that.
Shayla: In this exact room.
Matt: In this exact same room.
Shayla: What is your perception now of that?
Matt: I don't know, like I think . . . I'm sorry for saying that in front of you. It's . . . I feel like I need to apologize to you now.

Matt did not defend his previous actions. Rather, he earnestly and thoughtfully apologized for behavior that had seemed so funny to him a year before.

Finally, Raymond, a black student who had vigorously defended racial jokes as evidence of "racial progress," reported that he was now able to recognize the different tone black jokes and white jokes took. He explained:

There's only a few white jokes . . . It's hard to explain because . . . white jokes are . . . it's not to harm the character of a white person . . . You'll see like white jokes being like, "Why don't you go sell some insurance or something?" Like something that's a, you know, generalization . . . it's not usually an attack . . . 'Cause the stereotypes of the . . . society . . . that we live in . . . doesn't portray white as being a bad thing . . . even the stereotypes, they're all good.

Raymond still believed that racial joking should be socially acceptable, but he had a more critical lens though which to view these exchanges. He could identify and articulate distinct differences between white jokes, which reinforced positive or neutral stereotypes, and black jokes, which reinforced negative ones.

By the end of the year, students were feeling empowered to challenge racial humor, particularly students of color who were so often the targets of such jokes. Shannon (black and white) said when she hears jokes, "I always say something . . . like I just tell them that's rude or something." This contrasted with how she used to respond to these sorts of interactions: "I didn't say things as often as I do know. Before, I would just ignore it."

Ed (white) said when he heard students make fun of each other, "I interrupt people." While his actions sometimes caused people "to call me names and stuff," he said, "it don't really matter to me 'cause I don't really care what people think . . . I'll just be like, 'That's not nice. That's not cool, not cool at all.'" Jasmine (black) described a specific incident in which she challenged her classmates:

> There's this kid in my class—oh my gosh!—it's a Spanish class . . . and like there was a weird word we were pronouncing . . . and he's like why isn't it just [pronounced] how it's spelled? And [the teacher] is like, "Well that's just how it's pronounced." And [the student] was like, "No, it's because Mexicans are ignorant." And he made me so mad, I'm like, "Why would you say something that stupid?" He was just like, "I'm just kidding, why are you so mad?" I'm like, "Because you're just saying really stupid pointless stuff . . . " That kid made me mad! . . . He thought it was funny, and all his friends were like, "Oh ha, ha, ha it's a joke, it's funny." I'm like, "No it's not funny, it's stupid. That's hurtful."

Jasmine could have easily laughed along with these young men, but she did not. Instead, she acted as an ally and challenged the comment. Jasmine's actions were evidence that students were taking a stand against injustice, even when they were not personally the targets.[9]

Willie believed the actions of Intergroup students had already made a change in the school culture, especially in his grade. We were sitting at a fast-food restaurant when he reported:

Willie: Actually, I haven't even heard anything about any racist jokes ever since we talked about it. I haven't heard much of it.

Shayla: So why do you think that is? Is that coincidence or what? What do you think happened?

Willie: Um, I'm not sure. I think—well, I think it's kind of coincidence, but then at the same time, some people started seeing that it wasn't really funny and then like people in Intergroup, I'm sure—I'm sure more people would like tell them to stop or that's not funny or things like that. So I think we have, we kind of had a, I don't know how much of an impact on other people, but we—I think we had some type of impact on them.

While it is unclear whether the shift Willie witnessed was the result of Intergroup students alone, the fact that he believed he made an impact was significant. Before taking part in Intergroup, Willie told me that he was bothered by racial humor but was unsure of how he should respond. He now felt efficacious.

Students were also rethinking their casual usage of the N-word. Jasmine (black), who used the word often in her friend circle, was more aware of the impact this might have on her white classmates:

Jasmine: I think everyone says the N-word entirely too much . . . I know people shouldn't use it, but in reality like, being realistic, people are going to . . . 'cause I know I say it . . . I mean, I do the same thing, talk like, "Hey, what's up, my nigga?" I mean, I catch myself constantly, I'm just like, "Nig . . . hmm," and I'll stop saying it, but I still slip . . . [it's] habit.

Shayla: So what has made you decide that you should maybe try not to say it?

Jasmine: Like it feels like people look at me funny when I say it, like people that aren't black. Like if I say it and I'm like in a group of people that aren't my race, they just look at me funny like, "Did she just say that? Is it okay for us to say it?" I don't know. I feel like it just makes people uncomfortable . . . I think it confuses them. Like, "If I say it, will she be offended? Can I say it around her? Can I say it at all? Like will I get beat up if I say it?" . . . [So] I'm trying to stop saying it.

Ed (white) had a similar change of heart after hearing the perspective of his black peers. Prior to Intergroup, he argued that the N-word was not a racial slur but rather a way to describe ignorance. The following exchange highlights his change in thinking:

Shayla: So we talked about the N-word in our small group, and you said originally that you think about it as applying to anybody really, if you're ignorant and uneducated. And then it came up in the group somehow that, even though that might be true . . .

Ed: It was Willie (black) who brought it up . . . He said, true . . . that it could be true in some ways but . . . people usually direct it more towards the black people than anyone else.

Shayla: And what'd you think about that?

Ed: I mean, honestly, it's true. It's true . . . people seem to focus more on the negative about black people than the positive . . . I think what it honestly is, is how they used to be slaves and some white people, like the country people who are racists, don't want the blacks . . . They're thinking that blacks are gonna like switch roles and they're gonna rule over the white people and they're afraid, so they just want to . . . focus on the negative . . . I think that's how the whole system of picking on the black people by white people started.

Ed did not have a complete transformation. At different periods between his initial exchange with Willie and the post-interview, I asked what he thought about the N-word and he often reverted back to his notion that it applies to anyone "ignorant and uneducated." However, when reminded of this conversation, Ed was able to rethink his own assumptions. He credited Willie with revealing the ways in which the word was most often and hostilely directed at African Americans. Moreover, he was able to assess how contemporary and historical white racism worked to maintain a system in which white people, including his peers at Jefferson, picked on black people in order to retain their power and privilege.

Intergroup provided students with a space to talk openly and honestly about race in ways they previously had not. As facilitators, we did not present "right" or "wrong" perspectives; rather, we encouraged students to reflect on their own experiences, added new and relevant information, and asked questions that pushed them to think critically. In this way, the diversity of opinions already present in the school, which had been silenced by dominant post-racial narratives, were voiced.

Despite Willie's experiences, this small cohort of students did not interrupt racial segregation or stop racial discrimination at the school. In fact, during the second and third years of Intergroup, new students, as well as students from other integrated schools I worked at in subsequent years, reported that the problems were ongoing—racial jokes, slurs, and bullying remained cultural norms. However, these students were learning about the ways in which certain groups were unfairly targeted because of their social identities, they were challenging their own beliefs and biases, they were thinking much more critically about the world through the lens of race, and they were coming to understand how their decision, actions, and words contributed to a broader school culture in which discrimination had been made acceptable.

change takes time

THE PROMISE OF DIALOGUE FOR TEACHERS

I know that [race] is a factor here . . . 'cause I grew up on these back dirt roads . . . So when it came to the bus, the back half would be all white, and the front half would be all black . . . We all get along, we all know each other . . . we never had any problems, it was never any confrontations. It was just like they say, you know, at the lunch tables . . . So I knew that there was some things . . . I just didn't have quite the perspective of how bad it was. I thought we were more of a blended community [now] than what we really are . . . I think that there probably was a problem [then], but I was just naive to it.

—Ms. Flournoy, white teacher

I would like to see more risk . . . I guess to actually look at data and be willing to admit that what we're doing isn't as effective as it could be.

—Ms. McWilliams, white teacher

The seven teachers who participated in the Race in the Classroom professional development also reported significant changes in awareness and action. Although they were still struggling with how to effectively change their practice and felt they needed much more time together than we had, after the PD, they were thinking more deeply about how race mattered in their own lives, they were more aware of Jefferson's racial disparities and hyperracial culture, they were interrupting racial bullying between students, and they were redesigning their curriculum and lesson plans.

Although none of the teacher participants had thought of themselves as color-blind before the PD, the culture of silence in the district meant most were nonetheless oblivious to the realities of race at Jefferson. The PD was designed to raise their awareness in multiple ways. In our first session we provided teachers with a summary of basic demographic data, graduation rates, standardized test scores, and suspension rates by race, gender, and economic status. The handout, which also included a summary of the school climate and culture gathered through participant observation and interviews, sparked much conversation and provided a number of opportunities for teachers to begin thinking differently about race.

As Ms. Mitchell explained, "One of the things I found really useful was just the knowledge of those demographics, those stats that you gave, which were really eye-opening to me." In particular, she was interested in the fact that "black students are graduating at a higher rate but their grades overall are lower, and that many of the black students are of a higher economic demographic than many of our white students." This information "just really verified for me that we have a unique situation here, and that many of our problems are not the causes but more the effects. They're symptoms of something larger, and nobody ever wants to talk about it."

Ms. Flournoy, also found the data " . . . a little surprising. It was. I didn't really get it. I just didn't understand why there was huge gaps in many of the data. I mean it's like—whoosh! . . . Like, the population of Jefferson is what, 30 percent black or somewhere around there, but the referrals are 60 or 70? Whoa! That's a huge difference." For most of the teachers, this was the first time in their careers they had been provided with such information, thought about race in this way, or discussed these issues with colleagues. The data we provided did not identify causes. However, in the conversations that followed, teachers asked why there were such stark inequities and what the solutions might be. As Ms. McWilliams put it, "Okay, so why is it like this and what are we going to do about it?"

One possibility teachers were just beginning to consider was that they bore some responsibility for racial disparities. Ms. McWilliams said:

> So I still [have not] wrapped my head around what all [this] entails, but having the data that you provided gives me a baseline for understanding . . . [the] big picture . . . Maybe [our interventions] . . . need to be more teacher-based . . . because if realistically kids aren't bothering to try because they don't feel cared for, invested [in], and supported. I think that's the one thing I got that was a . . . like, whoa, ah-hah feeling.

Once teachers had "the numbers," it was much more difficult for them to place blame on black administrators or use color-blind frames to avoid race. As Ms. Mitchell reflected, "I just think it's the unspoken. You know even teachers . . . feel like there are certain racist administrators who favor black students over white . . . but the numbers don't really bear that out. But there's that perception."

The PD also allowed teachers like Ms. Mitchell to further look at the subtle ways in which black youth were framed as "problems" in Jefferson:

> I don't think it helps that at 3:00 p.m. somebody gets on the PA and says basically, "Get the fuck out of the building" . . . you know, in a mean tone. And you know who's usually in the building at that time, in the main hallway, that are being directly spoken to that way? . . . I don't think I need to [tell you]. You already know. If you walk down there, it's 99 percent black students in the hallways . . . I don't know if they're waiting . . . for a ride, waiting for parents to get home, waiting for a sibling . . . I have no idea . . . But . . . you know when people talk like that and we know it's directed at a certain group and it seems like it's because of mistrust. I don't see how you can interpret it otherwise.

Ms. Mitchell's nuanced observation was not based on numbers or data, but instead on the ways in which implementation of school policy was racially coded. She was observing who was in the hallways after school, thinking about why they might be there, listening to how they were being talked to, and making connections to the overall treatment of that group in the school more broadly.

Over the course of the PD, we asked teachers to keep journals and gave them writing prompts after each session. After one such assignment, Ms. Mitchell observed her "struggle connecting with certain kinds of kids, particularly . . . the male black students" and wondered if her own life experiences had played any part:

Ms. Mitchell: I really don't have any good [black] friends in my life. Ac-
quaintances, sure. People I talk to . . . And I'm just like, "Gosh . . . but why not? You know . . . what message am I sending? Am I sending out a vibe? And if I'm sending out a vibe amongst adults, am I sending out a vibe to students?" . . . I think there's merit to the idea that we all are somewhat racist, sexist, ageist, you know. We're all of them at different points.

Shayla: Is that something you had always kind of accepted or is this new?

Ms. Mitchell: It's kind of a newer realization 'cause I think your first initial response is [denial] . . . But yeah, yeah, all of us a little bit . . . Certainly all teachers are ageists at some point (laugh), you know, against teenagers.

Ms. Gorski was also thinking about how racial biases among adults affected students:

Ms. Gorski: I didn't know that [the cafeterias are segregated]. I thought—
I thought it was just . . . I don't even know what's going on in the lunchrooms, you know . . . But I mean . . . which of the issues . . . are just student issues, and which ones are factored in by the teachers, you know? I mean do we teach them to be racist?

Shayla: Did you teach them not to be?

Ms. Gorski: Well, can you? I mean, that would be modeling, right? So . . .
teachers have to be fair to all of the students, right? . . . But kids are smart. They can tell when somebody says, you know, "Well I expected

that of you." They know it. So I don't know—I don't know how the teachers can [un]teach racism if they're racists themselves, you know.

Shayla: And you think some of the teachers are?

Ms. Gorski: Yeah. Yeah . . . same as me. At least the same as me. At least I've let go of some of it.

Ms. Gorski was wrestling with her responsibility in helping students address racial bias. Like so many educators, she wanted to believe that racism was something learned through direct, hateful action at home, but was considering that silence might be just as powerful in reinforcing bias, particularly at school. She wanted to believe that students should work out their issues among themselves, but also knew it was unfair to ask them to do something even adults seemed unable to. Most interesting, though, was that Ms. Gorski accepted that she held racial biases that likely shaped her practice.

Ms. McCandless was similarly asking herself more probing questions about how bias might be influencing her practice. She had previously believed Jefferson was a place in which all students were treated fairly by educators and peers:

> Like I'm still having a hard time . . . Naomi [the facilitator], she said, "What if what the students say happened was the truth? What if that is the truth?" And I'm still fighting that . . . but I can see how that question would be very helpful in a lot of areas . . . What if it is true? What if I was unfair? What if? . . . I don't even know . . . [T]hat's one of the things I'm taking away.

Ms. McCandless struggled to accept that race affected school outcomes because that would mean the school system was racially biased, or worse, that she might be. However, rather than deny the possibility that bias was real, she viewed Naomi's question as an invitation to reflect on her relationship with black male students:

> I have one class every year that's like this . . . group of African American boys who are crazy and they call themselves out . . . and I just deal with it, and they know I love them and we just get through the year. But I always know that there's something that I should be dealing with. Like what can I do? . . . I feel like they just bulldoze my whole class. They just take over. And I don't

get mad, I'm not bitter about it, but at the same time I'm not thinking, "Well, this is their culture."

What Ms. McCandless revealed challenged the narrative of many white teachers who often argue against realties of racial bias by claiming: "I love all my babies." She realized that love was not enough to successfully teach her black male students. She generally had positive relationships with these young men. She liked them. Yet she did not feel that she was prepared to effectively manage her class when groups of black boys were present, nor was she giving these students what they needed academically. By the end of the PD, she was able to admit that if she cared about her students in the ways she said she did, she needed additional support to improve her practice.

As the PD sessions progressed, teachers stopped denying their struggles with race and instead began openly and collectively wrestling with what they could do to overcome them. As teachers learned about inequality, segregation, racial humor, and their own racial biases, which, in part, sustained these systems, they became committed to, as one teacher put it, learning how to "infiltrate" them. They asked each other how they might do this, given the limited diversity of their own social circles and the resistance of the district. These teachers were taking admirable steps in becoming the kind of reflective, honest, critically thinking educators that students at Jefferson needed. In particular, they made concrete changes in how they responded to racial bullying between students and how they approached their curriculum and lesson planning.

Ms. Flournoy offered a particularly poignant example in a follow-up interview. Her transformation was sparked by Khalif (Arab) who, I was unaware, had been in her seventh-grade class four years earlier. During the joint student/teacher session, Khalif recounted a story to the group in which he had been bullied and harassed by his peers in Ms. Flournoy's class. He looked Ms. Flournoy in the eye and said that what had been most disturbing to him was that she had done nothing—a truth that horrified her. In the following exchange a few weeks, later Ms. Flournoy revealed what that realization was like for her:

Ms. Flournoy: Talking with . . . the group and the other teachers and . . . opening my eyes and opening my ears, just those few weeks [of the PD], I saw a lot more that I just must have let go over my head. Like when Khalif came in, he was in my seventh-grade, and I remember them saying things like that [about him being a terrorist]. I felt sooo bad!

Shayla: What did you think about it when he was in seventh grade?

Ms. Flournoy: 'Cause he was laughing it off. I actually have . . . (gets up to find phone, brings it back and shows me a picture of Khalif) . . . There he is in seventh grade! . . . But he was wrapped up, with the scarf . . . They were kind of like, joking around with him and doing this and that. So to me, I just thought they were all joking around. It's kind of funny I still have that [picture] . . . I didn't get it . . . I just didn't get it.

Shayla: So what do you think about it now? So what did you learn?

Ms. Flournoy: They hurt him. And then he learned to develop a defense mechanism by being very well-versed in sarcasm.

Ms. Flournoy realized there had been many days like this over the years, in which she had failed to respond to racial harassment. She had not done so intentionally, but because it was easier to assume that if students were laughing, nothing was wrong. After her conversation with Khalif, she realized that laughter was often a cover for deeper pain. A week later, another opportunity presented itself for her to interrupt racial bullying. She responded very differently:

> I don't know if you recall when, um . . . Osama bin Laden [died] and I told you the story about [a] student . . . telling Mohammad across the room, "Well I'm sorry for your loss." And I could just see Mohammad's face . . . It was a boy who is mixed, he's Japanese and Korean, and then another boy who is a black boy. And they're both making comments to him, so you got three races making comments. Oh, boy! And I took them in the hall and just said, "You know, that's totally racist." "Oh, he's our friend. We're just joking, and he knows we're joking." I said, "That would hurt me!" I kind of yelled at them a little bit. But then they came out and they apologized. So . . . like I said, it was Khalif who brought that to my attention. And I looked right into Mohammad's eyes and I could see that he's not liking this . . . I think I would

have, I . . . may have not said anything before . . . I may have said, "Guys, just stop." That's what I may have said then. And then would have continued on what I was doing. This time I made a point of it: "No. This is racist."

Ms. Flournoy immediately applied what she had learned. Instead of passing over a racially charged incident, she now directly addressed the racist nature of the comment and interrupted the negative racial culture of students.

Teachers also reported making changes to their curriculum and pedagogy. For example, Ms. Stovall asked if I would come to all of her ninth-grade classrooms during the civil rights unit to do dialogues with students about contemporary prejudice at Jefferson. She helped them come up with their own ground rules in advance of the session. During the class, Ms. Stovall and I sat in a circle with the students and talked about race relations in the school, in much the way we had done in Intergroup and the teacher PD. Afterward, we discussed how she might facilitate such conversations in the future using some of the techniques Naomi and I had modeled.

One of the teachers was working with her colleagues to develop lessons in which students were learning about race. When teaching advanced students several years before, she had done a lesson on the N-word. Recalling that day, she said, "It was probably the only day in twelve years that I really felt like there was teaching and learning and exchanging, and it was like the perfect day. And it was surrounding that topic." Nonetheless, she had not done it again, because she had believed her regular students were not mature enough to handle the conversation and because she felt that race was such a taboo in the district. The PD changed her mind. At the time of the post-interview, she was developing a curriculum:

Teacher: One of the major units is "cause and effect" and there's a writing prompt that we're going to be doing . . . There's an article called "The Black Table Is Still There." It's about somebody going back years later to their junior high . . . and there was a black table and now it's still there. And so we take it a step further and there's not just a black table, there's a black cafeteria. And so, you know, one of the writing assignment or options will be to write a cause and effect. The cafeteria thing, is it the cause or is it the effect and then trying to find the solutions so . . . that's gonna be one of the paper options.

Shayla: That's great. I mean, I think that's like a perfect example of how you really take the curriculum that's already there and just incorporate . . . this kind of stuff.

Teacher: That's what we're doing . . . we're taking . . . these hot-button topics and incorporating them, finding essays and articles and things for the students to read, but also then we're teaching grammar, we're teaching writing, we're teaching argument, we're teaching all these things using . . . topics that kids need to know about and write about and think about and that really aren't talked about . . . I think that can really open up a conversation in a classroom, you know, using that article to kind of have that discussion and then have them figure it out . . . So I am taking things from [the PD] and you know, applying.

Ms. McCandless was also considering how she could improve some of the conversations she had already been trying to have with students about race:

> I used to think that I was able to talk about race, and I felt like I was kind of into that zone more than other teachers. But then when I had that one class, I felt—I don't know . . . I was willing to take the risk to kind of change it a little bit and say, "I know we talk about race a lot, but how do you feel about talking about race?" And so . . . having that be a blowup where some kids say they don't like it at all and they hate it and they feel yucky and then the different opinions, and then bringing up lists of slurs and, ugh, like I just . . . I recognize that there's a difference between talking about the literature and talking about how we feel about talking about the literature.

Ms. McCandless was observing something that students had already noted in previous chapters—her lessons had not been dialogues. When she actually attempted to push students to discuss how race was relevant to their own lives, rather than simply asking them to discuss its relevance to a book they were reading, she realized that she was not as adept, skilled, or comfortable as she had previously believed. She knew she needed to be doing more. In the post-interview, she said that in the PD she had learned how to "set ground rules better, proactively prepare students for issues that might come up," utilize strategies to "open . . . and then get into something for center time . . . and then . . . wrap up," and the importance of "closure. I don't do closure." She was eager to continue learning how to do it better.

While teachers did not get all they needed or wanted from the five-session PD, many said they left with a better understanding of their own biases and new ideas for improving their practice around issues of race. Moreover, they had built new relationships of support and accountability with each other. They sought each other out to get feedback on assignments they had created and to reflect on interactions they had with students. They had developed a community of practice, a cadre of like-minded colleagues committed to improving their teaching around issues of race.

A SPACE IS NEEDED

I guess what I feel like is that I should know what to do now, but I still don't. There! Not that I think I should've gotten everything I needed to know out of five weeks, but I just think that I kind of have this feeling that if I had paid more attention or if I had developed . . . if I go back and read everything that I've ever gotten in college and otherwise, with this new frame of mind . . . I feel like I could really make a difference.

—Ms. McCandless, white teacher

I wish we had classes like that . . . it would be sweet.

—Danny, white student

I wish we had more time.

—Ms. Gorski, white teacher

At the end of Intergroup and Race in the Classroom, teachers and students were requesting more. They wanted to spend more time together, they wanted to continue thinking and talking about race in a safe and facilitated space with the community we had formed, and they wanted more guidance about how to change the culture of their school.

For most of the students, Intergroup was the only place in their lives where they were having substantive conversations about race or other pressing issues. As Shannon (black and white) explained, "It's really nowhere else that people are gonna talk about this stuff, like you're not doing it in class. A lot of people don't talk about it with their friends or at home." She worried that if the school did not provide such spaces students would have nowhere else to explore issues of race and identity. Kwesi (black) agreed, "I feel like we should have a class. I just feel like everybody should be exposed to this, everybody in school should be exposed to this kind of program in some kind of way . . . because this could all tie into how we deal with each other in the world . . . This could be put in our curriculum, like this should be a separate class on, they should even call this like 'life issues.' I'm telling you this is great."

Similarly, Nathan (Asian and white) said, "A lot of students need Intergroup to enlighten themselves. 'Cause a lot of students here are, not just close-minded, but are ignorant in that fact. . . . like they only know what they were told." He worried that if adults and teachers did not provide such opportunities, his generation would go out into the world believing that the hyperracial ways they were interacting were acceptable.

Leah (white) said that she learned more in Intergroup that was relevant to life than in all of her academic classes. Her actions showed it. During her senior year, she served as an Intergroup peer facilitator; the year after she graduated from high school, she continued coming to Intergroup every week; and the year after that, she was hired as a paid facilitator for the program. As an adult, she has been a vocal activist for social justice.

Teachers were also brainstorming ways to continue the conversation. While they were more comfortable talking about race and were moving beyond color-blind frames, after ten hours together they were only just beginning to get what they needed in order to transform their classrooms and their school. Teachers kept asking if we were going to continue to work in the district; if we were going to do another round of professional development; and if we would be available to help them with issues that might arise in the future. In fact, Ms. McWilliams wanted "to have an actually paid position to do this." Ms. Mitchell felt the same:

> I mean, I think a lot of us would have liked to have gone on longer, you know, because I think we were just starting to get to that comfort level. I think that we had a lot more questions and situations and I think spending more time kind of addressing people's individual . . . you know, working on their individual issues in the classroom. Like I'd like a book of whatever it is you guys have, to make my classroom more like . . . incorporating dialogue.

Ms. McCandless said she could envision, "Intergroup for teachers . . . once a week!" Teachers especially appreciated that our work was not a one-size-fits-all model, but was specific to Jefferson. As Ms. Flournoy explained, "The fact [of] it being in my school, it's totally different than me going to take a workshop . . . where they're talking about the general population. I mean, you were able to bring statistics to us and show us different things. Bring students to us . . . I just like it a lot better that way. That's why I think at the end of our last session, I was asking you if you plan on doing this again next year."

The repeated question of teachers and students about how this work would continue, what the plans were for the following year, and how they could keep meeting, strongly challenged the narrative of "the Jefferson Way." It pushed back against the notion that people were unwilling, unable, and uninterested in talking about race. Instead, these participants demonstrated a hunger for spaces in which they could learn about and take action around injustice. Their interest was evidence of the promise and possibilities of intervention of this nature if done at scale. It also pointed to the sustained commitment needed to make real transformation in schools around race, and the lack of opportunities most educators and students have to do so.

Jefferson was an integrated school in which building administrators said they wanted to celebrate diversity, and many teachers thought of themselves as racially conscious. Yet most stakeholders had never actually reflected on issues of race, never talked about race, never viewed their practice or experiences through the lens of race—not because they were unwilling to do so, but because there simply has not been space for such endeavors in our public education system. These teachers and students made clear that in order to have the kinds of equitable, integrated schools we say we want, we must approach education and school reform much differently than we have.

CONCLUSION

Rethinking Reform

> Schools, for many of us who spend time in them and write about them, remain places of hope—they offer the possibility of new realities. Focusing on schools encourages us to emphasize the becoming and the emerging—the inevitability that racial understandings and racial rules must all be learned, that race does not exist inert and separate from us, and thus that racial lessons might be learned differently. Examining schools challenges us not merely to document what is but to begin to imagine how it might be better.
>
> —Amanda Lewis, *Race in the Schoolyard*[1]

Over the past decade, I have spent significant time in schools studying and working with students, teachers, and administrators around issues of race. I have worked in large diverse high schools like Jefferson, all-black middle schools, and majority-white elementary schools. I have developed and facilitated professional development workshops, afterschool programs, countywide diversity forums, and trainings for pre-service teachers. Currently, I am directing a multiyear project to improve racial and economic justice in a majority-black, low-income district.

While this book is about an exurban community that challenges the assumption that "low-income" is a synonym for "black," the story told on these pages is a common one. American schools overall are failing to deal with race at every level of the system. Every school I visit struggles to navigate race and inequality. Every school I have worked in has troubling racial gaps in achievement and discipline. I have experienced firsthand the barriers and roadblocks to addressing racial bullying. I have seen districts

★ need to turn dialogue into some small act

229

★ never talks about the issue of gender throughout the book
gender is marginalized b/c females are not taken seriously
(devaluing the importance & value of women)

adopt interventions and programs that come and go, leaving not only little improvement—save the abstract commitment of a few progressive teachers—but actually significant destruction in their wake. I have seen stereotypes about "poor black kids" reinforced by presentations meant to help educators learn how to better serve these populations. I have heard teachers complaining about the latest multicultural initiative as a waste of time, or even "reverse racism." I have seen educators blaming "those kids" for the racially inequitable outcomes in our schools while denying that they bear any responsibility. And I have witnessed students laughing and joking in interracial groups while making racially biased comments. Every time I talk to students, parents, or educators about my research and my work, people tell me that my findings resonate with their own experiences.

Recently, I was with a group of pre-service and first-year teachers. These educators worked in elementary, middle, and high schools, in integrated suburban districts and urban majority-black districts. They were all eager to learn how to be effective teachers for the students of color they most struggled to engage. On a whim, I asked them to visualize their most challenging student—what was this student's race, gender, socioeconomic background? What kind of neighborhood did he or she live in? I then asked them to think of a close friend in their own lives who shared the identities of the student they struggled with. As I anticipated, virtually no one could think of a close friend similar to the challenging students— almost all of whom were either students of color, low-income students, or both. The white educators did not have meaningful relationships with people of color; none of the teachers had friends from vastly different educational backgrounds; and few had close friends of different social classes. Almost all the teachers' close friends were like them—racially, economically, and politically.

This activity illuminated a reality about our education system that I have observed for years: we are asking educators to do something in their work that most of us have not done successfully in our lives. We are asking teachers, who, like the rest of us, live in a country that is highly segregated, to connect with students from racially and economically different backgrounds and understand their families, their experiences, and their needs. We are asking them to successfully teach diverse students when most have not managed to make a close friend across race and when little in their histories or education has prepared them to do so. We are telling them they must figure out how to close racial gaps in achievement and discipline when most of them have never even thought at any length or depth about race. Often, I think teachers, students, and administrators are being set up to fail.

In our K–12 schools, institutions of higher education, and national reform efforts, we have given educators virtually no skills to understand cultural differences, prejudice, or structural inequality, and yet we continue to blame the major problems of our schools on teachers or marginalized students and their families for not working hard enough. I would argue that hard work is not actually the problem of our schools when it comes to inequality—at least, not as we tend to measure it. The problem is that we have created an education system wholly uninterested in considering what it would mean to value students who learn, speak, behave, dress, look, and think differently than the average white, middle-class kid. So most teachers—unprepared to think or talk about race and paralyzed by fear that they will be labeled racist—ignore signs of conflict, struggle to connect with students of color, and fail to make their courses relevant to their students' lives. Despite their best intentions, their interactions with young people, and each other, frequently result in creating and maintaining racial disparities.

Students, too, contribute to this outcome. Most engage in hyperracial practices that hinder their ability to develop positive racial identities or form meaningful relationships across difference. In the absence of constructive guidance from adults, they use racial humor and claims that "everyone gets along" as a smokescreen for prejudice, thus perpetuating racial hierarchies and biases in ways that echo the discrimination of decades past.

In *Race in the Schoolyard*, Amanda Lewis conceptualizes schools as "race-making institutions" that reinforce racial categories. She argues that "race (in terms of meaning and identity) and racial inequality (in terms of access to resources) are reproduced in day-to-day life in schools . . ." and that "race is not merely a fixed characteristic of children that they bring to school and then take away intact, but something they learn about through school lessons and through interactions with peers and teachers." Schools are places that reinforce and reproduce what it means to be black or white, Asian or Latino.[2]

What Lewis observes can be seen in the perpetuation of stereotypes, prejudices, and notions of identity that reinforce ideas that black students are inherently "bad," "ghetto," and "intimidating"—or as Faye Harrison notes, symbols of the "social bottom"[3]—while white students are inherently "good," "smart," and "well-behaved."

These practices have led to a school system in which racial hierarchies persist, marginalized students remain marginal, and racial gaps in educational outcomes are not closed. As Jefferson exemplifies, these narratives flourish and go unchallenged even in integrated schools in which students of color are not living in poverty and even when people think of themselves as racially tolerant.

And yet, I have seen the promise and possibility of addressing race head-on in schools like Jefferson. I have seen transformation in how young people and adults feel, think, act, teach and learn. I have found that the shell of racial reproduction is not all that hard to crack. Despite the belief of many that we cannot talk openly about these subjects, I have encountered numerous students and educators longing to have real conversations about the racial disparities they witness and the interactions they are having in schools across race. Even through moments of frustration, tension, misunderstanding, and discomfort, when given the time, structure, and space to do so, most teachers and students want to talk about race.

However, while the shell is easy to crack, it is very difficult to break. The pull in the direction of silence, avoidance, and denial is strong. Beyond the walls of classrooms with chairs arranged in circles, there is significant pressure to act as though race were not an issue, or an issue only with regard to quantitative data—to ignore the everyday "hits of racism" as Stephanie (white) called it that maintain the racial status quo in our schools.

Unfortunately, school reform in our country is heading down a path in which initiatives that address race have little traction. The national focus on penalizing teachers for low test scores, closing failing public schools and opening failing charter schools in their wake, all while continuing to cut funding for education, has left little room for discussion of race relations.

RETURNING TO JEFFERSON

The year after the research for this project concluded, Jefferson hired a new superintendent, a white woman. I was invited to meet with her to discuss the findings of my research and the work I had done at JHS. When I walked in the room, she introduced herself and immediately got down to business. "So what's going on with race in my district?" she asked. Her tone clearly suggested that she had the potential to be a different kind of race leader. After we had talked for two hours, she said she hoped the district could continue proactively addressing race. She said, "This is important work. We need to deal with these things. How can we make this happen?" Feeling rather bold, I responded, "You're the superintendent. If you can't make it happen, I don't know who can." Within a few months, she had scheduled a meeting for me to present some of my findings to the school board. That year, she also sent two Jefferson administrators to participate in a countywide training on race. Jefferson was taking concrete steps to consider how they might address that which for decades they had actively worked to ignore. But it was not enough.

I returned to Jefferson again two years later, in 2014, at the request of one of the assistant principals, Ms. Billingslea, who had been part of the countywide PD, and two of the teachers from the Race in the Classroom PD three years before. They invited me to help Jefferson with the Race Card Project—a national initiative organized by Michele Norris of National Public Radio in which individuals write six words about race on a card. Teachers were going to engage every student in the school in this activity as part of a country-wide initiative.

On one hand, the fact that Jefferson was doing such a project at such a scale indicated that it had made significant strides in addressing race. This was not its first effort. The previous year, Ms. Billingslea had taken what she had learned in the PD back to Jefferson, where staff had since committed many of their meetings to engaging in activities to foster dialogue about race. Nonetheless, the few hours I spent at Jefferson made clear that engaging seven of eighty educators in the Race in the Classroom PD and forty of the fifteen hundred students the Intergroup afterschool program had not been enough to significantly change the culture and climate of the school.

Rather than lively dialogue about how to lead race conversations with students, there was silence in the room. I knew for a fact that there were lots of teachers at Jefferson open to talking about race. They had done so with me from 2009 to 2012 in their classrooms, in the teachers' lounge, and over lunch. But you would not know it from the palpable tension. They were scared to talk about race publicly, in a large group, with their colleagues—many of whom they still did not know—and their boss—the twentieth principal in as many years. Unfortunately, I was not surprised.

The overwhelming majority of teachers still had not had significant conversations about race. They were not comfortable with their own racial identities, they had not considered their views on racial inequality, and they still were not aware of how race affected the lives of their students. Moreover, they had no idea what their colleagues thought about race or what they would think of them if they spoke up. As I suspected, Jefferson had a long way to go, not because the school was so far behind, but because doing the work of race in schools is more difficult than most imagine.

Nonetheless, even in this context, there were a few moments of hope in which a couple of brave, committed teachers took real risks with their colleagues and shared a personal story about race. Even more teachers had conversations with their students in their classrooms about the Race Cards. These moments, if seized, could change Jefferson, and schools like it, for the better.

MAKING CHANGE IN SCHOOLS

What was it that kept Jefferson from making more significant change around issues of race? What must be in place for work of this nature to energize more than a few committed educators before petering out? What makes it possible to fully address race in schools? Interestingly, while there are undeniably many factors that contribute to success, the essential components don't have much to do with race at all.

Commitment from the Top Down

One of the biggest challenges to talking about race in schools is that it simply has not been made a priority by education leaders. Most educators do not feel they have the time, resources, or permission to address race. Thus the first step we must take is to create institutional cultures in which those in leadership positions—politicians, school reformers, superintendents, and school boards—make race a priority and make addressing it an expectation. Without the backing of those in leadership positions, classroom teachers are risking too much in talking race. They fear they will not be supported should parents or other teachers complain; they worry that they will be labeled racist if they are the ones who bring up race; and they fear they will be seen as taking limited time away from concerns deemed more important—testing, accountability, the Common Core curriculum. The culture of schools must be one in which talking openly about race at every level of the system is supported, nurtured, and expected.

Systematic and Authentic Examination of the School

The second challenge to intervening successfully in issues of race is that most schools and districts believe they can do so by adopting a ready-made program. The reality is that the overwhelming majority of "diversity trainings" are not successful in changing the culture of schools in part because they are not created with the specific needs of particular schools in mind. While many of the challenges schools face are universal, the contexts in which they are seeking to address these issues are all unique. To the extent that my work with schools has been successful, it has been in part because of the anthropological, ethnographic approach I have taken. I have spent significant time studying the schools in which I work, endeavoring to understand the specific challenges they face, what the power structure is, what the teachers worry about, and where the resistance lies.

School systems that are serious about doing race work must first get serious about studying the racial dynamics of their organizations and communities. They must talk to students, teachers, parents, administrators, paraprofessionals, custodians, and other stakeholders to gather accurate information about the specific challenges they face. They must analyze their demographic, achievement, and disciplinary data. And they must ask critical questions about why they struggle in the ways that they do. This information should then be used to inform the content and pedagogy of any proposed intervention.

Longitudinal, Sustained, and In-Depth

The third challenge educators face is that school reform initiatives tend to take on a "flavor of the month" model. Addressing race cannot be successful if it is treated as the latest fad in education. It is not possible to unlearn color-blindness, and all that comes with it, in a lecture—even an eight-hour one. It is not possible to change one's teaching after a one-time workshop. Educators will not become efficacious at engaging students in conversations about race in a single school year. Doing the work of race in schools requires sustained, longitudinal commitment. Teachers and administrators have to be able to count on it. They have to know that this is what education is about—every day, every semester, every year.

Too often, disgruntled educators co-opt or derail initiatives to address race by being the loudest in the room. Their actions are rooted not only in resistance, fear, and denial but also in the reality that usually if teachers put up enough of a fight, they can thwart efforts to make change. This is particularly true because most initiatives, even those going well, do not last long. If educators can grumble and drag their feet for a year about having to address race, knowing that the next year the district will move on, these initiatives will never gain traction.

Rooted in Relationships and Community-Building

Despite the many programs to improve education in the United States, the fact is that programs do not fix schools, people do. This is especially true when it comes to issues of race. While it is important for schools to have curriculum, policies, and practices that make race and inequality central, mandating that teachers do a Race Card Project with students, or read a book by an acclaimed scholar, or learn about African American families, will not be enough to change the climate of race in schools.

The most significant transformations I have witnessed are those that happen over time, after educators work together, come to know each other, and engage in dialogue, sometimes for years. It can take a facilitator as much as a year of being regularly present in a school to build enough trust and safety to actually have honest, reflective conversations about race. It can take two years to get enough buy-in from willing teachers to interrupt the resistance of naysayers or try out a new lesson plan. If educators do not like the person leading this work, do not feel that person is on their side, or do not see that person as a source of support and as someone they can confide in, it is highly unlikely that they will make significant changes to their pedagogy, curriculum, or interactions with students or each other. Every year, it is made clearer to me that people are not converted through programs, they are converted through relationships. This is not only true between educators, students, and families, but also between educators and whoever is leading professional development or interventions around race.

A Combination of Personal Reflection, Knowledge, and Action

In a recent PD I was facilitating, a teacher raised her hand, frustrated. She wanted to know when we were going to stop wasting time asking teachers to talk about themselves and start talking about students. She wanted me to tell her what to do with black kids in particular. Perhaps I had a checklist or information sheet on "black culture," she wondered. Her questions were evidence to me of the deep need for personal reflection and growth in the work of race.

In order to engage effectively with issues of race, teachers must "do their own work," as my colleague Dr. Melanie Morrison, director of Allies for Change, often says. This means thinking about your own racial identity, how you interact with people from different racial backgrounds, and the stereotypes and biases you hold about race so that you can interrupt them. Too often, professional development skips the work of learning about self and goes straight to the work of learning about others with little success.

At the same time, the focus cannot be on personal reflection alone. Some of the most problematic exchanges I have witnessed between students and teachers around race are rooted in teachers' lack of broader knowledge about the history, culture, sociology, and politics of race. When educators do not know much about race or diversity—for example, why income, housing patterns, and school demographics are so often racialized; when they don't know their disaggregated data—who is doing well, who is dropping out, who is being suspended; when they have not taken the time to step outside of their comfort zone and learn another language, visit a church in a community where they are a minority, or eat diverse foods; when they aren't paying attention to major issues of race in the news and the world—like the killing of Trayvon Martin and Michael Brown or the Supreme Court decision overturning the Voting Rights Act—they cannot teach their students to do so. It is not possible to give young people something we do not have or, as Gary Howard notes, to "teach what we don't know." Teachers must learn more so that they can teach more.

But knowledge is not enough, either. Educators also need specific skills and plans of action for what to do next. They need ideas about how to change their lessons. They need models of how to interrupt discrimination when they witness it and opportunities to practice doing it, with constructive feedback. They need spaces to look at their data and compare it to their practice. The most intellectually committed, reflective, knowledgeable teachers are of no service to students if they do not put what they know and think into practice. Teachers often need help doing this.

Far too often, schools work to maintain our social system as it is—one in which being black seems impossible to disentangle from being marginalized; one in which the racial biases that students come to scl grown in families and communities, are left unchallenged anu .... rupted; one in which educators easily fall into traps of blaming "those kids" and their families. In the current political climate, in which "education" is thought to be synonymous with standardized achievement and "value-added," it can seem as though issues of race and relationships are merely a distraction from what "really matters." However, the challenges we face to providing young people from all backgrounds with equal opportunities to be successful cannot be disconnected from how they are treated every day in our schools. Rather than viewing schools as public, democratic institutions in which teachers actively work against inequality to develop well-rounded, critically thinking, engaged citizens who are able to build relationships with those from very different backgrounds, current reform efforts are serving only to privatize, standardize, corporatize, and penalize public schools.

When we do not talk about race, when we ignore it, when we fail to interrupt racial discrimination and incorporate diverse perspectives in our curriculum and pedagogical approaches, we are teaching young people that racial inequality is acceptable. We are telling them we sanction an education system that only values and successfully educates students from certain groups. We are teaching them that the status quo is not a problem.

However, as the experiences of teachers and students at Jefferson have revealed, we have many race problems in our schools and in our country. These conflicts, tensions, and misunderstandings underlie the inequitable outcomes that consume reformers. They are more complicated and deeply rooted than any standardized test can measure. Solving them will take more creative solutions than anything currently being proposed. If we truly seek to create racially just schools, we will need to take seriously the reality that the data that concerns us is attached to real people, and that the needs, skills, experiences, histories, and social interactions of these people must be the focus of our efforts.

Unfortunately, as it stands, schools are dealing little with the things that really matter. However, we could change course. We could craft national policies that encourage the interrogation of race in schools. We could begin a federal "Race to the Top" initiative that is actually concerned with substantively addressing *race*, not just test scores. State boards of education could mandate that schools deal with race and other social justice issues and that teachers have competence in these areas, just as they have created standards for curriculum and teacher certification. States could create teacher evaluations that actually ask students what is happening in classrooms, or that require that teachers observe and learn from each other. District administrators could use the time and money they devote to professional development each year to create a model that actually provides teachers with the resources, support, and training necessary to do better with and for their most marginalized students in ongoing, collaborative ways. High schools and middle schools could develop courses like Intergroup, or mandate that teachers incorporate content and dialogue in their classes about race and relationships. Administrators could engage teachers in team meetings to intentionally build community among staff, attend to student culture, analyze disaggregated data, or systematically consider ways to provide opportunities for students to work together across racial lines. Teachers could mobilize their unions to demand more—more training, more information, more skills around issues of race. Teachers could collectively and systematically interrupt the problematic ways in which students interact across race, not by using punitive measures, but by engaging them in conversations that debunk stereotypes and prejudices. Schools of education could take seriously the need to train pre-service teachers around bias and inequality and provide them with techniques, skills, and internships to address these issues.

And as a nation, we could decide that our dual goals of raising student achievement and raising good people require that we deal head-on with race. We could change the narrative of school failure from one that blames *those kids* to one that looks critically at *our schools*. There is a lot we *could* do, but first we must decide we *want* to.

APPENDIX

Discussion Questions

Prologue

1. Recall the conflicts students in your school have had in the past few years.
   - How did race play into those conflicts? (Keep in mind that race may have been relevant in ways that were ignored or overlooked at the time).
   - How did your school respond to these conflicts? Did you do so in ways that provided opportunities to identify and work through the roots of these disagreements?
     - If so, how can you make sure to replicate this process in future situations?
     - If not, how might you respond more productively next time?

Introduction: The Continuing Significance of Race in America's Integrated Schools

1. What are the racial and economic demographics of your classroom, school, and district?
   - How has your student and teacher population changed over time?
   - What has been the source of this change?
   - If there have been demographic shifts, how have educators, students, and community members responded to them?

- What narratives exist in your district about the neighborhoods, families, and homes your students come from?
- How do these narratives compare to factual information about the neighborhoods, families, and homes your students come from?
2. Are there achievement and discipline gaps by race (or other identities) in your school?
    - What are the gaps?
    - Are educators aware of these gaps?
    - How is your school working to close these gaps?
    - How successful have these efforts been?

Part I: Students

Chapter 1: Racial Humor

1. How do students from different racial backgrounds interact across race at your school?
    - Do students make "joking" comments to each other that have racial undertones?
    - Do students use racial slurs?
    - If so, which groups of students tend to be the targets in these exchanges?
    - Which groups of students tend to be the perpetrators?
    - How do students from different backgrounds feel about these exchanges? How do you know this?

Chapter 2: Racial Performance

1. How are the terms *acting black* and *acting white* used by students at your school? How are these terms used by educators?
2. How do students in your school perform their racial identities?
    - How are these performances evaluated by students?
    - How are these performances evaluated by educators?
    - How does race play into these assessments?

Chapter 3: Intimidation and Fighting

1. How is the learning environment affected by racial intimidation or violence?
2. How do you see internalized racism play out in your school?

Chapter 4: "Full-Blown Racists"

1. In what ways is your school racially segregated?
2. What messages are white students in your school getting about race from their families, communities, teachers, and the broader society?

Part II: Teachers

Chapter 5: See No Evil, Hear No Evil, Speak No Evil

1. How do teachers in your school respond to hyperracial exchanges between students?
   • Why do teachers respond in this way?
   • If there are barriers to responding, what could you do to overcome them?
2. What efforts have educators made to engage students in conversations about contemporary issues of race in your school?
   • How successful have these conversations been?
   • What could you do to encourage more conversations about race?

Chapter 6: The Cycle of Mutual Disrespect

1. How is the term *racism* used by students and educators in your school?
   • What might this language indicate about your school culture?
2. What are some examples of racial bias among educators in your school?
   • How are students judged by educators when they walk into a classroom?
   • How do students respond to the judgments educators make about them?
   • What steps could you take to begin interrupting negative judgments?

Chapter 7: Reframing Race

1. Do you think of yourself as color-blind, color-conscious, or color-confused? Why?
   - What could you do to become more racially conscious?
2. What frames do you use to avoid talking about race? Why?
   - What frames do your colleagues use to avoid talking about race?
   - How could you practice having more honest conversations about race in your school?

Part III: Administrators

Chapter 8: "No One at the Table"

1. What are the racial demographics of your staff?
   - Does this accurately reflect the diversity of your student body, community, and the broader society?
2. What efforts are you making as a school to hire, retain, and promote a racially diverse teaching and administrative staff?
   - How successful have these efforts been?
   - Are there ways they could be more successful?
   - If you have not made any efforts, why isn't this a priority in your school?
3. How are staff of color valued in your school?
   - How have you created structures in which the voices of staff of color are heard?
   - How have you created a system in which race is an issue that everyone is expected to address and contend with?
   - What have you done to ensure that staff of color are not used as scapegoats for racial problems (or as solely responsible for their solutions)?

Chapter 9: "The Jefferson Way"

1. What is the overall culture of your district when it comes to issues of race?

- Is it one of silence? Avoidance? Open dialogue?
- Is your school welcoming of students and families from diverse backgrounds or resistant to their presence?
2. How do you use data to inform practice in your school?
   - Is data disseminated and accessible to educators?
   - How does data (or the lack of data) shape educators' perceptions of the students in your school?
3. How are multicultural holidays celebrated in your school?
   - Who is responsible for these celebrations?
4. What kind of professional development has been offered at your school around issues of racial justice?
   - Have these offerings reinforced or interrupted stereotypes about students and families of color?
   - What has been the takeaway of these initiatives?
   - What could you do to make sure that professional development offerings address your specific needs as a school?

Part IV: Intervention

Chapter 10: Learning Not to Be Racist

1. Where are the safe spaces in your school in which educators can talk about issues of race?
   - If you do not have any such spaces, how could you create them?
2. Where are the safe spaces in your school in which students can talk about issues of race?
   - If you do not have any such spaces, how could you create them?

Conclusion

1. Do you have a close friend with social identities similar to your most challenging students?
   - If so, what have you learned about yourself in that relationship?
   - If not, why do you think this is?

- What could you do to cultivate more relationships with people similar to the students you find challenging?
2. What racial lessons do students learn at your school?
   - What do they learn about who is likely to succeed and who is likely to fail?
   - What do the learn about who is well behaved and who is poorly behaved?
   - If you are unsatisfied with what they might be learning, is there anything you could do to impart different lessons?
3. Which of the tips for "Making Change in Schools" does your school currently practice when it comes to issues of race?
   - What would it take for you to begin doing the things suggested?

Notes

Introduction

1. Gary Orfield and Chugmei Lee, "Historic Reversals: Accelerating Resegregation and the Need for New Strategies," *UCLA Civil Rights Project/Proyecto Derechos Civiles* (August 2007), http://civilrightsproject.ucla.edu/research/k-12-education/ integration-and-diversity/historic-reversals-accelerating-resegregation-and-the-need -for-newintegration-strategies-112-education/integration; Gary Orfield, "Schools More Separate: Consequences of a Decade of Resegregation," *Civil Rights Project, Harvard University* (2001), http://civilrightsproject.ucla.edu/research/k-12-education/ integration-and-diversity/schools-more-separate-consequences-of-a-decade-of -resegregation/orfield-schools-more-separate-2001.pdf; John R. Logan and Brian J. Stults, "The Persistence of Racial Segregation in the Metropolis: New Findings from the 2010 Census," *Census Brief Prepared for Project US2010* (2011), http://www .s4.brown.edu/us2010/Data/Report/report2.pdf; Steven G. Rivikin, "Residential Segregation and School Integration," *Sociology of Education* 67, no. 4 (1994): 279–292.
2. During the 1950s, whites began fleeing U.S. cities for racially homogenous suburbs in huge numbers, isolating people of color in disinvested inner cities. See William H. Frey, "Central City White Flight: Racial and Nonraical Causes," *American Sociological Review* 44 (1979): 425–448. Two decades later, the U.S. Supreme Court ruled in *Milliken v. Bradley* (1974) that school segregation was not illegal if it was the result of residential segregation rather than explicitly discriminatory school policies. The *Milliken* ruling essentially tied the hands of municipalities attempting to integrate schools. See Joyce Baugh, *The Detroit School Busing Case*: Milliken v. Bradley *and the Controversy Over Desegregation* (Lawrence, KS: University Press of Kansas, 2011). Forty years later, some studies have found that schools are as segregated as they were prior to the 1954 *Brown v. Board of Education* decision.
3. Logan and Stults, "The Persistence of Racial Segregation in the Metropolis"; Matthew Hall and Barrett Lee, "How Diverse are U.S. Suburbs?" *Urban Studies* 47, no. 1 (2010): 3–28; William H. Frey, "Melting Pot Cities and Suburbs: Racial and Ethnic Change in Metro America in the 2000s," *Metropolitan Policy Program at Brookings, State of Metropolitan America*, May 2011.
4. Daniel Lichter et al., "National Estimates of Racial Segregation in Rural and Small-Town America," *Demography* 44, no. 3 (August 2007): 563–581; Alan Berube

et al., "Finding Exurbia: America's Fast-Growing Communities at the Metropolitan Fringe," *Metropolitan Policy Program, Living Cities Series* (Washington, DC: The Brookings Institute, October 2006); Bernadette Hanlon, Thomas Vicino and John Rennie Short, "The New Metropolitan Reality in the U.S.: Rethinking the Traditional Model," *Urban Studies* 46 (2006): 2129.

5. Myron Orfield and Thomas Luce, "America's Racially Diverse Suburbs: Opportunities and Challenges," *Institute on Metropolitan Opportunity, University of Minnesota Law School*, July 20, 2012, 2.

6. Frey, "Melting Pot Cities and Suburbs."

7. Deirdre Pfeiffer, "African Americans' Search for 'More for Less' and 'Peace of Mind' on the Exurban Frontier," *Urban Geography* 33, no. 1 (2012): 67.

8. Orfield and Luce, "America's Racially Diverse Suburbs," 12.

9. Nate Berg, "Exurbs, The Fastest Growing Areas in the U.S.," *The Atlantic, City Lab*, July 19, 2012, http://www.citylab.com/housing/2012/07/exurbs-fastest-growing-areas-us/2636/.

10. Lichter et al., "National Estimates of Racial Segregation," 577.

11. Deirdre Pfeiffer, *Sprawling to Opportunity: Los Angeles African Americans on the Exurban Frontier* (PhD diss., University of California, Los Angeles, 2011), 348.

12. Reynolds Farley, Sheldon Danziger, and Harry Holzer, *Detroit Divided* (New York: Russell Sage Foundation, 2000); Katherine S. Newman, *Declining Fortunes: The Withering of the American Dream* (NewYork: BasicBooks, 1993); Lois Weis, *Working Class Without Work: High School Students in a Deindustrializing Economy* (New York: Routledge, 1990).

13. Although Jefferson had many middle-class trappings, as Mary Patillo (*Black Picket Fences: Privilege and Peril Among the Black Middle Class* [University of Chicago Press, 1999]) notes, "'middle-class' is a notoriously elusive category . . ." (p. 13). A number of professors and graduate students affiliated with universities in the area and other professionals lived in Jefferson and sent their children to Jefferson schools. However, many residents were able to afford their lifestyle through blue-collar work in the service and manufacturing industries. Thanks to strong unions, these jobs historically provided good salaries, benefits, and pensions to black and white families, allowing them access to middle-class incomes without high levels of education. See Thomas Sugrue, *The Origins of the Urban Crisis: Race and Inequality in Postwar Detroit* (Princeton, NJ: Princeton University Press, 1996).

14. Berube et al., "Finding Exurbia," 2.

15. U.S. Department of Education, "Expansive Survey of America's Public Schools Reveals Troubling Racial Disparities: Lack of Access to Pre-School, Greater Suspension Cited," March 21, 2014, http://www.ed.gov/news/press-releases/expansive-survey-americas-public-schools-reveals-troubling-racial-disparities

16. Anne Gregory, Pedro Noguera, and Russell J. Skiba, "The Achievement Gap and the Discipline Gap: Two Sides of the Same Coin?" *Educational Researcher* 39, no. 1 (2010): 59.

17. Diane Ravitch, *The Death and Life of the Great American School System: How Testing and Choice Are Undermining Education* (New York: Basic Books, 2010).

18. Charles M. Payne, *So Much Reform, So Little Change: The Persistence of Failure in Urban Schools* (Cambridge, MA: Harvard Education Press, 2008), 169.

19. Lisa Delpit, *Other People's Children: Cultural Conflict in the Classroom* (New York: New Press, 2006); Gloria Ladson-Billings, "But That's Just Good Teaching! The Case for Culturally Relevant Pedagogy," *Theory into Practice* 34, no. 3 (1995): 159–165; Amanda E. Lewis, *Race in the Schoolyard: Negotiating the Color Line in Classrooms and Communities* (New Brunswick, NJ: Rutgers University Press, 2003); Angela Valenzuela, *Subtractive Schooling: U.S.-Mexican Youth and the Politics of Caring* (Albany: State University of New York Press, 1999); Margaret Mead, *The School in American Culture* (Cambridge, MA: Harvard University Press, 1951). George D. Spindler and Louise S. Spindler, *Fifty Years of Anthropology and Education, 1950–2000: A Spindler Anthology* (Mahwah, NJ: L.Erlbaum Associates, 2000).

20. Valenzuela, *Subtractive Schooling*; Pedro A. Noguera, *The Trouble with Black Boys: Essays on Race, Equity, and the Future of Public Education* (San Francisco: Jossey-Bass, 2008); Ladson-Billings, "But That's Just Good Teaching!"; James A. Banks, *Educating Citizens in a Multicultural Society* (New York: Teachers College Press, 2007); Adrienne Dessel, "Prejudice in Schools: Promotion of an Inclusive Culture and Climate," *Education and Urban Society* 42, no. 4 (2010): 407.

21. Pierre Bourdieu, *Distinction: A Social Critique of the Judgment of Taste* (Cambridge, MA: Harvard University Press, 1984); Pierre Bourdieu and J. C. Passeron, *Reproduction in Education, Society and Culture* (Beverly Hills, CA: Sage Publications, 1977).

22. Robert M. Emerson, Rachel I. Fretz, and Linda L. Shaw, *Writing Ethnographic Fieldnotes* (Chicago: University of Chicago Press, 1995).

23. Leith Mullings, "Interrogating Racism: Toward an Antiracist Anthropology," *Annual Review of Anthropology* 34, no. 1 (2005): 684.

24. John U. Ogbu, *Black American Students in an Affluent Suburb: A Study of Academic Disengagement* (Mahwah, NJ: L. Erlbaum Associates, 2003).

25. Sherry B. Ortner, *Anthropology and Social Theory: Culture, Power, and the Acting Subject* (Durham, NC: Duke University Press, 2006), 73.

26. Frederick Erickson, "Transformation and School Success: The Politics and Culture of Educational Achievement," *Anthropology & Education Quarterly* 18, no. 4 (1987): 353.

Chapter 1

1. Antonio Gramsci, Quintin Hoare, and Geoffery Nowell-Smith, *Selections from the Prison Notebooks of Antonio Gramsci* (London: Lawrence & Wishart, 1971); Simon Gunn, "From Hegemony to Governmentality: Changing Conceptions of Power in Social History," *Journal of Social History* 39, no. 3 (2006): 707.

2. Mark A. Ferguson and Thomas E. Ford, "Social Consequences of Disparagement Humor: A Prejudiced Norm Theory," *Personality and Social Psychology Review* 8, no. 1 (2004): 79.

3. Randall Kennedy, *Nigger: The Strange Career of a Troublesome Word* (New York: Pantheon Books, 2002).

4. Paula S. Rothenberg, *White Privilege: Essential Readings on the Other Side of Racism* (New York: Worth Publishers, 2008), 10.

5. Beverly Daniel Tatum, *Can We Talk About Race? And Other Conversations in an Era of School Resegregation* (Boston: Beacon, 2007), 33.

6. Michelle Alexander, *The New Jim Crow: Mass Incarceration in the Age of Colorblindness* (New York: New Press, 2010).

7. Michael Billig, "Humour and Hatred: The Racist Jokes of the Ku Klux Klan," *Discourse and Society* 12, no. 3 (2001): 287; Simon Weaver, "Jokes, Rhetoric and Embodied Racism: A Rhetorical Discourse Analysis of the Logics of Racist Jokes on the Internet," *Ethnicities* 11, no. 4 (2011): 413.

8. Simon Weaver, "Jokes, Rhetoric and Embodied Racism: A Rhetorical Discourse Analysis of the Logics of Racist Jokes on the Internet," *Ethnicities* 11, no. 4 (2011): 431.

9. John Burma, "Humor as a Technique in Race Conflict," *American Sociological Review* 11, no. 6 (1946): 714–715.

10. Mark A. Ferguson and Thomas E. Ford, "Social Consequences of Disparagement Humor: A Prejudiced Norm Theory," *Personality and Social Psychology Review* 8, no. 1 (2004): 79.

11. Ibid.; Dennis Howitt and Kwame Owusu-Bempah, "Race and Ethnicity in Popular Humor," in *Beyond a Joke: The Limits of Humour*, eds. Sharon Lockyer and Michael Pickering (New York: Palgrave Macmillan, 2005), 45–62.

12. Ferguson and Ford, "Social Consequences of Disparagement Humor," 91.

13. Billig, "Humour and Hatred," 267–289; Chandler Davidson, "Ethnic Jokes: An Introduction to Race and Nationality," *Teaching Sociology* 15, no. 3 (1987): 296–302.

14. Billig, "Humour and Hatred," 268.

15. Ibid., 286.

16. Leon Rappoport, *Punchlines: The Case for Racial, Ethnic, and Gender Humor* (Westport, CT: Praeger Publishers, 2005), xiii.

17. Ibid., 2.

18. W.E.B. Du Bois, *The Souls of Black Folk: Essays and Sketches* (Chicago: A. C. McClurg & Co., 1903).

Chapter 2

1. John Hartigan, "Culture Against Race: Reworking the Basis for Racial Analysis," *South Atlantic Quarterly* 104, no. 3 (2005): 557.

2. Erving Goffman, *The Presentation of Self in Everyday Life* (New York: Doubleday, 1990), 2.

3. Carla O'Connor, "Comment: Making Sense of the Complexity of Social Identity in Relation to Achievement: A Sociological Challenge in the New Millennium," *Sociology of Education* 74 (2001): 160.

4. Pierre Bourdieu, *Distinction: A Social Critique of the Judgment of Taste* (Cambridge, MA: Harvard University Press, 1984); Pierre Bourdieu and J. C. Passeron, *Reproduction in Education, Society and Culture* (Beverly Hills, CA: Sage Publications, 1977).

5. James W. Ainsworth-Darnell and Douglas B. Downey, "Assessing the Oppositional Culture Explanation for Racial/Ethnic Differences in School Performance," *American Sociological Review* 63 (1998): 536–553; Signithia Fordham and John U. Ogbu, "Black Students' School Success: Coping with the Burden of Acting White," *Urban Review* 18 (1986): 176–206; Roland Fryer, "Acting White: The Social Price Paid by the Best and Brightest Minority Students," *Education Next* 6, no. 1 (2006): 52–59; Angel L. Harris, "I (Don't) Hate School: Revisiting Oppositional Culture Theory of Blacks' Resistance to Schooling," *Social Forces* 85 (2006): 797–834.

6. David A. Bergin and Helen C. Cooks, "High School Students of Color Talk about Accusations of 'Acting White,'" *Urban Review* 34 no. 2 (2002): 113–134; Prudence L. Carter, *Keepin' It Real: School Success Beyond Black and White* (New York: Oxford University Press, 2005); Erin McNamara Horvat and Carla O'Connor, eds., *Beyond Acting White: Reframing the Debate on Black Student Achievement* (Lanham, MD: Rowman & Littlefield, 2006).

7. Carter, *Keepin' It Real*, 9.

8. Charles A. Gallagher, "Miscounting Race: Explaining Whites' Misconceptions of Racial Group Size," *Sociological Perspectives* 46, no. 3 (2003): 383.

9. Benedict Anderson, *Imagined Communities: Reflections on the Origin and Spread of Nationalism* (London: Verso, 1983), 6.

10. Andrew Shryock, *Off Stage/On Display: Intimacy and Ethnography in the Age of Public Culture* (Stanford, CA: Stanford University Press, 2004), 10.

11. Joe R. Feagin and Melvin P. Sikes, *Living with Racism: The Black Middle-Class Experience* (Boston: Beacon Press, 1994).

12. Lillian B. Rubin, *Worlds of Pain: Life in the Working-Class Family* (New York: Basic Books, 1976).

13. C. J. Pascoe, *Dude, You're a Fag: Masculinity and Sexuality in High School* (Berkeley: University of California Press, 2007).

14. Richard Majors and Janet M. Billson, *Cool Pose: The Dilemmas of Black Manhood in America* (New York: Maxwell Macmillan International, 1992).

15. L. Janelle Dance, *Tough Fronts: The Impact of Street Culture on Schooling* (New York: Routledge, 2002), 18.

16. Ibid., 52.

17. Ann Arnett Ferguson, *Bad Boys: Public Schools in the Making of Black Masculinity* (Ann Arbor: University of Michigan Press, 2000); Pamela Perry, *Shades of White:*

White Kids and Racial Identities in High School (Durham, NC: Duke University Press, 2002).

18. Eduardo Bonilla-Silva, *Racism Without Racists: Color-Blind Racism and the Persistence of Racial Inequality in the United States* (Lanham, MD: Rowman & Littlefield, 2010).

19. For more on racial performance, see Carter, *Keepin' It Real.*

20. Edward W. Morris, *An Unexpected Minority: White Kids in an Urban School* (New Brunswick, NJ: Rutgers University Press, 2006), 81.

Chapter 3

1. bell hooks, *Teaching to Transgress: Education as the Practice of Freedom* (New York: Routledge, 1994); Bakari Kitwana, *The Hip Hop Generation: Young Blacks and the Crisis in African American Culture* (New York: Basic Civitas, 2002); Tricia Rose, *Black Noise: Rap Music and Black Culture in Contemporary America* (Hanover, NH: Wesleyan University Press, 1994); S. Craig Watkins, *Representing: Hip Hop Culture and the Production of Black Cinema* (Chicago: University of Chicago Press, 1998).

2. Dick Hebdige, *Subculture: The Meaning of Style* (London: Methuen, 1979), 94.

3. Mary E. Pattillo, *Black Picket Fences: Privilege and Peril Among the Black Middle Class* (Chicago: University of Chicago Press, 1999), 118.

Chapter 4

1. Beverly Daniel Tatum, *"Why Are All the Black Kids Sitting Together in the Cafeteria?" And Other Conversations about Race* (New York: Basic Books, 2003).

2. John Hartigan, *Racial Situations: Class Predicaments of Whiteness in Detroit* (Princeton, NJ: Princeton University Press, 1999); George Lipsitz, *The Possessive Investment in Whiteness: How White People Profit from Identity Politics* (Philadelphia: Temple University Press, 1998).

3. Michèle Lamont, *The Dignity of Working Men: Morality and the Boundaries of Race, Class, and Immigration* (Cambridge, MA: Harvard University Press, 2000).

4. Lillian B. Rubin, *Worlds of Pain: Life in the Working-Class Family* (New York: Basic Books, 1976), xxxi.

Chapter 5

1. Mica Pollock, *Colormute: Race Talk Dilemmas in an American School* (Princeton, NJ: Princeton University Press, 2004).

2. John U. Ogbu, *Black American Students in an Affluent Suburb: A Study of Academic Disengagement* (Mahwah, NJ: L. Erlbaum Associates, 2003).

3. Douglass E. Foley, *Learning Capitalist Culture: Deep in the Heart of Tejas* (Philadelphia: University of Pennsylvania Press, 1990), 102.

4. Michael Billig, "Humour and Hatred: The Racist Jokes of the Ku Klux Klan," *Discourse Society* 12, no. 3 (2001): 269.

5. Pollock, *Colormute*, 218.

Chapter 6

1. Angela Valenzuela, *Subtractive Schooling: U.S.–Mexican Youth and the Politics of Caring* (Albany: State University of New York Press, 1999).

2. Michelle Alexander, *The New Jim Crow: Mass Incarceration in the Age of Colorblindness* (New York: New Press, 2010).

3. Jonathan Gayles, "Playing the Game and Paying the Price," *Anthropology and Education Quarterly* 36 no. 3 (2005): 250–264.

4. Lisa Delpit, *Other People's Children: Cultural Conflict in the Classroom* (New York: New Press, 2006), xxiiii.

Chapter 7

1. Nina Eliasoph, *Avoiding Politics: How Americans Produce Apathy in Everyday Life* (Cambridge, UK: Cambridge University Press, 1998), 6.

2. Frances Kendall, *Understanding Whiteness: Creating Pathways to Authentic Relationships Across Race* (New York: Routledge Taylor & Francis Group, 2006), 48.

3. Gloria Ladson-Billings, *The Dreamkeepers: Successful Teachers of African American Children* (San Francisco: Jossey-Bass, 1994), 33.

4. Lani Guinier and Gerald Torres, *The Miner's Canary: Enlisting Race, Resisting Power, Transforming Democracy* (Cambridge, MA: Harvard University Press, 2002), 42.

5. Pedro A. Noguera, "Schools, Prisons, and Social Implications of Punishment: Rethinking Disciplinary Practices," *Theory into Practice* 42, no. 4 (2003): 341–350; Carla O'Connor and Sonia DeLuca Fernandez, "Race, Class, and Disproportionality: Reevaluating the Relationship Between Poverty and Special Education Placement," *Educational Researcher* 35, no. 6 (2006): 6–11.

6. Gary R. Howard, *We Can't Teach What We Don't Know: White Teachers, Multiracial Schools* (New York: Teachers College Press, 2006), 56.

7. Eduardo Bonilla-Silva, *Racism Without Racists: Color-Blind Racism and the Persistence of Racial Inequality in the United States* (Lanham, MD: Rowman & Littlefield, 2010), 30.

8. Ibid., 28.

9. David L. Harvey and Michael H. Reed, "The Culture of Poverty: An Ideological Analysis," *Sociological Perspectives* 39, no. 4 (1996): 465; Oscar Lewis, *Five Families: Mexican Case Studies in the Culture of Poverty* (New York: Basic Books, 1959).

10. Julie Landsman, *A White Teacher Talks about Race* (Lanham, MD: Rowman & Littlefield, 2001), xi.

11. Melvin L. Oliver and Thomas M. Shapiro, *Black Wealth/White Wealth: A New Perspective on Racial Inequality* (New York: Routledge, 1995).

12. John U. Ogbu, *Black American Students in an Affluent Suburb: A Study of Academic Disengagement* (Mahwah, NJ: L. Erlbaum Associates, 2003).

13. Adolph L. Reed, *Class Notes: Posing as Politics and Other Thoughts on the American Scene* (New York: New Press, 2000); Lillian B. Rubin, *Worlds of Pain: Life in the Working-Class Family* (New York: Basic Books, 1976); Sherry B. Ortner, "Identities: The Hidden Life of Class," *Journal of Anthropological Research* 54, no. 1 (1998): 1–17.

14. E.P. Thompson, *The Making of the English Working Class* (New York: Vintage Books, 1963).

15. James T. Patterson, *America's Struggle Against Poverty in the Twentieth Century* (Cambridge, MA: Harvard University Press, 2000).

16. David S. Dobbie, "More Than the Sum of Their Parts? Labor-Community Coalitions in the Rust Belt" (PhD diss., University of Michigan, Ann Arbor, 2008).

17. Frances Fox Piven and Richard A. Cloward, *Poor People's Movements: Why They Succeed, How They Fail* (New York: Vintage books, 1979), xii.

18. Guinier and Torres, *The Miner's Canary*.

19. Paul E. Willis, *Learning to Labor: How Working Class Kids Get Working Class Jobs* (New York: Columbia University Press, 1977).

20. Philippe Bourgois, *In Search of Respect: Selling Crack in El Barrio* (Cambridge, UK: Cambridge University Press, 2003); Melville Herskovits, *The Myth of the Negro Past* (New York: Harper, 1941).

21. Geneva Gay, *Culturally Responsive Teaching: Theory, Research, and Practice* (New York: Teachers College, 2010); Gloria Ladson-Billings, "But That's Just Good Teaching! The Case for Culturally Relevant Pedagogy," *Theory into Practice* 34, no. 3 (1995): 159.

22. Karolyn Tyson, "Notes from the Back of the Room: Problems and Paradoxes in the Schooling of Young Black Students," *Sociology of Education* 76, no. 4 (2003): 326.

23. Lisa Delpit, *Other People's Children: Cultural Conflict in the Classroom* (New York: New Press, 2006), 283.

24. Mica Pollock, *Colormute: Race Talk Dilemmas in an American School* (Princeton, NJ: Princeton University Press, 2004), 16.

25. Christopher Ingraham, "Three Quarters of Whites Don't Have Any Non-White Friends," *Washington Post*, Wonkblog, August 25, 2014, http://www.washingtonpost .com/blogs/wonkblog/wp/2014/08/25/three-quarters-of-whites-dont-have-any-non -white-friends/?wpmm=AG0003386.

Chapter 8

1. Harry Wolcott, *The Man in the Principal's Office* (New York: Holt, Rinehart and Winston, 1973).

2. Gloria Ladson-Billings, "Is the Team All Right? Diversity and Teacher Education," *Journal of Teacher Education* 56, no. 3 (2005): 229–234; Tia C. Madkins, "The

Black Teachers Shortage: A Literature Review of Historical and Contemporary Trends," *Journal of Negro Education* 80, no. 3 (2011): 417–427; National Collaborative on Diversity in the Teaching Force, "Assessment of Diversity in America's Teaching Force: A Call to Action," (Washington, DC: National Educational Association, 2004); Ana Maria Villegas and Danne E. Davis, "Approached to Diversifying the Teaching Force: Attending to Issues of Recruitment, Preparation, and Retention," *Teacher Education Quarterly* 34, no. 4 (2007): 137–147.

3. Meredith Mountford, "Motives and Power of School Board Members: Implications for School Board-Superintendent Relationships," *Educational Administration Quarterly* 40, no. 5 (2004): 704–741.

4. James Ryan, Katina Pollock, and Fab Antonelli, "Teacher Diversity in Canada: Leaky Pipelines, Bottlenecks and Glass Ceilings," *Canadian Journal of Education* 32, no. 3 (2009): 591–617.

5. Nandhini Rangarajan and Tamkia Black, "Exploring Organizational Barriers to Diversity: A Case Study of the New York State Education Department," *Review of Public Personnel Administration* 27, no. 3 (2007): 249–263.

6. A number of studies and reports have noted the frequency of principal turnover across the nation. See, for example, Ed Fuller and Michelle D. Young, "Tenure and Retention of Newly Hired Principals in Texas," *Texas High School Project, Leadership Initiatives Issue Brief 1* (University Council for Educational Administration, University of Texas at Austin, 2009); Susan M. Gates et al., "Mobility and Turnover Among School Principals," *Economics of Education Review* 25, no. 3 (2006): 289–302; Karen Hickman, "High School Principal Retention—Defying the Odds: A Qualitative Case Study of Five Principals in a High Needs School District," (PhD diss., University of Houston-Clear Lake, 2011); Michelle Partlow, "Contextual Factors Related to Elementary Principal Turnover," *Planning and Changing* 38, no. 1–2 (2007): 60–76; Michelle Partlow and Carolyn S. Ridenour, "Frequency of Principal Turnover in Ohio's Elementary Schools," *Mid-Western Educational Researcher* 21, no. 2 (2008): 15–16 and 21–23; Sara Ray Stoelinga, Holly Hart, and David Schalliol, "The Work of Chicago Public Schools' Principals: Leading in a Complex Context with High Stakes," (Chicago: Consortium on Chicago School Research, University of Chicago Urban Education Institute, 2008). In addition, the National Center for Education Statistics, has begun tracking principal attrition and mobility; see Danielle Battle, "Principal Attrition and Mobility: Results from the 2008–2009 Principal Follow-Up Survey, First Look," Washington, DC: National Center for Education Statistics, 2010.

7. Ann Arnett Ferguson, *Bad Boys: Public Schools in the Making of Black Masculinity* (Ann Arbor: University of Michigan Press, 2000); Anne Gregory, Pedro Noguera, and Russell J. Skiba, "The Achievement Gap and the Discipline Gap: Two Sides of the Same Coin?" *Educational Researcher* 39, no. 1 (2010), 59; Pedro A. Noguera, *The Trouble with Black Boys: Essays on Race, Equity, and the Future of Public Education* (San Francisco: Jossey-Bass, 2008).

8. Michel Foucault, *Discipline and Punish: The Birth of the Prison* (New York: Vintage Books, 1995), 104.

9. U.S. Department of Education, "Expansive Survey of America's Public Schools Reveals Troubling Racial Disparities: Lack of Access to Pre-School, Greater Suspension Cited," March 21, 2014, http://www.ed.gov/news/press-releases/ expansive-survey-americas-public-schools-reveals-troubling-racial-disparities.

10. Gary R. Howard, *We Can't Teach What We Don't Know: White Teachers, Multiracial Schools* (New York: Teachers College Press, 2006), 123.

11. Blair Mascall and Kenneth Leithwood, "Investing in Leadership: The District's Role in Managing Principal Turnover," *Leadership and Policy in Schools* 9, no. 4 (2010): 367–383.

Chapter 9

1. Harry Wolcott, *The Man in the Principal's Office: An Ethnography* (New York: Holt, Rinehart and Winston, 1973), 322.

2. Billy Young, Jean Madsen, and Mary Ann Young, "Implementing Diversity Plans: Principals' Perception of Their Ability to Address Diversity in Their Schools," *NASSP Bulletin* 94, no. 2 (2010): 146.

3. George Lipsitz, *The Possessive Investment in Whiteness: How White People Profit from Identity Politics* (Philadelphia: Temple University Press, 1998).

4. Karen Travers and Jake Tapper, "Obama: 'Day of Reckoning' for U.S. Economy," *ABC News*, February 24, 2009, http://abcnews.go.com/Politics/President44/story ?id=6950691.

5. Ruby K. Payne, *A Framework for Understanding Poverty* (Highlands, TX: Aha! Process Inc., 2005).

6. Joel E. Dworin and Randy Bomer, "What We All (Supposedly) Know About the Poor: A Critical Discourse Analysis of Ruby Payne's 'Framework,'" *English Education* 40, no. 2 (2008): 101; David L. Harvey and Michael H. Reed, "The Culture of Poverty: An Ideological Analysis," *Sociological Perspectives* 39, no. 4 (1996): 465; Oscar Lewis, *Five Families: Mexican Case Studies in the Culture of Poverty* (New York: Basic Books, 1959); Oscar Lewis, "The Culture of Poverty," *Society* 35, no. 2 (1998), 7.

7. Paul Gorski, "The Classist Underpinnings of Ruby Payne's Framework," *Teachers College Record* (February 9, 2006); Paul C. Gorski, "Peddling Poverty for Profit: Elements of Oppression in Ruby Payne's Framework," *Equity and Excellence in Education* 41, no. 1 (2008): 130–148; Dworin and Bomer, "What We All (Supposedly) Know About the Poor," 101; Jennifer Ng and John Rury, "Poverty and Education: A Critical Analysis of the Ruby Payne Phenomenon," *Teachers College Record* (July 18, 2006).

Chapter 10

1. Gary R. Howard, *We Can't Teach What We Don't Know: White Teachers, Multiracial Schools* (New York: Teachers College Press, 2006), 123.

2. Shayla R. Griffin, Mikel Brown, and naomi m. warren, "Critical Education in High Schools: The Promise and Challenges of Intergroup Dialogue," *Equity & Excellence in Education* 45, no. 1 (2012); Michael S. Spencer, S. Abdullah, Mikel Brown, and Shayla Griffin, "Outcome Evaluation of the Intergroup Project," *Small Group Research* 39, no. 1 (2008): 82–103.

3. Maurianne Adams, Lee Ann Bell, and Pat Griffin, *Teaching for Diversity and Social Justice* (New York: Routledge, 2007); T. F. Pettigrew, "Intergroup Contact Theory," *Annual Review of Psychology* 49, no. 1 (1998): 65; David Schoem and Sylvia Hurtado, *Intergroup Dialogue: Deliberative Democracy in School, College, Community, and Workplace* (Ann Arbor: University of Michigan Press, 2001); Ximena Zúñiga, Biren (Ratnesh) A. Nagda, Mark Chesler, and Adena Cytron-Walker, "Intergroup Dialogue in Higher Education: Meaningful Learning about Social Justice," *ASHE Higher Education Report* 32, no. 4 (2007).

4. Paulo Freire, *Pedagogy of the Oppressed* (New York: Continuum, 2000).

5. Lani Guinier and Gerald Torres, *The Miner's Canary: Enlisting Race, Resisting Power, Transforming Democracy* (Cambridge, MA: Harvard University Press, 2002).

6. Adams, Bell and Griffin, *Teaching for Diversity and Social Justice*, 31.

7. Freire, *Pedagogy of the Oppressed*.

8. Zúñiga et al., "Intergroup Dialogue in Higher Education," 1.

9. Faye V. Harrison, "Introduction: Expanding the Discourse on 'Race,'" *American Anthropologist* 100, no. 3 (1998): 609; Robert Dean Reason, Elizabeth A. Roosa Millar, and Tara C. Scales, "Toward a Model of Racial Justice Ally Development," *Journal of College Student Development* 46, no. 5 (2005): 530.

Conclusion

1. Amanda E. Lewis, *Race in the Schoolyard: Negotiating the Color Line in Classrooms and Communities* (New Brunswick, NJ: Rutgers University Press, 2003), 190.

2. Ibid., 188.

3. Faye V. Harrison, "Introduction: Expanding the Discourse on 'Race,'" *American Anthropologist* 100 no. 3 (1998): 612.

Acknowledgments

Some children learn to read and write easily. I was certainly not one of them; I was made a writer by the dedication, determination, and commitment of my mother—a woman who continues to amaze me. My earliest memories of writing are of her red pen correcting my spelling, helping me restructure sentences, and pushing me to think more critically. She made me rewrite, redo, and rework until it was truly my best. Until I went to college, my mother read every paper I wrote—going through it with that red pen, making me redo it again and again. It was this commitment, rooted in her immense love for me, that laid the foundation for this project. This book has truly been a collaboration between the two of us three decades in the making.

Caroline Chauncey has been a passionate shepherd of this project as we worked together to get it over the finish line. She has been everything I could have hoped for in an editor and has made this a much better book in many ways.

I have had the wonderful honor of getting to work with dedicated, passionate, innovative scholars who have been great role models and provided intellectual feedback and positive support. Jelani Cobb and Stephen Knadler, two of my earliest academic mentors, made me feel at a young age that my voice was important. Andrew Shryock, Michael Spencer, Carla O'Connor, Damani Partridge, and Laura Lein. have all pushed me to think deeply about my work while smiling, laughing, and making me feel like maybe this journey does not have to suck your soul dry.

I would also like to thank those who have provided academic and technical support, especially Letha Chadiha, Lorraine Gutierrez, Laura Thomas, Todd Huynh, Sean Joe, Hoa Nguyen, Sharon Clark, Samantha

Drotar, Natasha Johnson, Ilean Baskerville (for her amazing transcription services, which truly saved the day), and Jasmine Gary (for her last-minute policy expertise).

I came to this project as a practitioner doing youth work and inter-group dialogue in high schools. Michael Spencer, Charles Garvin, Mikel Brown, Naomi Warren, Noel Folks, Linda Hibbs, Adrienne Dessel, Kelly Maxwell and Susan King have been amazing colleagues, teachers, and friends along the way. Their collaboration made me a better facilitator and sparked my interest in the questions that guided this book. I also want to thank Melanie Morrison, who has been a constant cheerleader for this project while challenging me to be my best self in the work we do together.

This project would not have been possible without significant financial support. The National Science Foundation, Rackham Graduate School, and Andrew W. Mellon Foundation have all provided me with fellow-ships that allowed me to do the research for this project. The University of Michigan's Center for the Study of Black Youth in Context provided me with a generous post-doctoral research fellowship that allowed me to write this manuscript. I am also grateful to the Graduate Employees' Organiza-tion and the American Federation of Teachers Michigan for fighting for good funding and a living wage for all graduate employees, lectures, and educators.

I am immensely grateful for my community outside the academy, which has kept me nourished spiritually, emotionally, and physically. I would like to thank my father, Thomas Jefferson Griffin II, for his un-wavering conviction that his children truly are the best in the world and my siblings—Maiessha Griffin, Trevor Griffin, Cory Griffin, Margarette Griffin, and Victoria Griffin—for cheering me on, making me laugh, and continuing to remind me that I will never be the funniest, smartest, or wittiest among them. I would like to especially thank Marggy and Tori for offering to do the "grunt work" of transcription before realizing what they had gotten into, and Trevor for continued tech support. And to my extended family, the Sallees, Griffins, and Dobbies, who continually bring me joy and give me support and practical advice. To my family by proxy, the Dorns, you have truly treated me as one of your own and given me assistance through this process in the form of good food, good laughs, and borrowed children.

My academic friends have kept me going in more ways than they know; especially the "Core Four" and "We All We Got": LaFleur Stephens, Jennifer Maddox, and Latoya Branch—the three women who started this journey with me and are still my close friends; and "Michigan's Finest": Davin Phoenix, Keith Veal, Kenyatha Loftis, Maria Johnson, Menna Demessie, Gbenga Olumolade, Andrea Benjamin, Tonya Rice, and Kyla McMullen.

To those who have been with me since my youth and remain my best friends and biggest supporters: Qrescent Mason, Robyn Morris, Tarani Merriweather Woodson, and Darrika Van. And to the amazing community of friends I have cultivated in Michigan, who have entertained my conversations about schools, written with me at coffee shops and in living rooms, and cheered me on: Jennifer Bahns, Roxana Zuniga, Al Defreece, Nate Walker, Clare Pritchard, Andy Pritchard, Nikhol Atkins, Danielle Atkinson, Jamilia Harnois, and Jodi Willard.

I am forever indebted to the many people who agreed to read early drafts of this manuscript and give me detailed feedback, especially Melanie Morrison, Dave Dobbie, John Pahle, Pamela Griffin, Tarani Merriweather Woodson, Naomi Warren, and Mikel Brown.

Perhaps most importantly, I would like to thank the truly amazing students, teachers, and administrators I have had the honor and pleasure of getting to know over the past decade, especially Shannon Johnson, Rona Lohry, Ronald Norwood, and Kyle Sherrod. You are amazing young adults! In particular, I want to thank everyone at Jefferson High School, who not only gave me access to their school and lives, but also welcomed me with open arms. Know that after three years of working at Jefferson, my biggest conclusion is that I really like you all.

And finally, to my beloved David S. Dobbie. You are my "biggest" supporter, my most important adviser, and my best friend. You literally got me through this process by being a sounding board, notetaker, editor, proofreader, great friend, and loving husband. You enrich my life, bring me joy, and continually motivate me to be a scholar-activist. Your steady support, calm disposition, sense of humor, and pure genius sustain me in this work and in our life together. Through your own commitment to social justice and education, you inspire me to leave the world a better place than I found it.

About the Author

Shayla R. Griffin received her PhD and MSW from the joint program in Social Work and Cultural Anthropology at the University of Michigan–Ann Arbor and her bachelor's degree from Spelman College in Atlanta, Georgia. Her work focuses on issues of race and class in K–12 schools.

Griffin has extensive experience in dialogue facilitation, diversity training, and social justice education. She has worked with high school students, college students, and hundreds of K–12 teachers around issues of race, class, gender, and sexual orientation. In addition, she consults with a number of nonprofit organizations on issues of social justice.

Griffin has taught courses on race, social justice, and diversity at the University of Michigan for the Program on Intergroup Relations, the School of Social Work, and the Department of Anthropology. She has been the recipient of a number of research grants, including the National Science Foundation Graduate Research Fellowship and the Andrew W. Woodrow Mellon Graduate Fellowship in Humanities. From 2012–2014, she was a post-doctoral research fellow in the Center for the Study of Black Youth in Context at the University of Michigan. Currently, she is the Diversity and School Culture Consultant for the Washtenaw Intermediate School District (Michigan) and director of Creating Culturally Proficient Communities, a five-year initiative to improve racial and economic justice in Ypsilanti Community Schools (Michigan). She resides in Detroit.

Index